P9-CKW-009

BONDS
THAT MAKE US
FREE

BONDS
THAT MAKE US
FREE

HEALING OUR RELATIONSHIPS,

COMING TO OURSELVES

C. TERRY WARNER

SHADOW
MOUNTAIN

Page 56: "Little Gidding" from *Four Quartets,* © 1942 by T.S. Eliot and renewed 1970 by Esme Valerie Eliot, reprinted by permission of Harcourt, Inc.

© 2001 The Arbinger Institute, Incorporated

All rights reserved. No part of this book may be reproduced in any form or by any means without permission in writing from the publisher, Shadow Mountain®. The views expressed herein are the responsibility of the author and do not necessarily represent the position of Shadow Mountain.

Visit us at shadowmountain.com

Library of Congress Cataloging-in-Publication Data

Warner, C. Terry.
  Bonds that make us free: healing our relationships, coming to ourselves / C. Terry Warner
      p.   cm.
Includes index.
  ISBN 1-57345-919-4 (hardbound: alk. paper)
  1. Interpersonal relations. 2. Emotions. 3. Attitude (Psychology)
I. Title.

HM1106 .W37 2001
158.2—dc21

                                                            2001002811

Printed in the United States of America   54459-0189R
Malloy Lithographing Incorporated, Ann Arbor, MI

10   9

For Susan
my soul mate
here and hereafter

~

CONTENTS

Preface

People can change fundamentally—in their hearts and not just in their outward behavior. I have been led to this conviction partly as a result of having lived through the transformation experiences of many individuals. I say *lived through* because I had very little to do with the change they made. They brought it about themselves. That's what has delighted me about the work I have been privileged to participate in. The possibility of overcoming very deep personal and interpersonal problems lies within the power of each of us.

Not many people believe this. Most are convinced that our genetic structure and life experiences have dictated the kind of people we have become. Hence any changes we might make will be behavioral, not emotional and attitudinal. Even those self-help programs that paint seductive pictures of a transformed life generally turn out, when studied closely, to focus more on outward rather than inward change.

Why then, if we are able to change fundamentally, don't we do it? Why do we get and keep ourselves stuck in anxiety, suspicion, resentment, or anger if we all have the power to do otherwise? The answer to this extraordinarily challenging and fascinating question is that we devise and hang on to our emotional problems *for a purpose*, a purpose more important to us than our happiness. And we deceive ourselves about the fact that this is what we're doing. We participate in the creation of our emotional troubles and deny we've had any part in it. In regard to our troubling emotions and attitudes, we are our own worst enemies.

Just about as far back as our civilization's intellectual memory extends, thoughtful people have tried to understand why we would do such a thing. For what possible reason would we keep ourselves from making the beneficial personal changes of which we are capable? This is the issue that first got me intrigued with the subject of this book. It seemed to me that a sound answer to this question would show us how to stop deceiving ourselves about what we're doing and make the changes necessary to our well-being. Though my field was a theoretical one, my ultimate aim was to help people, beginning with myself.

So, aided by others whom I will speak of in the Acknowledgments section, I sought for this new kind of psychology. I worked at it for years, primarily at Brigham Young University and also at Linacre College, Oxford University. Often I seemed to make progress and received much encouragement from other professionals. But my associates and I kept discovering, when we paid close enough attention, that each new theoretical "breakthrough" suffered from the same problems as its predecessors. Finally it dawned on us that our own self-deceptions were twisting our understanding of the issues. We could see that self-deception wasn't something our little band of self-deceivers was likely to understand. We had no chance of achieving our goal until we became more honest with ourselves. So our quest became a personal and ethical one; we quietly and individually sought to become better human beings than we had been.

As solutions to the theoretical problems gradually became clear, we were led to develop a method of teaching that emboldened people to see their own lives clearly and honestly. It began in response to requests of psychologists and leaders of business and other organizations. That led to teaching groups of individuals and couples, and then to training others to teach also. We called ourselves The Arbinger Institute.

To our amazement we found, right from the first, that almost all of the participants in our classes experienced, in small degree or great, something of a fundamental change, a change of heart. Without guidance or pressure from the teacher, but simply by considering the true stories and explanations that were shared, the participants would often realize the truth about their part in a troubled relationship, and often they would want to share the story. Their complete honesty with themselves enabled them to see how they had been responsible for the thoughts and feelings that had been troubling them. In the discovery of the truth and then in the telling of it, their hearts began to change.

You might think that studying this topic would be a somber experience, but it wasn't. Those who listened to the personal stories responded with laughter. They laughed joyously rather than derisively, not *at* those who told their stories, but *with* them. For they recognized themselves in each other's stories: every story was, except for details, their own story too. By resonating with the storyteller they recalled situations in their own lives that they had previously not remembered truthfully. They discovered, with relief and joy, that their fears about themselves and resentments toward others—the very emotions that had troubled them—were gone.

∽

I have tried to write this book in the spirit of the Arbinger classes I have described, partly by including a number of the many rich stories that individuals have shared over the course of nearly a quarter of a century. If you ponder them, these true stories are likely to serve you better than the explanations that connect them. (Sometimes I have changed names and other details, including names of my children, to protect the privacy of individuals.) And your own stories, which will come to you with the force of truth, will be most important of all. Moreover, the effect of your own stories will be enhanced if you write them down; pieces of personal history honestly written can work therapeutic miracles. If you are like the participants in the classes and scores of thousands who have read the materials I will share, you will begin to see your own life differently as you contemplate what you read, and you will feel yourself being changed in the process.

I should add a word about the explanations that surround the stories; they make this book different from other works on similar topics. As people gain a deep, true understanding of their attitudes and actions, their self-deceptions fade, and they can begin to see clearly how to move forward on their own. On the other hand, if they're merely told what to do, they can't act independently; they must either blindly accept what they've been taught or just as blindly reject it. A correct understanding of why we feel and think and act as we do helps to set us free. Developing that understanding is the point of the explanations.

It is because we want to promote this independence that my colleagues and I regard ourselves as ordinary teachers rather than givers of advice. When people obtain their own independent understanding of the truth, they can go beyond what they've been taught. If a price must be paid to obtain that understanding, then a teacher who cares will not deprive the student of the opportunity to pay that price by making the way forward seem easier than it is.

∼

My heart goes out to two kinds of readers, both of whom may have particular difficulty coming to grips with what I will say.

First are those who want to deal with the material intellectually, as a way of muffling their own inner voice. This has sometimes been my own besetting self-deception—to think self-understanding is to be achieved by reason rather than by honesty. It has often kept me in my own darkness. I could be most miserable at the very times when I was most convinced I was right. In portraying human problems and possibilities as I have in this book, my concern has been not to persuade you of my views, but to prepare you to discover the truth within yourself. So, to those who like me might tend to intellectualize the ideas presented here, I invite you to give up that defensive strategy and, like our research team, seek instead to become more honest with yourself. The simple, clean truth about ourselves has more therapeutic power than any psychological theory.

The other readers for whom I am concerned suffer from feelings of deep inadequacy, convinced that nothing they do can make them worthwhile and acceptable. They have already taken on themselves more than their share of blame. To those burdened souls, talk of personal responsibility for our emotional problems sounds like the very sort of condemnation they have made a habit of heaping on themselves. As far as they can see, they've exhausted the "personal responsibility" approach, and they long to affirm themselves.

We will discover in this book that the self any of us doubts, feels ashamed or guilty about, perhaps even wishes to annihilate, *is not really who we are,* but a fear-driven phantasm, not grounded in reality. Until we make this discovery, the early chapters, where we will talk about the origin of this phantasm and the destruction it causes, may leave us feeling hopeless. They may stir up old feelings that we can't "measure up."

If this happens to you, override your discouragement and press on. Your self-doubts, if you have them, aren't about *you* at all, but about a misconception of yourself, a false self-image, that you can be rid of—provided you give way to the truth and not your fear of it.

∼

We live in a culture zealous about self-awareness, self-esteem, self-gratification, and other ways of focusing upon self. Beware of these. Beware too of material that invites you to throw over deep religious and moral values, which invariably contain more wisdom than any self-improvement program that seeks to challenge and replace them. Beware of prescriptions for life that encourage self-seeking and confrontation; they rest on failed assumptions and soon lead to escalated conflict and pain. Beware of programs that create artificial communities and encourage public disclosure of personal information, invite physical contact, or develop emotional dependency.

Also beware of people who are anxious to tell you how you ought to live. Instead, test everything, including what is said in this book, against your own thoughtfully considered experience. If you are honest about that experience, what is true will ring true—you will not have to rely on my say-so or anybody else's. No self-proclaimed human authority will serve you better than your own straightforward sense of what is right.

Finally, beware of any humanly devised material or training that encourages devotion to *itself.* Our families deserve our devotion, as do our honorable occupations and the deep truths by which the good things in our heritage have been achieved. What you are about to read is intended to reawaken commitment to such people and principles.

The necessity for all these cautions explains why those of us who have been engaged in sharing the materials found in this book adopted the name *Arbinger.* It is a variant of the word *harbinger,* which means *herald, forerunner,* or *precursor*—someone who goes ahead and announces or paves the way for what's coming. It would not be accurate to describe this book as supplying the truths upon which we must build our lives. Instead it shows how we can put ourselves in that receptive, honest, and discerning condition that will enable us, any of us, to find these truths on our own.

~

ACKNOWLEDGMENTS

No book ever had more generous supporters or keener collaborators than this one. I mention first my co-workers in the Moral Studies Group at Brigham Young University and in the Arbinger Institute: the late Arthur Henry King, James Robertson, Duane Boyce, Terry Olson, Lyn Mattoon, Dennis Packard, Richard Williams, Jim Faulconer, Alice Johnson, Jim Ferrell, and David Warner, as well as my generous Oxford colleague, Rom Harré, and my research assistant during my time at Oxford, Glen Cooper. To our intense discussions over many years I owe the development of many of the ideas expressed here. Lyn Mattoon's collaboration on the form and flow of the manuscript helped significantly, and her sound literary judgment made it clearer than it would otherwise have been.

Countless contributions have been made by my research assistants, students, and fellow faculty at BYU (notably the members of the Early Bird group), by my Arbinger colleagues and clients, by my associates at the Anasazi Foundation, and by numerous correspondents and friends. They have shared their insights and personal stories and provided oft-needed encouragement. Though these make up a number far too long to list individually, I think they each know of my gratitude. As she has done with many other aspects of my work, Kimberly White produced the indexes with her unfailing accuracy, thoroughness, and dispatch. Josh Stott, Cherie Loveless, Katie Warner, Jim Murphy, and especially Kathy Grant did first-rate work that assisted materially at various stages of this project. And besides some of those I have already mentioned, Jane Birch, Karen Merkley, Alan Melby, Brooke Bentley, Steve Preston, Danny Warner, Jeff Nielsen, Chris Wallace, Don Norton, Cynthia Collier, Leena Pullenin, Giles Florence, and Carol Tavris made valuable manuscript suggestions.

I am grateful beyond measure to my Arbinger compatriot Paul Smith, whose constant labors have freed me to write, and to the numerous BYU administrators, notably Robert K. Thomas, Dallin H. Oaks, Dennis Packard, Jim Faulconer, Cody Carter, and Dennis Rasmussen, who for nearly three decades have generously supported and encouraged my theoretical work.

To all the good people at Bookcraft and Shadow Mountain in many departments I extend my appreciation. Thank you to Sheri Dew, Cory Maxwell, and Brad Pelo, whose intrepid persistence finally persuaded me to turn my unfinished manuscript, *Bonds of Anguish, Bonds of Love,* into an honest-to-goodness book after nearly twenty years. And I extend particular thanks to my wise and convivial editor Emily Watts, and her fellow editor Jay Parry, for their expert and gentle guidance.

Most of all I express my gratitude to Susan and our children, who exemplify the life I aspire to and voluntarily do double duty as my champions and best critics.

CHAPTER 1

LIFE'S SWEETNESS LOST

A Day When I Lost It

Susan and I named one of our sons *Matthew*, which means "gift of God." During the early months of his life I would dance around his crib in my pajamas, singing. Some of the songs I made up as I went along, some I had learned from my mother, and one my grandfather had taught me many years earlier:

> Matthew, Matthew was a fine old man,
> Washed his face in a frying pan,
> Combed his hair with a wagon wheel,
> And died with a toothache in his heel.

Susan would laugh. It was the best of times.

Thirteen years later Matthew appeared one afternoon at the bathroom doorway and yelled, "When're you going to get it fixed, huh, Dad?" The downstairs toilet had been broken for several days, which meant Matthew had to use the bathroom upstairs where I was changing the baby's diaper.

I closed my eyes for a moment and took my time acknowledging his presence. My ears began to heat up a little. How dare he talk to his father that way?

I didn't raise my voice. Instead I set the reeking diaper in the diaper pail and observed my son standing stiffly in the doorway, arms crossed, waiting for an answer. I said, very slowly, "I am not going to answer a question put to me in that tone of voice."

"So you're not even going to talk to your own son, huh?"

I did not say the next thing that came into my mind, which

was, "I'm not going to talk to my son until he can speak respectfully to me." Nevertheless, he responded with a defiant "Oh yeah?" in his eyes. For a fleeting moment this reminded me of his bright eyes and spirited bearing when, at the age of nine, he sang "Wells Fargo Wagon" in the university musical. How had that charming child turned into a teenager whom, for that moment at least, I would have been happy to have out of my sight?

Summoning up my patience, I briefly considered explaining how I had tried to fix the toilet that very afternoon—but then decided he didn't deserve the courtesy of an answer. The growing pressure of my silence was making him squirm. "Fine!" he finally exclaimed, and he huffed out the door, through the house, and down the driveway toward the Hickmans'. Probably to use their bathroom.

"Oh, brother!" I heard myself say.

Hadn't I answered with perfect self-control? Hadn't Matthew become even more impudent? What more can a father do when his son acts like that? I picked up the baby and told myself to forget about the whole episode.

Not half an hour later I heard Matthew talking with Susan in the laundry room. He was complaining that I was so far gone I wouldn't even talk with my own children. Susan didn't say anything in response—she didn't even try to correct him! All I could hear besides Matthew's complaints was the hum of the dryer and the clicking of the snaps on the clothes going round and round inside. Couldn't Susan see he had her eating out of his hand?

I decided to get myself downstairs to make sure the broken toilet wasn't overflowing. I didn't want to give Susan and Matthew more evidence against me than they already had. On the way down I nearly tripped on a pile of clothes Matthew had left on the stairway landing. For a fleeting instant I felt like yelling, "What are these clothes doing here?"

But I didn't yell. Suddenly, quite unexpectedly, all my resentful thoughts gave way to silence. As quickly as I took my next step, I could see for the first time what I had been doing, as if light had broken through a crack in the ceiling of my mind. I had been looking upon my own son as my enemy! How could I have done that? How could I have been finding satisfaction in catching him in a fault? How could I have demeaned a person I loved so well?

I knew the conventional wisdom—you need to come down hard on a boy who acts defiantly, not let him get away with it, give him a swift kick in the pants, take away his privileges. But had I done any of those things, I would have felt even worse than I did. The truth that mattered was not that he had been mistreating me—perhaps he had, but that's not what stopped me in my tracks. The truth that mattered was that I had been mistreating him.

How Could This Have Happened?

Matthew had been a toddler when his sister Emily was born. While Susan was in the hospital, he and I had gone everywhere together and had become perfect friends. No one had ever looked at me more knowingly. We played in the afternoon when I was supposed to be preparing for my classes and did errands in the early evening as long as the Spring light lasted. We were easy and generous with one another. Though only one year old, he understood everything.

Why wasn't I easy and generous now? Why hadn't I put my arm around my son and admitted how inept I am with mechanical devices? I could have asked him to help me figure out how to fix the toilet; we might have done it together. I could have apologized for my bad feelings. I had often seen others defuse tense situations in just this way and had even done so myself at other times. Why had I been so quick to take offense this time?

Never mind about Matthew's clothes cluttering the landing. I was tripping over truths about myself that lay strewn all around my memory. My thoughts and words in the bathroom had been mean and petty. I had congratulated myself for not yelling at Matthew, but hadn't my pious scorn and silence put him down as ruthlessly as a slap in the face?

If only I had responded differently to him, he would have responded differently to me. I knew this.

The more I reflected on my history with my son, the more those truths disturbed and disheartened me. They reminded me how much lighter and finer and happier things could be between us. They showed me how much of what I prized most in life I had lost.

I could only ask, How could I have fallen so far? Why had I made myself so unhappy?

I could not answer these questions. I only knew that somehow, as I had gained in life experience, I had declined in sensitivity and wisdom. If the episode in the bathroom was any indication, I had grown temperamental and petty. Getting older had made me less mature. I had actually believed that if things were ever going to be right between Matthew and me again, it was he who needed to change, not I. This wasn't the truth; I was the one who had to change. Why would I, an apparently intelligent and well-adjusted man, mistreat the boy I loved and make myself unhappy in the process? How could the life I had shared with this boy have lost its sweetness?

Memories of the experiences that had imparted that sweetness made the exchange with Matthew all the more grim by comparison. I was capable of so much better. The more I thought about my better possibilities, the more sorrowful I became. I had failed to be the person I knew myself capable of being—the person I am when I feel most whole and alive and in harmony with myself.

Nothing in my experience has been a greater source of sadness than this discrepancy, this distance, between the person I am when

I am true to what I know to be right and the person I become when I am not.

∾

TROUBLED FEELINGS—
THE UNIVERSAL AFFLICTION

We have all had experiences like mine with Matthew. We have felt hurt or provoked or upset by the people around us—angry, for instance. Or resentful. Or envious. Or intimidated. Or fearful. Or humiliated. Or disgusted by something done to us. We feel helpless to rid ourselves of these feelings.

We don't rid ourselves of this sense of helplessness by trying to ignore the supposed offenses of others or attempting to distract ourselves from our feelings. The unfairness, indifference, disrespect, rudeness, or cruelty troubles us through and through— sometimes only faintly but always unmistakably. The pain, which is real, seeps into and taints every sector of life. Unclouded happiness seems impossible.

Everyone who has ever been stuck in such troubled thoughts and feelings knows how they make a shambles of our inner lives. A "gas law" of emotional disturbance operates here, which might be formulated as follows: "Any inner space, no matter how large, will be filled by any agitation, no matter how small." The feelings that we blame on others, and that seem to ruin everything, rudely refuse to be evicted once they take up residence in us. Even though we retreat to the bedroom and lock the door, figuratively speaking, we sleep in terror, knowing those feelings are somewhere wandering about in the house. Families who live on strained terms discover that their impatience and frustration contaminate every project they undertake, whatever the setting—cooking in the kitchen, repairing something in the workshop, reading in the bedroom, even trying to play a game together. It is difficult to overestimate the corrosive power of agitated feelings.

A Few Examples

I cannot help thinking of individuals I know who have struggled under the oppressive weight of some negative, troubled emotion or attitude. Their problems range from everyday unhappiness to what clinicians would call pathologies. No doubt you can also think of people you know—or of yourself. Keep in mind that this condition is as common as breathing air. Each of us, to one degree or another, deals with troubled thoughts and feelings.

A homeowner constantly critical of everyone in the neighborhood;

A schoolgirl envious of her more popular classmates;

An office worker who gets passed over for promotion because she's constantly down on herself;

A family member who refuses to do his part of the household chores and complains against those who press him to help;

A teacher who belittles his students if they don't answer his questions to his satisfaction;

A woman who nags her husband;

A businessman preoccupied with his appearance and possessions and overanxious to impress.

When such ordinary people are described in a little more detail we can see that some of them live with considerable frustration, disappointment, or pain.

I recall Mandy, for example. Her father, a construction supervisor, had died of a stroke when she was fourteen. When she was a little girl, he had always worked long hours, often on jobs far away. He took Mandy's older brother, Jeddy, with him on school holidays. Her mother encouraged it because "the boy needs his father's influence." When little Mandy asked to go, her father would say, "Not a good place for girls." In the summer he would get away overnight for hunting or fishing, sometimes with a friend and usually with her brother. But he'd say to Mandy, "You're too little," or "I need Jeddy to clean the fish." About the time Mandy turned ten her little sister, Nessie, was born, and her father was promoted and didn't have to leave the house so early or work so late. He would throw Nessie in the air and crawl around with her and kiss her good night; when Mandy tried to kiss him, he said, "You're too old for that." As she grew in years she would feel "down" for long periods, and at those times especially it would take very little to make her feel rejected. If someone didn't give her full attention, she would try to get out of the situation as quickly as she could. At those times, she said, her resentment over being rejected would glow in her like hot coals. She would often brood about what her father had done to her.

∼

Another person I think about is Norm, a successful business owner with great drive and energy. He controlled his costs and his people with equal impatience. It did not surprise me to learn that his inner life was blighted by troubled relationships with his chief lieutenants. Despite his power, Norm could not find a way to make his employees more committed and cooperative, and he carried his aggravation home from the office every night. "I haven't really been with my wife for nearly a year," he told me. "When we go to bed she reads and I just lie there and stare at the ceiling and relive my frustrations."

～

I got to know Ruel not too long after he took a job in sales, thinking he might be able to break out of a pattern of "bad luck" in trying to find a job at which he could be successful. After receiving his training, he didn't immediately get himself out the door to make sales calls. Instead, he spent his days listening to motivational tapes—getting prepared, he told himself, so that he could succeed when he did go. On the surface he appeared cheerful enough, but as I got to know him I discovered him to be preoccupied with wounded feelings and discouraged thoughts— the customers would be unreceptive; the manufacturer had done a poor job on the product and it would be hard to sell; his own family and life circumstances had not prepared him properly to get on in the world successfully.

～

Victoria had reared her two now-teenage children in an authoritarian and controlling spirit. They had become touchy and belligerent—so much so, she said, that "they wouldn't listen to me on anything. I couldn't control them anymore. I had no idea where to start getting our household into order—I didn't even know how to talk to them." She felt completely stymied.

You get the idea. I am not focusing on the emotional and attitudinal problems of unusual people, different from the rest of us. I'm talking about troubles that belong in some form and at some time to just about all of us, the kind of troubles that we worry and talk about in our families and with our confidants or that we're ashamed to admit to anyone.

"Stuck"

Many have told me of doing everything humanly possible to change a negative attitude or rescue a spoiled relationship, only to fail again and again and finally give up hope. This seems to me the saddest part of being driven by negative emotions or attitudes: We cannot see how to stop. We feel stuck. What a savage irony! We have been endowed with the capacity to imagine a happy and fulfilling life for ourselves, but we cannot see how to make it that way.

Most curiously, we will look in vain for an adequate name for the "stuck" condition I have been describing. Though clearly a pernicious and, in its extreme varieties, a devastating kind of emotional "dis-ease," it has no name in common usage that captures it in all its scope. And this is true of other important aspects of this stuck condition, including (as we will see later) its origins and its consequences in our relationships with others. We have no names for them. Having no concepts or words for picking them out of the flow of experience, we remain largely ignorant of their true character and therefore helpless to understand ourselves when things go wrong. We are blind to the nature of our most troublesome personal difficulties.

So we need to find language to talk about being stuck in negative emotions or attitudes. I will call them "negative," "accusing," "afflicted," "anguished," and "troubled," aware that none of these words quite captures all I want to convey.

This is what I mean by "feeling stuck": *experiencing other people or circumstances as having more power over our own happiness than we do.* We believe they have the ability to cause troubling feelings in us that we cannot do anything about, no matter how we try. We wonder how we can ever be genuinely happy, inwardly peaceful, and fulfilled. Obviously we can't as long as we continue feeling offended or provoked or hurt, but we cannot stop feeling that way because we can't see how to stop. Can we ever get out of this box once we find ourselves in it?

I am reminded of a condition I suffered with much of my life: My flesh would itch intolerably as if it were lined, on the *inside* of my skin, with a wire-brush blanket, fiery in all its tips. Scratching would bring me no relief at all—in fact, it made the itching worse. Our troubling attitudes, emotions, and moods resemble that itching; seldom is there anything we can think to do that actually succeeds in preventing them or expunging them. Even "power emotions" like anger and hatred carry with them a sense of powerlessness to stop, a feeling that other people are provoking us, "making" us angry or hateful by what they say and do.

The predicament I have been describing is as old as time. On no subject has more diverse advice been given. Every profound ethical or spiritual teaching speaks of it under some label or other. So do many of the more superficial teachings that focus on success. Some of these offer strategies for cultivating tranquillity amidst affliction or adversity. Some show us a path of love they claim will lead us away from fear and frustration. Some, with a much different approach, encourage us to assert ourselves and defend our rights in order to keep others from aggravating and taking advantage of us. Some supply negotiation techniques for winning the respect, deference, or cooperation of others. Some recommend suspicion, pessimism, or resignation as tactics to make us less vulnerable to offense.

Generally speaking, such prescriptions for happiness don't work very well. They don't work because they fail to show how our hearts can be changed, and with "hearts" I include the troubled emotions and attitudes that keep us "stuck." That failure is fatal, because *without a change of heart whatever we do will carry the smell of our manipulative, selfish, or fearful intent, and other people will readily discern it.* (The "mature" and "soft" way I spoke to

Matthew in the bathroom is a case in point. Instead of caring about him, I was accusing him to make myself look good, and he could tell.) The self-help movement that began in the latter half of the twentieth century suffers particularly from this flaw, for the personal and interpersonal skills it seeks to cultivate are almost always designed to get us more of what we think we want, rather than to bring about a change of heart.

Much of the time, the advice we give one another, like the advice of experts, is based on misguided diagnosis. Our advice trusts the experience of those who feel "stuck" to identify the cause of the trouble. But when we are "stuck," we think, falsely, the problem lies with other people, when the truth is that the problem lies within ourselves. We develop strategies for relieving ourselves of our unwanted feelings without retracing the path that got us into them in the first place. Lacking a sound diagnosis as a starting point, we aren't likely to come up with treatments that will help fundamentally.

On the other hand, a sound diagnosis can lead to a cure. It was so with my terrible itching. It had grown worse during a nearly two-year period in which I struggled to recover from the effects of a rare strain of hepatitis, a disease that attacks the liver. My wife, Susan, went to work with her characteristic tenacity to find a cure. She took note of the fact that my mother and sisters experienced the same itching in the later stages of pregnancy because of a condition called cholestasis, wherein the liver does not function well and allows bile into the bloodstream. So she reasoned that, being related to them, I too had a liver that did not function very well, especially under the added stress of my illness. She put me on a strict diet, which I have followed faithfully since. And *voilà!* The itching subsided almost completely. Finding the truth about the source of the problem pointed the way to the cure—which in this case did not relieve the itching so much as prevent it from occurring.

Yielding to the Truth

Learning the truth about a problematic condition in our physical bodies enables us to take steps to find the remedy. As they say, the diagnosis is half the cure. *But with emotions and relationships, the truth is the cure.* In the realm of emotions and attitudes, as we will discover in this book, honest self-understanding liberates us from our stuck emotions.

For example, realizing what I had done to Matthew shocked and discouraged me—but it also brought an end to my piously punishing attitude. I couldn't admit the truth to myself and continue hardening myself toward him. Difficult though it was, that moment of truth following our bathroom confrontation inaugurated better times for us.

Mandy, who felt unloved for much of her life, thought her troubles stemmed from having been rejected by her father. But she came to realize, as we will see in chapter 13, how much she was responsible for her feelings, and how badly they had skewed her memories of her childhood. And that recognition of the truth freed her from her emotional troubles.

Norm, the business owner who controlled his employees, did something similar. As we will discover in chapter 14, he saw the way he treated people in a new, truthful light and suddenly could understand why they resisted his influence. They quickly became more important to him, and because of this change in him, they began to respond to him cooperatively.

Victoria, who had the nonresponsive teenagers, achieved in her family what Norm did at work, at least for a time (see chapter 12). She realized that she had tolerated only one way of doing things—her own—and had constantly chastised and corrected family members who deviated. With this realization came a change in her feelings and a desire to listen to her children rather than berate them. But she relapsed, and the old troubling emotions and sour relationships returned. Her failure to maintain her change of heart will prove to be as instructive to us as the change itself.

In due course, we will examine the details of these and many other personal stories to see that even when our emotional burdens seem very heavy, we can rid ourselves of them and recover from any subsequent relapses. And we will also learn why so many who desire to do this do not succeed, so that we can avoid their mistakes.

~

Because honest self-understanding plays such a crucial role in a change of heart, I will avoid speaking of the solutions to our emotional problems at first and concentrate instead, in the first six chapters, on the sources and character of those problems. Then, in chapters 7 through 14, I will discuss the remedy. Until we get hold of the truth about our condition, our continuing self-misunderstanding will guide us to do things that only make matters worse—like my desperate scratching of that fiery itch.

When I was small, growing up in San Francisco, my father brought home a toy from Chinatown, a woven tube six inches long and about as big around as one's index finger. He called this toy "Chinese handcuffs." When you put a finger in each end of the tube and then tried to draw your fingers out, the tube would tighten. The more you pulled, which seemed the logical thing to do, the tighter it would grip. But when you understood why it gripped, you saw that pulling outward was not logical at all, but illogical. You needed to press inward so the fibers would relax; then you could draw your fingers out.

Just so, when we learn how our troubled emotions and attitudes have a stranglehold on us because we have misunderstood their grip on us, we will give up our futile strategies for escaping them. Our new understanding will have loosened that grip. Being honest with ourselves is the key.

But while we are stuck in troubled thoughts and feelings and need relief, the remedy we will learn about in this book will appear illogical—the way the secret of the Chinese handcuffs seems to those who haven't yet comprehended it. Reading the book can fix that problem. As it unfolds, chapter by chapter, our misunderstanding of our emotional troubles should decrease, and when it does, the remedy will make perfect sense.

To this prediction, I add a cautionary note. When the self-understanding comes—and we will recognize it—we will not have completed our work. On the contrary, we will have just begun. The good part is that, at that point, our frame of mind and our feelings will enable us to be taught by our experiences what we need to know for our next stages of growth—provided, of course, that we want to learn. I will address this subject toward the end of the book, after we accomplish its primary purpose, which is learning the truths about ourselves and others by which we can get ourselves unstuck.

CHAPTER 2

LIVING
A
LIE

How We Betray Ourselves

We are seeking to understand the source of our troubled, afflicted emotions and attitudes and the way they foul our relationships with others. Here is a clue: those times when we feel most miserable, offended, or angry are invariably the occasions when we're also most absorbed in ourselves and most anxious or suspicious or fearful, or in some other way concerned about ourselves. Why is this? Why do we get so caught up in ourselves and so ready to take offense at what others do?

Going Against Our Sense of Right and Wrong

To answer these questions, we first need to learn about something we all experience but seldom notice. I call it *self-betrayal.*

Often we have a sense that something is right or wrong for us to do—a sense, for example, that we should or shouldn't treat some person or other living thing in a certain way. We have only to pay attention in our everyday experiences to notice ourselves having such feelings about how we ought to act.

We might, for example, feel called upon to smile when someone smiles at us, choose words carefully so that someone can better understand what we're trying to say, help a child who's having trouble, keep from cutting across someone's new lawn, share what we're eating with someone else in the family, visit a person who's had a recent setback or who's simply lonely, or let another driver move into the flow of traffic. Those of us who live in an urbanized and impersonal world may have gotten out of the habit of acknowledging the needs and feelings of others in public settings. But even in such settings, we can often catch ourselves having a sense of what we ought to do, if we just pay attention.

Self-betrayal occurs when we go against the feelings I have just described—when we do to another what we sense we should not do, or don't do what we sense we should. Thus self-betrayal is a sort of moral self-compromise, a violation of our own personal sense of how we ought to be and what we ought to do. For example:

> Entering her workplace, a senior manager sees discouragement in the face of a groundskeeper and feels she ought to reach out briefly and express her appreciation and support. Instead she hurries on to do her business.

∾

> A busy man driving home late at night notices the gas gauge dropping near empty. Almost imperceptibly, yet unmistakably, he feels he ought to fill the tank for his wife so she won't have to do it the next day. But he doesn't.

∾

> Despite repeated scoldings and many warnings from her mother, a teenage girl has left her room in an awful mess. The exasperated mother feels impressed that instead of berating her daughter again she should welcome her cheerfully and listen to her concerns. But when the girl enters the house, the mother finds herself saying the same blistering words as always.

∾

> A teacher makes a Friday afternoon appointment to see a parent whose daughter has been struggling in school. But friends invite him to play tennis. A feeling that he ought to keep his commitment squeezes at him, just for an instant. But he ignores it and calls to cancel the appointment with the parent.

Our Living Connection with Others

From where does our sense of right and wrong come? In general, from other beings around us—other people and even animals (and, as I believe, God, though faith is an issue I will reserve for the Epilogue). For example, in the expressions on others' faces, the tone of their voices, and their posture and gestures, we find indications of their emotional needs and feelings, and this gives us a sense of how we ought to treat them. To recognize another individual as a person, even if we don't see a face or hear a voice, is to know that we should treat him or her differently from the way we would treat a mannequin or a statue. There's nothing mysterious about any of this; perceiving the cues or signals from others that guide us in how to treat them is basic to just about all we do in life. It is as commonplace, almost, as breathing.

Often we call our sense of right and wrong *conscience,* though that name doesn't capture the way it arises from our living connection with other beings (we will speak of this further in chapter 7). Think about the senior manager who discerned an opportunity or need to reach out to her fellow employee, or the man who, remembering his wife, imagined her having to fill the gas tank the next morning. It would not be exaggerating to say that, at the moment of sensing what was right to do, each of them was *alive to* another human being, aware of and sensitive to his or her inner life and feelings. (It would not make him or her less alive and aware if he or she happened to be wrong about what this other person needed on that particular occasion, just as it would not make me blind if I mistakenly thought the dog I saw was a cat.)

Our own humanity is intimately bound up with our capacity to sense something of others' needs and feelings. That is why I call the violation of that sense *self-betrayal.* We may or may not betray someone else when we do wrong by others, but we always betray the most sensitive and humane part of ourselves.

This living sense, in connection with others, of what is right or wrong for us to do is not necessarily binding upon other people, and in this it's unlike any moral rule. It may not even apply to us on other occasions.

The right and wrong we sense in our living connection with others differs from what we generally have in mind when we speak of right and wrong. The meaning we usually give these words is tied to certain rules of behavior we have learned, many in our childhood, and some through our social and professional associations as adults. Such rules express the behavior that members of the group expect of one another. Here are some examples: "Do not tell a lie." "Show up on time." "Don't talk with your mouth full." "Don't speak unless you're spoken to." "Speak kindly to others." And so on. In ordinary usage, *right* means conforming to such rules; *wrong* means violating them.

But such rules can be conformed to hypocritically, and this makes them different from the gentle guidance we receive when we look at, listen to, or think about others. For example, we can tell the truth to make ourselves look good, act politely to hide an evil intention, and even speak kindly to make another person squirm. (I did something very close to that when I responded to my son Matthew; see page 3.) That is because rules tell us what to do, not the reasons we should have for doing it. By contrast, our living sense of how we should respond to others requires something more, and that something more is wholeheartedness, consideration, and respect. It requires us not just to *act* honorably or kindly, but to *be* honorable or kind. Rules work like unwritten contracts, specifying the minimum we should do in regard to one another. But the personal obligations we feel to one another, soul to soul, call us to give of ourselves without reserve. Anything less, as we shall discover in this book, is self-betrayal. That is perhaps what the Baal-Shem, the founder of the Jewish religious movement known as Hasidism, meant when he said that sin is *anything you cannot do wholeheartedly.*

SELF-JUSTIFYING STORIES

The fact that self-betrayals are ordinary and commonplace might make them seem almost normal and, in the broad scheme of things, relatively harmless. But, in fact, they wreak devastation. We cannot betray ourselves without setting in motion all manner of emotional trouble. This is demonstrated by the experience of a businessman named Marty, in his early thirties, who told the following story:

> The other night about 2:00 A.M. I awoke to hear the baby crying. At that moment I had a fleeting feeling, a feeling that if I got up quickly I might be able to see what was wrong before Carolyn would be awakened. It was a feeling that this was something I really ought to do. But I didn't get up to check on the baby.

The matter did not end there. Marty didn't quickly forget about this small episode. He *couldn't* have simply forgotten about it. Here he was, a man expecting himself to get up, thinking that his wife would benefit from his doing so, and knowing in his heart that it was the right thing for him to do. And yet not doing it. He had to deal with this dishonorable situation somehow. But how? How could someone like Marty get away with not doing what he knew he should do?

The answer to this question is very important to understand. Somehow, Marty had to minimize the obligation he was placing upon himself, or in some other way make it seem right *not* to do what he felt summoned to do. He had to find some way to rationalize his self-betrayal.

Marty continued his story:

> It bugged me that Carolyn wasn't waking up. I kept think-
> ing it was her job to take care of the baby. She has her
> work and I have mine, and mine is hard. It starts early in
> the morning. She can sleep in. On top of that, I never
> know how to handle the baby anyway.
>
> I wondered if Carolyn was lying there waiting for me
> to get up. Why did I have to feel so guilty that I couldn't
> sleep? The only thing I wanted was to get to work fresh
> enough to do a good job. What was so selfish about that?

From the instant he decided not to get up, Marty began to make it seem as if what he was doing wasn't his fault. He reminded himself that he had to make a presentation the next morning—he couldn't afford to miss his sleep on that particular night. He noticed irritating or difficult elements of his circumstances, such as Carolyn's failure to wake up. Maybe she was only pretending to be asleep, he thought, waiting for him to get up and take care of the problem. Such matters hadn't even crossed his mind before the self-betrayal. But now he suddenly could think of nothing else. He remembered things he would otherwise have forgotten entirely, such as Carolyn's not having changed the baby just before putting her to bed.

So here was the mental situation he created for himself: Just seconds before, as he had awakened to his infant daughter's crying, he had focused on the baby's need and, if only fleetingly, on the possibility of saving Carolyn from the inconvenience of having to get up. *But now he focused on himself.* He became irascibly alert, collecting data as though he would be required to submit a depo-sition to the family court for his pretrial hearing on charges of spousal abuse and child neglect. One moment he was lying there pleasantly enough, and the next he was agitated, rationalizing his conduct and accusing his wife. Though in itself subtle and all but unnoticed, his self-betrayal quickly spawned a jumble of troublesome feelings. As my four-year-old daughter Emily said when asked to explain temptation: "You know what's right and you know what's wrong, and you get a fuss in your mind."

If the prompting to attend to the baby had not come to him, Marty would not have had any reason to engage in this kind of mental research. He would have had no need to collect facts with which to defend himself. It would not have occurred to him to assemble a story that would portray him as justified or excused in what he did. But once the prompting came and he failed to follow it, finding excuses for not getting up became his biggest concern and commanded all his attention. He wove these excuses into a story that, in his own mind, proved he was justified in not doing what he felt he ought to do. That story got him off the hook.

Marty's story is reminiscent of mine as I stood with Matthew in the bathroom and collected all the facts I could to justify myself in refusing to understand and sympathize with him. My story, too, grew out of a self-betrayal. I mentioned that the toilet in the basement bathroom had been broken for several days. I had felt I ought to attend to it immediately, but I didn't—that was how I betrayed myself. Predictably, between my initial self-betrayal and eventually getting around to trying to fix the toilet, I got caught up in all sorts of rationalization. Repairing it was just one more obligation on a list already longer than I could manage—a list I rehearsed more than a few times in my mind. Why couldn't someone else in the family step up to some of the maintenance tasks around the house? How could I be expected to master the complex mechanics of the toilet when I had my work, my family, and various community and church responsibilities to worry about? I was certain that anyone looking on, observing my depiction of myself struggling valiantly against all manner of adversity, would sympathize and take my side!

By our self-betrayals Marty and I each plunged ourselves into a desperate project of weaving a story by which we might justify ourselves. We needed to make the wrong we were doing seem right— or at least not our own fault—especially in our own eyes. Marty blamed Carolyn and his boss and the baby; I blamed Matthew and Susan and everyone else who had expectations of me. We both felt overwhelmed with responsibilities and fatigue. In the life-stories we were composing, the fault for our failure to do as we knew we should lay elsewhere, not with us. We insisted that we were doing all that we could reasonably be expected to do.

We All Understand about Living a Lie

I have discovered that everybody knows how this works. I once gave a talk at a training school for mentally challenged children. I decided to try to explain the idea of self-betrayal as simply as I could, together with the ways that we rationalize and blame other people. One boy of about twelve said aloud, "Oh, you mean living a lie." Yes, that was exactly what I meant.

When I tell a self-betrayal story to a group I am just beginning to teach, I may ask what they think might have gone through the self-betrayer's mind. Occasionally someone will say, "Guilt" (a subject I will speak of in chapter 6). But most of the time the answer I get is, "Rationalization." Then I will ask for examples of sentences that someone like Marty might actually say in his mind. Here are some samples of their responses:

"Carolyn's not having a difficult time in her job like I am."

"I can't handle the baby as well as she can."

"If I do this once it will set a bad precedent. I'll be expected to do it all the time."

"She's the one who wanted to have the kid in the first place."

The term *self-justification* seems just right for accurately describing such contorted efforts to make what's wrong seem right, or at least not our fault. *Justification* means trying to make something straight or to bring it into line—for example, we justify the text we are typing on the computer when we enter the command that straightens up one or more of its edges. When Marty tried to justify himself, he strove to make his crooked decision, which went against his conscience, seem straight. He worked at making the case that his decision to stay in bed lined up with what was right. Carnival fun houses sometimes sell glasses that make the world appear crooked. Self-justification, as we have seen, is like putting on glasses to make our crooked behavior appear straight.

"For the justification of sins," Leo Tolstoy wrote, "there exist false arguments, according to which there would appear to be exceptional circumstances, rendering the sins not only excusable, but even necessary. These false justifications may be called 'snares.'" They are lies that catch and trap us. We get caught in our own snares when we start presenting ourselves as if we are excused or justified in what we're doing when in reality we're not.

An expressive word for Marty's commitment to the lie he was living is "self-deception." "It is no doubt an evil to be full of faults," Blaise Pascal wrote in the seventeenth century, "but it is a still greater evil to be full of them and unwilling to recognize them, since this entails the further evil of . . . self-delusion."

BLAMING EMOTIONS AND ATTITUDES

The blaming that self-betrayers do as they shift responsibility for what's going wrong to someone else consists of more than rationalizing words. It includes feelings, like Marty's and mine, of irritation, humiliation, self-pity, resentment, or frustration. Marty, for example, justified himself not only by thinking certain thoughts like "It's her turn" and "It's not fair." His self-justification required him also to adopt and indulge in negative emotions like those I've mentioned. Without such emotions he could not have convinced himself that he was being taken advantage of. His rationalization would have been no more believable to him than an actor performing *Hamlet* with the passion of a newscaster. We lie with our emotions and attitudes (and often even with our moods) as well as with our words.

The many kinds of emotions and attitudes with which we can do this are too numerous to itemize completely. But I include a partial list below.

Anger	Touchiness	Hesitancy to take initiative
Self-pity	Arrogance	
Crustiness	Boredom	Resentment
Suspicion	Discouragement	Contempt
Fear	Despondency	Indifference ("That person is not worth wasting my time on.")
Impatience	Humiliation	
Bitterness	Envy	

You will notice that these emotions and attitudes have in common some element of accusation. In addition, the list contains no attitudes or emotions that unite us with other people, but only ones that divide us from them. It includes no reference to love, delight, generosity, consideration, sympathy, or kindness. Nor does it refer to such empathetic and caring emotions and attitudes as grieving and sorrow, which are forms of emotional pain that contain no accusation.

Who Causes Such Emotions and Attitudes?

We have seen that when as self-betrayers we develop a self-justifying story, we don't merely *tell* ourselves a lie. We *live* the lie. We get completely caught up in the lie, emotions and all.

We can see this happening in the following exchange between a father and his daughter:

Louisa: Daddy, I can't figure this math problem out.

Howard [*her father, watching* Monday Night Football *and feeling that he should help Louisa*]: Sure you can. You've just got to struggle with it.

Louisa: But I've tried, and I'm getting nowhere. If you could . . . [*Louisa begins to cry, her head on her book.*]

Howard [*his eyes still fixed on the screen*]: You're trying to take the easy way. They wouldn't give you the problem if they hadn't taught you all you have to know to solve it. [*His voice rises as he turns to look at Louisa.*] Why do you wait until I'm right in the middle of watching my game? In fact, you should be in bed, young lady. Why did you leave your homework till the last minute, anyway?

Louisa: I didn't think it would take me very long . . .

Howard: Well, ask your sister upstairs. She had the same math last year. She knows it better than I do.

Louisa: But I've just got one question.

Howard [*his anger blossoming*]: Louisa, I'm tired of you trying to get me to do your work for you. Now, I've told you what you need to do to get it done and you're just avoiding doing it.

Louisa [*pouting*]: When Danny asks for help, you help him.

Howard: Oh, boy! Look, if you would do what you are

supposed to do, I would be glad to help you. There is a difference between helping Danny after he's struggled with something and helping you when you haven't made any effort on your own. You just want me to do your work for you.

Starting with Howard's self-betrayal, we can track the development of the lie he lived, beginning with his trying to brush Louisa off and ending with his full-blown anger.

Louisa didn't cause that anger, as Howard believed. It was his own doing. Nevertheless—and this is the crucial point—he *was* angry, genuinely angry. He wasn't merely pretending; he actually felt his anger well up in him. That's what made the lie so convincing—because his angry feelings were real, he was sure the person toward whom they were directed was causing them. But she didn't cause them. He did.

When we betray ourselves and shift responsibility onto others by means of our accusing thoughts and feelings, we, like Howard, believe it is *their* mistreatment of *us* that leads us to accuse them. This is the self-betrayer's lie. The truth—the profound, almost world-shaking truth—is that we accuse them because of *our* mistreatment of *them*. Seldom has this profound insight been more arrestingly expressed than by King Solomon: "A lying tongue hateth those that are afflicted by it" (Proverbs 26:28).

Fable
Our accusing, self-excusing feelings such as anger, frustration, bitterness, self-pity, and so on, are signals that we are in the right.

Fact
Such feelings are signals that we are in the wrong.

To a person who has accusing thoughts and feelings, the things I have been saying will seem unbelievable. "What if the accusing feelings are how I *really feel*? I'm not just pretending to have them. How can you say they are lies?"

As Howard's story shows, self-betrayers truly do have their accusing, self-excusing feelings. *But this does not mean that the feelings themselves are truthful.* We can take up a false position with our emotions and attitudes just as well as with our words. In my episode with Matthew, I claimed by means of my upset feelings to be suffering wrong rather than doing it. Feeling offended was my way of saying, "Look how you are hurting me!" My feelings were real but not truthful. Matthew wasn't making me suffer. My upset feelings were being caused by no one but myself.

Fable

When we're stuck in troubled feelings, we believe that all our feelings are true—that is to say, we believe that by our emotions at that moment we are making accurate judgments about what's happening. If I'm angry with you, I'm certain that you are making me angry.

Fact

Though we truly have these feelings, they are not necessarily true feelings. More likely I'm angry because I'm misusing you, not because you are misusing me.

Like Living in a Box

In his experience with Louisa, Howard created or projected an illusion around himself—an illusion that he was living with a daughter who had the power to make him irritable and impatient.

He projected this illusion by means of his accusing feelings. You might compare his projection of this illusion to the projection of the image of a sunset onto a screen. The projection is real; the sunset image is real; the screen is real—but the sunset is not. Similarly, Howard's feelings and the way he portrayed Louisa by means of these feelings were real, and Louisa too was real—*but a little girl who could make her father angry was not real.* The screen wasn't a sunset, and Louisa wasn't a person with the power to make Howard angry.

It takes a projection that is being cast by the right kind of equipment to create the illusion of a sunset on a screen, and it takes real feelings to create an illusion that others have power to offend and anger us.

Projecting such interpretations upon everything around us is in many ways like living in a box of our own making. The walls of the box surrounding us are like that sunset backdrop—they are the negative interpretation we project onto others. You might think of these walls as a falsification of reality—a distorted way of seeing, feeling, and thinking about other people that makes them seem offensive or malicious or otherwise untrustworthy. Remember, the people are really there, but we wall ourselves off from the truth about them by the false way we picture them.

I readily acknowledge that it seems preposterous, when we're beset by a troubled emotion, to say that our circumstances do not cause us to feel as we do. Think of Mandy, remembering years of resentment toward her father and certain she was neglected by him. Or of Norm, overwhelmed by the laziness and stupidity of the people on whom he relied. Surely, he would have said, he wasn't just imagining the pain his financial losses caused him.

Living in the box means being convinced that other people and our circumstances are responsible for our feelings and our helplessness to overcome them. What we can't see when we're in the box is that the way the world appears to us is our projection, and that we

FIGURE 1

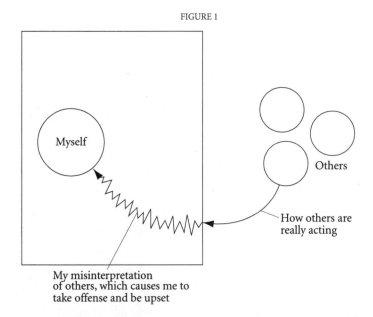

are making this projection to justify ourselves in self-betrayal. We cannot see that it's not others' actions but our accusations that result in our feeling offended.

◆

BUT HOW *COULD* I BE LYING TO MYSELF?

The idea that we deceive ourselves about our wrongdoing seems to go against our experience. After all, we're generally not aware of having gone through a process of first refusing to do the right thing and then of cooking up an excuse to get ourselves off the hook. So how can it be said that we are lying to ourselves?

It is true that we have no awareness of going through such a process. That's because we *don't* go through a process. We do not say to ourselves, on *any* level (even an "unconscious" one): "I'm going to hide from myself the fact that I'm doing wrong. I'm going to convince myself I'm actually doing the best I can."

But if we don't go through this sort of process, how do we manage to deceive ourselves about what we're doing?

The answer is this: The violation of our sense of what is right, the accusation of others, and the distortion of reality—all these are aspects of one and the same self-betraying act. They occur together, rather than in sequence. Seeing others accusingly and distortedly is *how* the act of self-betrayal is accomplished; it can't be done in any other way. We don't first notice our self-betrayal and then, in order to cover it up, try to find someone to blame and summon up an emotion with which to blame them. In its very first moment, self-betrayal brings with it the accusing feelings and the distortion of reality.

Perhaps an analogy will help. What happens in self-betrayal resembles the physiology of speech. When I talk, I bring my nervous system, vocal muscles, tongue, and lips into play in a technically skillful manner, but I do not intentionally try to make them work as they do. I don't even need to have any knowledge or awareness of these organs in order to use them to talk. What I *try* to do is speak, and my mobilization of the relevant organs is part of the way I manage to do it. Speaking and making these organs work as they do are two aspects of *a single act*—the act of speaking. The same is true of self-betrayal: *betraying oneself and blaming others are two aspects of a single act.* That's why we don't catch ourselves carrying out a process of lying to ourselves—there isn't any such process.

But What If My Accusation Is Correct?

Another puzzling feature of self-betrayal is the idea that justifying ourselves by accusing others of mistreating us must always be a lie. What if we really are being mistreated? Aren't we then telling the truth?

Recall my son Matthew yelling at me in the bathroom. I felt sure I was not making this up. As far as I was concerned, it was a fact. How could I have been lying if I was only blaming him for what he was actually doing?

Even if all I said about Matthew's behavior was true (and I can't be sure of that because self-betrayers don't see things clearly), there is still one thing that isn't true. It isn't true that he caused me to be upset. What facts I cited to myself, what truths I told, were only to justify myself in treating Matthew wrongly. In one of Dostoyevsky's novels, *The Devils,* a character named Stavrogin expresses the point I am making by saying, "All my life I have been lying. Even when I told the truth. For I never told the truth for its own sake, but only for my sake."

We can get the facts right and be wrong in contending that these facts excuse or justify us.

And What If I Can't Remember Betraying Myself?

Like me remembering my hurt feelings in the bathroom with Matthew, we can often trace an accusing emotion or attitude to some specific self-betrayal. But for many of our accusing emotions or attitudes we can identify no corresponding self-betrayal. Does this mean that in those cases they *weren't* caused by self-betrayal? Does it leave open the possibility that sometimes people *do* offend, discourage, distress, infuriate, or anger us after all? How else are such symptoms to be explained, if we can find no self-betrayal that caused them?

Imagine that you've betrayed yourself at work, treating another person harshly and mentally building a case all day to support what you've done. You come home upset. When you see your family members or roommates, you are *already* in an accusing, self-excusing frame of mind. They expect you to interact with them civilly, perhaps help with dinner, and support their plans for the evening; but given your emotional state, these expectations seem about as inconsiderate as they can be. Can't they see you've got troubles of your own? Can't they think of anyone but themselves?

In this situation you are learning of others' hopes and needs, and you are refusing to respect and honor them. That's self-betrayal. But it doesn't *seem* to you like self-betrayal because, in your accusing eyes, their perfectly reasonable expectations look like very unreasonable demands, made by extremely insensitive people. That's why you don't feel you're doing anything wrong when you refuse; what you do does not feel like self-betrayal. Why should you go out of your way for people who are so inconsiderate of your feelings? To you, this is just one more of those times when the people around you have asked more of you than they have a right to ask, and you have had to put your foot down.

When we're in a state of self-betrayal already, we so distort our sense of what we ought to do that we are led to further self-betrayals that in our minds are already pre-explained. That's why, when we look back over our experiences, we can often see the telltale signs of self-betrayal—the offended feelings, the resentment, envy, self-pity, or anger—without being able to recall any associated self-betrayal. The reason is, we didn't think of it as self-betrayal at the time; we were already self-deceived.

ᐭ

WHO WE ARE

Our *undistorted* sense of right and wrong calls us to do right toward others, to act as love dictates. Most fundamentally, we are beings bonded to one another by love. In self-betrayal we violate these bonds, deceive ourselves about who we really are, harden ourselves to what we feel is right, and live a lie. Our living connection with others calls us to let go of this lie and be who we really are.

Our sense of how we ought to treat others that comes to us via this living connection reveals what really matters most to us. It is not something we merely wish or desire. Believing it is part of our being. That is the reason why, when we betray ourselves, we violate ourselves so deeply.

It is also the reason why, when we act with integrity, according to what we genuinely feel is right, we have nothing to cover up. Since what we are doing is right in our own eyes, we don't have to spend any effort trying to make it *seem* right. We can pour our energies into what needs to be done without worrying about appearances or excuses. We need to concoct no self-justifying story, which is the telltale sign of self-betrayal, because we have no use for it.

Suppose Marty had gotten up to see what was wrong with the baby instead of staying in bed. Imagine him tiptoeing to the crib, covering the baby with a blanket, and softly singing the baby back to sleep. Would he have needed to produce a rationalizing story for what he was doing? Would he have been concerned about justifying himself? Not at all. Only people who are doing something that goes against their own sense of right and wrong have to spend time and energy spinning out a self-justifying story.

This book explores, among other things, the devastation of character and personality that self-betrayal brings. In the effort to make our wrongdoing seem right, we struggle to portray ourselves in our ongoing personal story as worthy of approval and respect. The very fact that we need to struggle for approval proves that we do not approve of ourselves. Having to convince ourselves of something means we do not really believe it. That is why we contort ourselves grotesquely, lose sight of who we really are, and tangle ourselves pathetically in a complicated falsification of our lives. Wang Yang-Ming, a Chinese teacher of wisdom, wrote: "The inferior man . . . attempts a hundred intrigues in order to save himself, but finishes only in creating a greater calamity from which he cannot run away." The self-betrayer could scarcely be better described.

We need now to study the ways in which self-betrayal defiles our sensitivity to others, inhibiting our capacity for love and joy in the process. It leaves us absorbed in ourselves and accusing, resentful, hardened, fearful, and perhaps even embittered toward others.

CHAPTER 3

THE SELF-ABSORBED WAY OF BEING

Two Ways to Be

When we betray ourselves, we undergo a transformation. By seeing others suspiciously, accusingly, or fearfully, we *become* suspicious, accusing, or fearful ourselves. By no longer seeing them with care, delight, and generosity, we ourselves *cease to be* caring, delighted, and generous. *The kind of people we are cannot be separated from how we interpret the world around us.* "Adam is Adam's world," wrote the philosopher Gottfried Wilhelm Leibniz. *Who we are is how we are in relation to others.*

I must have been about ten years old when I first caught hold of the thought that my character—the kind of person I was—might have something to do with how I thought about others. My family was living near San Francisco. My parents and another couple had gone out for the evening, and I was left in the other couple's apartment to sit up with their sleeping baby (which nowadays would be illegal, but it wasn't then). I took a book from the shelf and read. One of the sentences I encountered there made such an impression on me that I still can recall the book's color and heft, the names of its authors, Harry and Bonaro Overstreet (though I do not remember the name of the book itself), and the feeling I had as I read from it. The sentence seemed to stand out from the page about three-quarters of an inch and to be lit from behind. I was sure it had been written just for me. It said: "To the immature, other people are not real."

Those eight words pierced me. I knew that, aside from my mother, other people were not especially real for me. Their feelings and desires did not matter to me as much as my own; a lot of the time they didn't matter to me at all. Yet I was sensitive enough to be disturbed by my insensitivity. At that moment, it seemed to me supremely important to be a person who cared about people.

Each of us chooses whether or not to be an individual for whom others are real. As I indicated in the preceding chapter, we don't make this choice deliberately, in the same way we decide which color of sweater to buy. Rather, the choice is made subtly, in a process that cannot be distinguished from life itself, the process of responding or refusing to respond to others as we feel we should. *For to the extent that we act toward others as we feel we might, we open ourselves to their inner reality, and their needs and aspirations seem as important to us as our own.* We hope their hopes will be fulfilled and need to see their needs satisfied. Their happiness makes us happy, and we are pained to see them hurt. We resonate with them and delight in their prosperity. Few of us consistently live this way, it is true, but far fewer never live this way at all. At least some of the time most people have a resonant relationship with a child, a mate, or a beloved sibling or friend. Living resonantly is not limited to the most saintly among us.

Still, some embody this ideal to a remarkable and memorable degree. When our family moved to England for a year, a couple we scarcely knew, Julie and Joseph, found us a house to rent, picked us up at the airport, got us situated in the village, and befriended and encouraged our children. It was clear that they never considered any of this a sacrifice; everything they did for us they did joyfully. And even though they were busy with their own lives, they treated everyone else this way, too. If you have had the sort of feelings we enjoyed in their presence, you understand why, each time we prepared to leave them, we did so reluctantly. When we returned from England, our boys wanted to find a woman like Julie when they grew up and our girls a man like Joseph. Anyone who has never known such people is still basically unacquainted with humanity.

By contrast, to the extent that others are not real to us, we are guarded, alienated, and hardened. These words describe a more brutish way of being. They suggest something of the way we grow numb and anxious when we betray ourselves, as if darkness were descending and the landscape were becoming desolate, foreboding, and cold. We get wrapped up in ourselves, worried about gathering evidence of our worth, such as the company we keep or the possessions we have accumulated or the public image we have managed to project. We cannot spare ourselves to care very much about others' hopes and fears and feelings because of our intense preoccupation with our own.

When we live in this guarded way of being, we attend to others only when they can help us get what we want or when they stand in our way. This goes not only for the cashier at the store, the teller at the bank, and the neighbor next door, but also for the son or daughter we want to behave well in public and the spouse we wish would hurry up. While others are talking, we are thinking about what we want to say next or about what we have to do today. We see everything and everyone in terms of how they fit into our program, our agenda for ourselves. We have become absorbed in ourselves and commensurately suspicious, mistrustful, or fearful of others.

To live in the first, open, generous, resonant way is to live *for others*; in the second, accusing, self-absorbed, alienated way, *for ourselves*. There are no other possibilities. In a famous book published in 1923 entitled *I and Thou*, Martin Buber tries to express this important truth by inventing a special vocabulary. He applies the name *I-It* to the self-absorbed, guarded way of being into which, I have suggested, self-betrayers plunge themselves. By this term he suggests that when we live in this mode, we regard others as if they are objects existing primarily for our use. In contrast is the sensitive and responsive way of being, which he calls *I-You*, or *I-Thou*, signifying how we are when we regard others as having their own inward lives and when we respect their hopes and needs as we do our own.

Self-absorption diminishes our capacity to give ourselves with abandon to other people, to our work, to play, to God, and to the beauty of nature. One evening when I was nineteen, I was walking along upper Broadway in Manhattan with Suzanne Miller, talking and looking in store windows. I had met Suzanne in one of Stella Adler's acting classes at Stella's studio, which at that time was located on Central Park West. Suzanne had a fierce integrity and a vigilance against humbug in herself that impressed me from the first moments I knew her. These qualities had already exercised a strong influence upon me. Nevertheless, she caught me completely by surprise that night by asking me: "Do you love yourself in the theater or the theater in yourself?"

The question stopped me in midstep. I knew I couldn't answer it the way I wanted to be able to answer it. I didn't have to search my memory to discover that I couldn't; I knew it immediately— or possibly I should say, I knew it *already,* even before she asked. Indeed, I knew that this had been the question for me all my life, though I had refused to acknowledge it before. It wasn't a question about the theater only, but about my motivations for everything I had ever done. Did I love what I was doing, or did I love myself in doing it?

In that moment a choice lay clearly before me. I could spend my life assembling, feeding, and protecting the egotistical, ravenous, and addictive fiction I called my *self*—or I could refuse it every sort of nurture and let it die an unregretted death. I knew that unless I somehow could leave off my project of promoting and protecting myself and instead open myself to life, I would be doomed to a lifetime of self-involvement. I could see that self-absorption is poison to the spirit.

❧

BONDED, ONE WAY OR THE OTHER

When we actively relate to people as rivals or enemies, we foster the false belief that we and they stand independent of one another. The truth is that we bind ourselves to them as if by an invisible tether, and we do so by our negative thoughts and feelings.

Years ago, before it became fashionable for young people to dress in torn and faded clothes, a freshman student showed up at an honors program social at our university wearing dirty jeans and a logger's shirt. She stretched herself conspicuously on a couch and read James Joyce's formidable novel *Ulysses*. A "true intellectual," she thought herself above our frivolous socializing. But to make the point she had to come where we had all gathered; she needed us in order to show that she didn't need us. Like concern for others, self-concern is a way of relating to people.

I have already alluded to the manipulative quality of the I-It connection with others. We see them in terms of our own self-centered agenda; as far as we are concerned, they exist for our use. In relation to our quest to get what we want, they become (1) obstacles standing in the way, (2) vehicles able to help us, or (3) simply irrelevant. If we see them as obstacles in our way, we will tend to react to them in frustration and feel angry, resentful, irritated, or fearful toward them. If we see them as vehicles helpful for accomplishing our purposes, we will ingratiate ourselves with them and indulge them manipulatively—or punish them if they let us down. If we consider them irrelevant to getting what we want, we will treat them arrogantly, find them boring, or scarcely notice them at all. One way or the other, we become bullies, manipulators, sycophants, or snobs.

When we stand in relation to others or nature or God as an I to a You, the You is vibrantly real to us; we give ourselves to such a relationship with our whole being. But when we stand to others or nature or God as an I to an It, the It is an object in our eyes, a mere *he* or *she*—not a being whose own inner life is important to us. In this kind of relationship we cannot give ourselves completely. When others are Its to us, we ourselves are different from who we are when others are Yous for us. We are different depending on how we address, understand, appreciate, and respond to them. We cannot think of them as objects without becoming I-It, or as real persons without being I-You. We cannot find them irritating without becoming irritated persons ourselves, nor can we find them worthwhile without becoming appreciative persons ourselves. Who we are is who we are with others. How they seem to us is a revelation of ourselves.

Buber captures this idea with the hyphen inserted in each of the terms *I-It* and *I-You*. The hyphen in *I-It* makes this term a single word, to show that whenever this word applies, the *I* is not separate from regarding others as Its. So too for the hyphen in *I-You*; intrinsic to the *I* in this word is its way of perceiving others as Yous. Making each of these terms a single word signifies that the self cannot be pried apart from how he or she sees and feels about others. Personal identity and personal relationships are the same thing seen from two different angles. Buber's neat lexical invention helps us express and remember this important truth.

Here we discover something significant about the kind of profound personal transformation we are seeking to understand. *To the extent that we can come to see others differently, we can undergo a fundamental change, a change in our being, a change of our emotions and attitudes, a change of heart.*

SLIPPING AWAY

It is possible to observe a person slipping into the hardened, self-absorbed way of being. The process is apparent in the following story, told by a young teacher in the South named Jennifer.

> When my widowed aunt was in the hospital for major surgery I thought I ought to visit her. She needed some company, and I guess I was one of the few people who was likely to come around.
>
> But I didn't go. I was going to go this one night, but there was something good on TV, and I decided I'd only watch a little of it and then go. When I was watching I started thinking about how hard it would be to talk to her. I'm young and she's old, and it was pretty obvious I wouldn't be able to think of much to say.
>
> Another time I was going to go and I realized when I was thinking about it that it wasn't really my fault that I couldn't think of anything to say. She was just plain hard to talk to. She never spent a lot of time talking to me when I was growing up, and that's the reason we don't have much of a relationship. Besides, I knew she didn't think too highly of getting a college degree, which was what I was doing.
>
> So why should I feel guilty that I didn't visit her? I'm just as alone as she is, with my folks in the service and all. I figured it would be best if she went her way and I went mine. I guess we don't take to each other much.

Trace with me the germination and growth of Jennifer's accusing emotions—and her transformation into a somewhat different, I-It kind of person. The first pivotal moment came when she decided to watch "only a little" of that television show. A second one occurred when she failed to jump from the couch, grab her jacket, and head out the door. These were self-betrayals. They got her noticing defects in her aunt and other reasons that would explain why she was not getting up and going to visit her.

One of these reasons was that Jennifer and her aunt didn't know one another very well. Another reason was that her aunt had never reached out to her and made her feel welcome. "I started thinking how hard it would be to talk to her." It is clear from the tone of Jennifer's story that this thought brought with it an irritated, somewhat offended feeling: How else can a person respond when a relative treats her insensitively? The more Jennifer reflected on her history with this aunt, the more fussed she became.

Thus, by her efforts to defend her self-betrayal in her own mind, Jennifer blunted her sensitivity to her aunt—almost as if she had replaced what she knew of her aunt with a fictional picture that excused her own unwillingness to care.

We need to remind ourselves that Jennifer's urgent, self-absorbed need to justify what she was doing sprang into being when she betrayed her sense of what was right to do in regard to her aunt. By this act, she transformed her attitude and thus herself. That is an astounding thing to contemplate.

We might be tempted to take this fact as a reason for discouragement, supposing that a moral slip can plunge us irretrievably into darkness. But in actuality it is a source of hope. It means that by desisting from self-betrayal we can cease having any need to justify ourselves. We can escape our self-absorption. We can release ourselves from the *I-It* condition.

Many will recognize that *self-betrayal*, which is my term for the pivotal act by which we indirectly choose our way of being, captures what was once in more traditional terms meant by the word *sin*. For those who understand its meaning—and many in our culture do not—*sin* suggests something about our being, whereas the more superficial description that I have been using, "doing the wrong thing," does not. Because this act of sin or self-betrayal, properly understood, alters how we are, we do not simply *act* falsely when we betray ourselves or sin; we *are* false, false in our *being*.

This may explain in part why few people nowadays speak of sin: it lays responsibility for the kind of people we are becoming squarely upon ourselves and therefore challenges us, without tact or subtlety, to examine ourselves. This idea can be frightening when not adequately understood. Who wants to face up to the fact that they have themselves to thank for their present muddles and messes? Yet this idea is a key for solving the deepest and most difficult problems that we struggle with from day to day. If we care about one another, we must understand and teach it.

So as not to put people off unnecessarily, I have adopted the term *self-betrayal* to express in an acceptable way something of the meaning of the word *sin*. But ultimately the truth needs to be told. Everything depends upon what we are becoming, and what we are becoming depends upon how true we are to the deep, gentle, and irrepressible invitation to do right by our fellow beings and before God.

༄

WE ALL KNOW THE DIFFERENCE

When I read that line in the Overstreets' book—"To the immature, other people are not real"—the words smote me so swiftly and deftly that I felt sure I was being reminded of something I knew already. It had the ring of a truth I had been trying to remember, even at that tender age, a truth I was ashamed to have forgotten.

I have come to believe that every normal person has this knowledge, for the simple reason that our relationships with others cannot be separated from our identity as individuals. Though some of us may not have given any thought to it or been willing to admit it, we all have a sense of the two ways of being and the differences between them.

Sometimes when I teach these ideas I start out by explaining just a bit about the two ways of being and then ask those present to call out the words they might use to describe people who are either more *I-It* or more *I-You*. This is a sample list offered by one group:

I-It	I-You
worried about self	interested in others
scarcity-minded	abundance-minded
resents others' success	delights in others' success
insecure	secure, peaceful
sees others as rivals	sees others as friends
controlling	trusting
manipulative	sincere
concerned with quantity	concerned with quality
selfish	sharing
lonely	supportive
reactive	solicitous
guarded	open
anxious	assured
suspicious	trusting
fearful	serene
rigid	flexible
self-centered	other-centered
defensive	accommodating

Most people will enthusiastically acknowledge their own desire to possess the *I-You* qualities; whether they have thought of themselves as being moral or religious does not seem to matter. Moreover, when I ask individuals to tell me about the most influential person in their lives, they invariably choose someone generous and kind. These are the personal characteristics we most appreciate and prize in others, whether or not we manifest them ourselves.

Sometimes very crusty, old-line businesspeople weep when they realize how difficult they have been to live with. One of these, hardened from a career in the New York financial markets, said at the end of our time together, "I'm going to try softer."

But those are examples of people who changed their minds. There are some who, when they consider the issue intellectually, deny that it's good to be I-You. However, even they infinitely prefer those with I-You qualities, in spite of their unwillingness to admit it. Years ago we had as houseguests a prominent scholar and his youthful second wife. His marriage to her, about a year earlier, had rejuvenated him; even before their stay with us he had described her reverently as warm, sensitive, selfless, caring, spontaneous, genuine, and happy. When we met her, Susan and I felt we had seldom encountered a more open and welcoming individual.

The scholar had just read a paper I had written entitled "Anger and Similar Delusions," in which I asserted that negative emotions such as anger, resentment, envy, and hatred are not necessary—that we can live without them and that by indulging in them we deceive ourselves. He objected vigorously to these ideas. To take away these emotions, he contended, would be to strip us of the most vivid and interesting colors of our personalities. He did not see the contradiction in his position. The bright being sitting next to him was, by his own account, richer in humanity than anyone he had ever known, yet she possessed none of the emotional tendencies he insisted a richly human person must have.

We all know the difference between a person acting sensitively and a person hardened toward others. We all know when a person is open, welcoming, spontaneous, easy, and caring, and conversely when a person is defensive, insecure, conceited, fearful, controlling, manipulative, arrogant, or self-centered. Whether we ourselves are open to others or hardened, we recognize these characteristics. But when we are hardened, we cannot think very clearly about what we know.

What Makes Life Hard to Bear

The above list of I-It qualities illustrates the self-destructive character of the self-absorbed way of being. When we are caught up in it, we accuse others so as to excuse ourselves, and that makes it a *judgmental* way of being. We grasp at evidence that others are wrong and we are right, and that makes it a *comparative* way of being. We're certain that if they get what they want, we can't have what we want, so it is an *assertive* and *competitive* way of being. And we believe we suffer our setbacks and failures because of other people and achieve our successes in spite of them, making it also a *combative* and *controlling* way of being.

The qualities I just named—*judgmental, comparative, assertive, competitive, combative,* and *controlling*—were among those my scholar friend claimed he would have been proud to have. But notice, again from the list, the qualities inseparably connected to those qualities that no one considers desirable, such as *lonely, insecure, anxious,* and *fearful.* On the underside of all arrogant, self-promoting, and manipulative characteristics we will always find a deep lack of confidence that amounts to fear. If we pay attention only to the bravado surface of these characteristics we can think them to be less self-destructive than they are.

This, then, is the devastating effect of self-betrayal:

> To take up a hard, resentful attitude toward others is to have to live in a resented world, a world full of people who oppose and threaten us. How they are in our eyes is reflective of how *we* are.

> The punishment for self-betrayal is having to live, in this resented world, a life that's far more difficult than it needs to be.

By this I do not suggest that life is or should be easy. Life is often hard, sometimes very hard, for just about everybody. Indeed, for many it is fraught with affliction. But anyone who has witnessed freedom from self-pity among the sorely deprived people of the earth knows that life's being hard does not make it hard to bear.

For some years my wife, Susan, traveled throughout the world for an organization devoted to the welfare of children. She invariably came home deeply affected by her visits in the humble homes of the profoundly poor—in Africa, the Pacific Rim, Polynesia, South America, and Europe, including the Eastern European countries that emerged from the breakup of the Soviet Union. Many families she met were unable to acquire anything beyond what they needed to survive, and sometimes not even that. Yet they were invariably gracious, cheerful, solicitous, optimistic, thankful for all they had—which means free of envy—and devoted to one another. She went to minister to them and found them ministering to her. She went to teach and was transformed by what she learned.

Happiness, as Susan's international friends demonstrated by the dignity with which they carried themselves through their constant trials, is more like a decision than a condition. It is a decision anyone can make, anywhere, and at any time. For it is not the enjoyableness of objects or activities or opportunities that makes us happy or unhappy; rather, our happiness, rooted in our relationships, makes objects and activities enjoyable. Things, events, and opportunities have no value in and of themselves; they get their value from the significant part they play in our key relationships with others.

Thus life's being hard does not force us to adopt a resentful attitude. Life becomes hard to bear only when we, as self-betrayers, cast ourselves in a victim's role by regarding others as our victimizers and nurse our misfortunes as if they were badges of honor. I think of self-betrayal as a form of subtle self-destruction because it obliterates the open and generous individuals we can and ought to be—and all for this paltry mess of pottage, the unsteady and impermanent feeling of justification in wrongdoing.

∽

WHICH PART OF ME WILL DIE?

As we contemplate the I-It and I-You lists, we notice that the differences between the characteristics on the two lists are more than outward, behavioral manifestations. These differences are inward and deep—matters of the condition of the heart. We change in fundamental ways in our passage from I-It to I-You.

And indeed this is the only kind of change that can get us "unstuck" from our anguished attitudes and emotions. When we betray ourselves, we set in motion a transformation toward the self-absorbed and alienated way of being. If we could not reverse the effects of that transformation, self-betrayal would be the greatest of all disasters.

One day some years ago, Keith, the creative director of a major advertising agency, phoned me for advice. The team he headed had been responsible for an eminently successful advertising campaign for a client I'll call X Company. As a result of Keith's success, he had received an offer from an even larger and more prestigious advertising agency to become *its* creative director—to take one of the most coveted creative positions in one of the most successful organizations in his business. He told officials at X Company of his intention to switch firms and they said, "We'll switch with you"—meaning they would shift their business to the new agency that had offered Keith the job.

Disaster. Keith's present agency had unwisely become so dependent upon the X Company account that losing it would mean the agency would have to close some of its offices. Keith's friends and advisers insisted that he jump at this once-in-a-lifetime employment opportunity. But then he began to think about the many people an office closure would throw out of work, people he knew, people in the mail room, on the production teams and custodial crews, and so on, some of them struggling, some without any good employment options. What should he do?

I would not have advised him in such a personal decision even if I had been confident in my opinion. But I could respond to the tone of his voice. It evoked an image in my mind, which I described to him. In this image, an expensive book of photographs lay open on a table. The full-page picture on the right was of Keith surrounded by many admirers—he was the focal point; the picture was about him. The picture on the left, in which he did not appear at all, showed only the people he had been concerned about.

After I described the two photographs I waited through a long pause. Finally Keith said, "That's the most important thing anyone has said to me."

Then came another pause, even longer. "But it is such agony," he said.

"Perhaps a few lines from T. S. Eliot's *Four Quartets* might help," I responded. (In line 2, the word *pyre* means a pile of wood for burning someone or something.)

> The only hope, or else despair,
> Lies in the choice of pyre or pyre—. . .
> We only live, only suspire
> Consumed by either fire or fire.

"Keith," I said, "whichever choice you make, a part of you is going to die. The only question is, Which part?"

He did not take the job.

CHAPTER 4

MAKING VICTIMS OF OURSELVES

THE CORE OF ALL EXCUSES

Carol hated Saturdays because her husband yelled at the children when he supervised their household chores. She said this ruined her hopes for a day of cooperative work and loving play. When he would begin to yell she would roll her eyes and say under her breath (or sometimes a little louder than that), "Here we go again!" or "He's ruining everything just like every Saturday." As a victim of this domestic autocrat, she would often cry.

Then she came to a realization that astonished her. In a flash of understanding (not unlike mine when I realized what I had been doing to my son) she saw that the Saturday morning problems were not entirely her husband's fault.

> I told myself I was trying with all my might to make sure we had a good time together, but in reality I was looking hard for evidence that he was making it impossible. That's what surprised me so much. What was most on my mind was, "How can I be a good mother when the father acts like this?" Ironically, I could tell that my criticism not only hurt him but seemed to make him even more agitated and impatient. My criticism was contributing to the problem!

Carol's story shows clearly how three aspects of the self-betrayer's conduct always go together:

accusing others,

excusing oneself, and

displaying oneself as a victim.

We can't seek vigilantly for evidence that others are mistreating us, as self-betrayers do, unless we actively put ourselves in the victim's role. Our sense of suffering, or at least of being inconvenienced, clearly proves—at least in our own mind—that our accusation of them is justified. Furthermore, it is precisely by taking this victim role that we are able to excuse ourselves for not being more considerate. It makes no sense, we tell ourselves, to think we could respond more generously when we're being mistreated so!

The following chart illustrates the perfect correlation between various commonplace accusations that self-betrayers make and the resulting sense they have of being victimized.

Accusing Judgment	Sense of Being Victimized
"It's your fault."	"I'm suffering because of you."
"You're not being fair."	"I'm getting cheated."
	(Or, "Someone's being cheated and I'm offended by that.")
"Our suppliers are unreliable."	"We were prevented from meeting our production quotas."
"The instructions weren't clear."	"You made me foul up the job."
"You insisted on having this kid."	"Now my whole career's going to pot."

Fabricating Victimhood

Carol accused her husband and excused herself by thinking of herself as his victim and acting the part of the victim. This raises an issue that needs to be cleared up before we go any further.

There is a very big difference between <u>portraying</u> oneself as a victim the way Carol did and actually <u>being</u> a victim. To the extent that we are actually being victimized, we bear no responsibility for the bad things that are happening to us, such as being mugged on the street or falling ill or being discriminated against because of our gender, race, or religion. But we *are* responsible when we *present ourselves* as victims in order to excuse or justify ourselves. There are indeed real victims, but acting and feeling victimized does not make a person a real victim.

Carol's case illustrates this well. No doubt she honestly suffered from her husband's insensitive treatment of their children, and to the extent that she had no part in this, she must be considered a victim. But in addition she *amplified* the destructiveness of what he did by portraying herself as hurt, thinking obsessively about how he was wrecking their lives, and so on. How she might have felt if she had not done this, and what difference that might have made in her relationship with him, are subjects we will address later. At this point, however, we will simply note that both her feelings and her marriage would have been different.

One way we can make ourselves out to be victims is by failing in some aspect of life; our failure "proves" how badly we have been treated. We have all known someone like Heather, who "just knew" no man would want her. She was attractive enough, and fairly often men would make overtures. But she would interpret everything they did (even their innocent actions) as some form of rejection, until finally they would give up. Those who knew her best reported that finding evidence of rejection seemed to be her primary interest. "Yeah, see, he didn't call back," Heather might say. A roommate, trying to be helpful, would explain, "But he did; he left a voice-mail message with his number." "No, if he was really interested, he would have kept trying till he got me." Heather's tone in such reactions would be triumphant, as she once again successfully defended her theory of why her life didn't work. These losses in love established her as a Great Martyr, and in her mind this excused her from treating men considerately, as fellow human beings.

A businessman who coaches tennis in the summer says that after watching tournaments for many years, he came to an intriguing conclusion: Except in a very few matches, usually with world-class performers, there is a point in every match (and in some cases it's right at the beginning) when the loser decides he's going to lose. And after that, everything he does will be aimed at providing an explanation of why he will have lost. He may throw himself at every ball (so he will be able to say he's done his best against a superior opponent). He may dispute calls (so he will be able to say he's been robbed). He may swear at himself and throw his racket (so he can say it was apparent all along he wasn't in top form). His energies go not into winning but into producing an explanation, an excuse, a justification for losing.

It is no different for those who amplify their victimhood in everyday life. Their particular way of going against conscience and evading responsibility is to look for reasons why someone or something else is to blame for their loss. Their key concern is not with winning, enjoyment, or getting a job done but with being prepared with an excuse when they lose, so it will be clear that they have been unfairly deprived of what was rightfully theirs. Failing to win, succeed, or become important is acceptable to them as long as they collect evidence that they *deserve* to have won, succeed, or become important—and they would have done so if they had not been unlucky or treated unfairly.

Often such people go to extreme lengths. Some put themselves at a severe disadvantage, falling behind in the economic or social struggles of life, or making shocking sacrifices, in the way they suppose a genuine victim might be forced to do. There are people who make fools of themselves in public, lose a job, or even take their lives just to prove they are victims—just to prove that someone else (possibly the whole human race or even God) has treated them unfairly.

Losing out in the affairs of life is not the only way to display oneself as a victim. Victimhood can be just as readily displayed by those we think of as successful or powerful. The successful may view themselves as victims when they perceive others as trying to take advantage of them and then redouble their efforts to succeed. Hitler may be the most extreme instance of this. He called his autobiography *Mein Kampf*—"my struggle." He had originally planned the title to center on the idea of "a reckoning" or "a settling of accounts," but then put this idea into the subtitle instead. He wanted to convey in the title something about the wrongs he had suffered and the vengeance he was taking. He stands as an extreme example of people whose preoccupation with their own victimhood leads them to seek power so they "won't have to suffer abuses anymore" and so they can "give them (their abusers) what they deserve."

MAKING THE WORST OF THINGS

That we can use our victimhood as an instrument of blame has bizarre implications. Think of it: If I'm a self-betrayer, accusing others so as to excuse myself, I am able to feel right about what I'm doing only because I've got evidence that someone else is doing wrong. *My belief in my "goodness" depends upon my belief in someone else's "badness."* Amazing!

It is well to remind ourselves of a basic point we learned in chapter 2: We seek this diminishment of others and our own elevation not because of any wrongs *they* may be doing to *us*. We do it because of the wrongs *we* are doing to *them*. Our demeaning, judgmental, and cruel ways grow out of our own self-betrayal and not, as we almost always suppose, from any need to defend ourselves.

In this simple fact is embedded one of those cosmic truths that help us understand the causes of the miseries that human beings inflict on one another, such as prejudice, hate, bitterness, vengeance, and cruelty. *We can't feel justified in withholding kindness from others unless we find, or invent, some reason why they deserve it*—some deficiency or despicable characteristic that requires us to ignore or correct or chasten or punish them.

Instances of this truth can be found in every institution and context of life—in diplomacy, in labor relations, in classrooms and neighborhoods. I'll offer only a couple of examples here, since all the stories included in this book illustrate the phenomenon to some degree.

I recall one successful man telling about an acquaintance with whom he had attended college:

> His very existence irritated me. He drove a Porsche and dated the flashiest girls. I had to walk in the snow and couldn't take any girl out because I didn't have money to spend.
>
> Years later we moved into a neighborhood where he lived. He owned some small restaurants and drove three expensive cars. I began accumulating data. His wife, a real display piece, had had her teeth capped and had plastic surgery done in strategic places. She seemed to be interested in only one thing: spending his money. These things pleased me deeply.
>
> A while ago a neighbor asked if I knew him. "Is he the one with the hot dog stands?" I asked, in mock naïveté. The neighbor said that my old acquaintance had gone bankrupt. I put on a long, concerned face and said, "That's awful," but inside, I'm ashamed to say, I was just about bursting with secret glee.

Secret glee? Over the bad fortune of another person? Yes. If I'm a self-betrayer, the defeat of the person I'm envying shows how undeserving he or she must be, and in my mind this excuses my envy, my pettiness, and my unkindness.

A person who rejoices in another's troubles or failures will be disappointed when that person succeeds.

A good illustration of this is found in a story recounted by a young woman named Lauren:

> I was going to a dance but didn't have the dress I wanted to wear. I could picture it lying in a heap in the corner of my sister's bedroom, wrinkled, stained, and untouched since the day she borrowed it two weeks before. I was seething.
>
> Then I heard a knock at the door. It was my sister with my freshly cleaned dress in her hand. Did I thank her for her thoughtfulness? No, I immediately began to berate her instead. I demanded to know why she hadn't returned it sooner. Had she carelessly stained it so she had to have it cleaned? Or was she just inconsiderate about when I might need it again?
>
> Of course, she became defensive. "You should have told me you needed it earlier, or that you really didn't want to lend it to me."
>
> "I shouldn't have to beg you to return what's mine," I shot back.
>
> She threw the dress at me. "Take your stupid dress. I'll never borrow anything from you again!" And she stomped out.
>
> "See," I thought to myself, "she wasn't even grateful that I let her borrow it."

As self-betrayers we typically reject good fortune and find disaster useful, just as Lauren did. We do so because we are using our victimhood to justify or excuse ourselves. Portraying ourselves as victims validates the lie we are living, which is that someone else is doing us harm and that our role is strictly passive. Good fortune, on the other hand, takes away that validation—if those we accuse treat us well, we lose our excuse for treating them poorly. When we give in to pessimism, defeatism, or despondency, it is because adopting such an attitude helps us avoid responsibility for ourselves and supports our efforts to justify ourselves in our self-betrayals.

Lauren's story shows how, by our self-victimizations, we exaggerate others' destructiveness and our own helplessness. Mental health professionals often speak of clients "horribilizing" or "awfulizing" or "catastrophizing" their situation or the conduct of others, or of "minimizing" their own contribution to their problems. These invented and admittedly awkward terms attempt to capture the way we exaggerate the distinctiveness of others and the losses we think they are inflicting upon us.

We can see that it costs us a lot to secure evidence of our justification and personal worth. We have got to feel mistreated or inconvenienced or stoop to cowardice or petty self-absorption. The worse we think we're treated or the more we feel put upon or helpless, the more certain we are that we're doing the best that can reasonably be expected of us. *For self-justification, we are willing to pay almost any price—and very often the higher the price, the more justified we feel.* That's why we typically do not respond favorably when someone suddenly offers to reduce the price—like the sister who borrowed the dress and returned it clean. To us, such good gestures threaten to deflate our justification; we feel a keen pang of disappointment.

ॐ

A VIOLENT HEART

By making victims of ourselves, we accuse and abuse other people. We make them out to be heartless victimizers, and *that* is a very victimizing thing to do to them. We display ourselves as suffering at their hands. And we evade acknowledging our mistreatment of them by accusing them of mistreating us. Though motivated more by fear of them than malice, we nevertheless can do them damage.

You can see the violence in this. When the violence is not outwardly expressed in acts and in words, it is perpetrated in the mind and heart. Violence is a mark of the self-betraying way of life.

The violence can be subtle and difficult to detect. A man named Wally told this story:

> Once during a New Year's Eve party in our home most of those present took turns letting themselves be coached in singing by one of the guests who was a professional voice teacher. Despite widespread urging, I declined. I said I'd be too embarrassed. The jovial atmosphere seemed to vacate the room. After a bit, a few of the couples said they thought they should get home, and it wasn't even midnight. Only later did I realize that I was in effect saying to everyone present that I couldn't trust them enough to sing in front of them—they would judge me too harshly if I tried. My silent criticism of them made them feel uncomfortable, and they wanted to go home.

Would that all self-betrayers' violence were this mild. Unfortunately, it can also become aggressive and cruel. *Often we will do almost anything to hang on to our victimhood, even if it means destroying something we treasure.* Our need is to make whomever we are accusing as monstrous as possible.

The following story was told in a class by a man I'll call Merrill. I knew him well and much admired him as a husband and father. I mention my admiration to emphasize that self-betrayal is

not a condition reserved for people with evil intentions. It is a trap
we can all fall into. Merrill told the class:

> For a few years after we were married, my wife, Tammy,
> and I lived in a trailer court that was filled with families
> who also had young children. When our daughters, Kelly
> and Kimberly, were about three and two, we came home
> one day to discover that all their toys were missing. After
> we searched for a time, a five-year-old neighbor girl finally
> admitted that she had taken the toys and showed us where
> she had hidden them.
>
> At first Tammy and I weren't upset about the incident.
> It wasn't any big deal. But when word of what happened
> reached the five-year-old's mother, she denied that her
> child had taken the toys. The woman became so adamant
> that she told all the neighbors that our story was only a
> vicious rumor. She tried to poison our friends against us.
> Even her daughter's admission of the truth made no dif-
> ference; she didn't come to us and apologize. She made no
> effort to make sure there were no continuing hard feelings.
>
> I told Tammy I pitied this woman. "She's a sick human
> being," I said. But I have to admit I was angry.
>
> Two months later the little girl had a birthday party.
> Every single child in the trailer court was invited except
> Kelly and Kimberly. I was livid. Inviting all but two of the
> neighborhood children—what a cruel thing to do! A
> mature woman, supposedly, was taking out her guilt on
> two little kids!
>
> I was outside our home on the morning of the party,
> planting flowers and watching the children gather glee-
> fully at the woman's trailer for the party. Soon they were
> playing games. Then Kelly and Kimberly came out of our
> trailer and saw the children having fun. They naturally
> went over to join the group. I had a sinking feeling as I
> watched them go. I was afraid the worst might happen.
>
> It did. About the time my girls arrived, the other

children were invited into the trailer and the door was closed, leaving Kelly and Kimberly standing outside alone. A bit later the children emerged again, and my girls joined them. The girl's mother began passing out ice cream cones. I watched in stunned amazement as she carefully gave one to every child but mine. Kelly and Kimberly just stood there, puzzled.

Then the woman passed out balloons, again to all the children but two. All those children were dancing and jumping excitedly, and my two were standing alone in the middle, silent and still.

I was furious. These two little girls were innocent and helpless. What a monster this woman was! She was using these kids to hide her guilt and get at me and my wife! It was easily the most detestable thing I had ever seen.

When Merrill told this story in the class, he presented it as an example of self-betrayal, to illustrate the lengths to which people will go to justify themselves. Many people in the audience were impressed. "She must have been insane," someone said.

Then a question was raised that riveted the interest of everyone present. A woman asked, "Why were you so offended at that woman if you were as innocent as you say you were?"

"Obviously, she was misusing my little girls," Merrill replied.

"You said she tried to ruin your reputation," another person added. "Weren't you doing the same to her?"

"What do you mean? I don't understand."

"Well, you said you were angry at this woman."

"Yes, but . . ."

"And you said she never came to you to be certain there were no hard feelings. But did you ever go to her?"

"Well, no, but . . ."

"Honestly, didn't you have just a little sweet taste of revenge when you said she must be sick?"

"Look," Merrill said, "that woman had something to straighten out with me!"

"And what about your children going to the party?" another person interrupted.

"Well, what about it?"

"You knew they weren't invited."

"Yes."

"Then why did you let them go?"

Another person piped up. "I know why. You were angry with this woman. You knew what would happen. You knew your neighbor would treat them that way. You wanted her to. Then you would have proof you were justified all this time in hating her."

"You were using your children just as much as she was," said another.

"She mistreated them, but so did you. You let them go. You set them up."

Not for several days, Merrill told me, did the pain and sorrow he began to feel that evening start to subside. Later he wrote:

The realization of what I had done to my children stunned me. I had used them. As I stood in front of the group, facing the truth for the first time, I remembered seeing Kelly and Kim standing puzzled and hurt in the midst of playing, gleeful children. I was the one who had put them there. In a desperate and selfish effort to believe the feelings I had toward this woman were justified, I was willing to abuse my own children.

This was a tough experience for me. I learned from it how easy it is to blind ourselves to our own wrongdoing by pointing to the wrongdoing of others. I'm not an evil person. I'm not naturally given to cruelty. But in my quest to be justified in my own eyes, I used whatever means were available, even my kids. I didn't feel cruel, but what I did turned out to be the actions of a cruel person.

Am I a Monster Underneath?

Why would anyone, let alone a man of Merrill's sensitivity and dignity, ever do such a thing? Why would he misuse his children and pollute his own happiness just to prove himself innocent of what he was doing? Was justifying himself in his insensitivity to that woman worth sacrificing what mattered most to him? This seems especially puzzling when we remember that he had the power to stop doing it at any time. Surely he could see what he was doing. It doesn't seem to make any sense.

Nor does it make sense that any of us indulge in this kind of self-destructive behavior. Why don't we get fed up with the wretchedness of being angry, resentful, irritated, vindictive, petty, humiliated, offended, or whatever, and say to ourselves, "Living like this stinks! Who wants to wallow around in pain? I'm quitting! I'm tossing out these afflicting feelings—packing them around is ruining my life!" Why don't we just stop? Why do we relentlessly pursue such a misery-making course? Why work so hard to ruin our lives? When a situation gets painful in other areas of life, we flee. But when we betray ourselves, far from fleeing our misery, we can't let go of it, because we need it as evidence of our innocence. Of all humanity's mysteries, none seems more unfathomable than this systematic self-destruction of the soul. Why would it be more important to us to justify ourselves than to free ourselves from deep emotional pain?

What we have learned about self-victimization helps us understand this mystery. *Once we betray ourselves, accuse others, and box ourselves into the victim's role, we no longer see things the way they really are.* In our minds, there can be *only* two options: one is that we are right in accusing them, which means that they are guilty of all the trouble between us and that we are their victims; the other is that we're wrong and they aren't guilty after all, and this means *we're* guilty of the trouble and *they* are *our* victims.

Anxious to justify ourselves, we insist on the first of these possibilities—the people we accuse are wrong and we're right. But they don't accept this. They protest their innocence. They accuse us of treating *them* unfairly. In defending themselves against us, they constantly throw in our faces *their* insistence that they are not the monsters we claim them to be. On the contrary, they insist that *we* are the monsters.

Think what these accusations against us mean. Here we have been displaying ourselves as doing the best we can in spite of them. Their being in the wrong is our proof that we're in the right. But if it were to turn out that they were right and not monstrous after all, it would follow that we *could not* be right—we *could not* be the admirable people we've been portraying ourselves to be. Instead, we would be the monsters they claim we are. If that were so, our public portrayal of ourselves as justified and worthwhile would be nothing more than a façade. And underneath that façade would lurk a malicious and hypocritical person, willing to accuse others falsely, willing to make them look bad solely to make ourselves look good! What kind of moral scum, what kind of monster, would do such a thing?

You can see from this why, when we're in self-betrayal, we can't even conceive of not casting ourselves in the victim's role, even if it means making ourselves miserable. For as we have seen, *if we were to acknowledge not being a victim, in that very instant we would in our own eyes become a victimizing, hypocritical monster.* A hypocritical monster, moreover, who has been accusing others of being hypocritical monsters! If the woman Merrill accused turned out to be innocent of his charges, it would mean he sent his little girls off to be rejected by her! How could he stand himself? How could he endure this absolute obliteration of his self-respect? No wonder he painted himself as her victim in a hundred different ways—it was the only way to "prove" his innocence! It was the only way he could fight off the possibility that, underneath his public behavior, there lurked a monster too despicable even to contemplate.

The emotionally anguished life of a victim, fraught with accusing attitudes or emotions like anger, resentment, suspicion, fear, anxiety, and such, is the price we pay for avoiding the self-condemnation I have been describing. For some, that price becomes completely consuming—like carrying lifelong grudges for years, refusing ever to forgive, nursing and even cherishing resentment and vengeful feelings, even taking their own lives—because for them, in their self-betraying condition, everything depends on the others being shown to be wrong, so that they can be shown to be right.

The bitter nectar that is our victimhood, with all the sacrifices and losses it entails, has a narcotic effect. We acquire a taste for the momentary relief from responsibility and accountability it seems to provide—we don't have to face what we suspect might be awful truths about ourselves. We perversely find a kind of sweetness in the fact that it is so bitter.

∽

MORE ABOUT WHO WE ARE

Here's what's most ironic about all of this. The monster we vaguely suspect and fear we would be if our accusations of others and self-justifications turn out to be false—this monster doesn't exist! The despised qualities we struggle to cover up are fictional, exactly as fictional as the admirable qualities we are publicly trying to project. It is worth taking a moment to explain this crucial point.

We create this monstrous image of ourselves when we project an idealized image of ourselves. These two self-images come into being together. They can be thought of as two sides of a single coin. Before we betray ourselves, neither image exists for us—doubts about our worth have not arisen, and neither have we attempted to overcome such doubts. But with our self-betrayal, and our insistence that we are acting conscientiously and acceptably, comes the perception that we might not be that way at all, but just the opposite.

We've all known a teenage beauty who's convinced she is hideous. Or a macho daredevil and small-time terrorist driven to prove that he is not a weakling. Or a "supermom" keeping the family going by her indefatigable efforts and struggling to fight off depression over her inadequacies. The beauty would never have suspected herself hideous if she had not made her appearance a major issue by wishing to be gorgeous. The macho punk would never have doubted his strength and courage if he had not first indulged in fantasies of himself as strong and courageous. The mother who doubted herself to the point of depression would not have sunk so far had she never gotten herself into the business of proving herself a "supermom." All of these people would never have imagined the possibility of their monstrousness if they had never tried to prove themselves impressive.

So as self-betrayers we project an image of a deserving, worthwhile person, and then we struggle constantly to produce evidence that we're measuring up to that image. This is hard work and exceedingly stressful. We must conceal what we suspect we really are so as to keep from being "found out." But what we cover up when we hide behind this "false front"—when we publicly project an idealized and fictitious version of ourselves—is not real. We are no more the worthless person we are trying to hide than the impressively worthwhile person we are trying to hide behind.

We may then ask, If we are neither the ideal people we fancy ourselves to be, nor the worthless kind of persons we sometimes suspect we are, then what kind of persons are we? The answer comes in two parts:

First, we *are not* inherently evil, worthless, illegitimate, or even self-seeking, even in part. That idea is false. But such a view of humanity is a very widespread fiction, because we are all self-betrayers to some degree, and part of the self-betrayer's lie is to believe this fiction. Many of us do act evilly—indeed, some of us are in bondage to evil—but that is because of self-betrayal; it is not the expression of an evil nature that we are trying to hide and that we can never obliterate.

Second, we *are* infinitely worthwhile, but not because we are the idealized beings who appear in the positive self-image we project publicly. Instead, our measureless worth, which for me means our inherent goodness—has something to do with our capacity to respect and revere others. But that is a subject we will take up later in this book. We have little conception of how worthwhile we are because we are working so hard to prove how worthwhile we are! In the vast fields of our possibilities, many of us, shrouded in the fog of resentment and fear, hold out far too little hope for ourselves.

WHEN HELL ITSELF LOOKS LIKE THE SOLUTION

It will be helpful to trace out one more dimension of the way we victimize ourselves when we get locked into self-betrayal. We have learned how we get ourselves boxed in by our false interpretations of others and of ourselves. We think our attacks on others and our protection of ourselves are somehow fending off disaster and saving our necks when in actuality we're digging ourselves deeper into the box. We think that the world offers us solutions— solutions such as standing up for ourselves when we're caught in a conflict with someone or graciously giving in—but these, when pursued, only drag us further into bondage.

In C. S. Lewis's allegorical story *The Great Divorce,* there appears a series of "Ghosts"—spirits of people who have passed away—who refuse to enter into heaven. To them, it seems like hell. Why? Because heaven provides none of the proofs of their self-justification to which they have become addicted. No one there will mistreat them sufficiently.

When a Ghost arrives in heaven's outskirts, a "bright Spirit" is dispatched to lead him or her farther into heaven's interior precincts. The bright Spirits are former Ghosts who have given up their self-absorption and consequently have experienced love and joy. One of the male Ghosts refuses to go with his Spirit-guide because he knows that this guide led a far worse life on earth than he did. Consequently, the Ghost feels unfairly treated; he is not being given his due; his rights are being denied. He is confident that his guide has made it into heaven's inner circle by exploiting an "Old Boy" network. So, self-victimizingly, he decides to resist this discriminatory treatment; he refuses to cooperate with the Establishment. Not surprisingly, a note of triumph accompanies the bitterness in his voice when he announces his decision. He turns his back upon his happiness in the conviction that he is not only protecting himself from the abuses of these Spirits but is also taking a stand against the evils of favoritism.

A female Ghost is embarrassed to go with her attendant Spirit because it and the other Spirits radiate a brightness that exceeds hers. In life she was the sort of person who could be mortified by the thought of being inappropriately dressed for an occasion. The Spirit sent to help her invites her to fix her mind on something other than herself, but that only makes it plainer to her that the Spirit cannot understand the embarrassment she feels. "But they'll *see* me," she protests. "What does it matter if they do?" the Spirit asks. "I'd rather die" is her response, not realizing that what she really needs to do *is* to die, which is to say, to give up the fictional self she has always portrayed herself to be.

The Ghosts in Lewis's story are ensnared in bonds of anguish. Escaping their bodies in death is insufficient to liberate them from such bonds, because the bonds are not physical—they are emotional and spiritual. In each case, all that is required to ensnare them in these bonds is an obsessive preoccupation with justifying themselves. And it is because heaven threatens to destroy their carefully cultivated justification that it seems to them like hell. When the bright Spirits extend kindness, the Ghosts suspect malice. Yet the Spirits will not be manipulated; the Ghosts cannot use their old maneuvers to flatter or provoke. In desperation they want to curse their Spirit-guides and flee. They actively resist their salvation, convinced that they are saving themselves when in fact what they are struggling to save is only a false image of themselves.

Self-betrayers do not comprehend that what they need is the destruction of this fictional self. By trying to save themselves, they damn themselves. The phony self-image must die in order that they, as sensitive human beings, might live. As I said to Keith, the advertising executive whose story appeared at the end of chapter 3, "Whichever choice you make, a part of you is going to die. The only question is, Which part?"

Lewis's tale is not so much a story about the afterlife as it is an allegory about every person's possibilities in *this* life. What he calls heaven is more familiar to us as the people we encounter daily, understood without distortion. Lewis wants us to realize that *it is infinitely joyous (as well as completely safe) to rid ourselves of self-deception and see others and ourselves as we really are.*

ᗡ

UNDERSTANDING
CREATES COMPASSION

The idea that we can make victims of ourselves easily lends itself to misunderstanding. First of all, it does not mean that we who may be victims are necessarily responsible for whatever happens to us. As I said earlier, there *is* such a thing as being victimized, pure and simple, by some act in which we do not collaborate at all. But quite apart from such abuse, we can *use* the fact that we have been (or are being) victimized to excuse or justify ourselves in failing to live up to our own sense of right and wrong. Even if Matthew really did yell at me in the bathroom, it's a separate issue that I used that fact to blame him for the demeaning way in which I treated him.

We may have a hard time accepting this idea. We sympathize with a person like Mandy, the woman hypersensitive to rejection and subject to depression whose story I recounted in chapter 1. She connected her problems with her father's having largely ignored her when she was a girl, spending his time instead with her brother and sister. When we read her story, we doubt that we would have responded to these same childhood experiences better than she did, and in this we are almost certainly right. Life can be very, very hard. None of us gets through it without having to struggle with some form of the emotional and attitudinal difficulties we are discussing in this book. For that reason, we hesitate to think of ourselves—and Mandy, for that matter—as being responsible for deep fears and resentments.

But remember—and this is the first of two important points that needs to be made about this topic—by saying that Mandy is responsible, we do not lay blame and call her unworthy. We do not imply that she could have been expected to grow up in her family of origin without any resentment at all. Instead, we suggest that the harsh judgments contained in her resentful attitude were *her doing*—these judgments engaged her energy and intelligence and were therefore her responsibility.

That's Point One. Point Two is that Point One opens up hope. *Precisely because Mandy was responsible for doing what she did, she could stop doing it.* Whatever her father did was a separate matter. She bore no responsibility for that and had no power to change it; she could not change how her father had treated her. But she *could* change the resentful and despondent way she conducted herself afterwards, because she *did* bear responsibility for that. We will study this subject further in chapter 13. There we will discover that the most destructive part of her experience—the part that made her life hard to bear—was not what her father did to her, but what she did with what he had done to her. In other words, what made her life hard to bear was the unforgiving and resentful way she felt toward him.

Simply by understanding these points, we become able to see that *self-betrayers do not accuse others and make themselves miserable maliciously. A real fear motivates them—a real fear of something that is not real.* They struggle anxiously with what they falsely believe to be threats needing to be dealt with. In the world as they construe it, they act purely in self-defense.

If we fail to understand this truth about those who are caught up in self-betrayal, we will think them the monsters they fear they might be, maliciously motivated underneath a "righteous" public façade. We will condemn them in the way they fear they'll be condemned. We will make ourselves their enemy. *But if on the other hand we understand how threatening the world seems to them, we will set ourselves free of our accusing, judgmental attitude.* We will become, as onlookers, more open, truthful, and considerate in our way of being, more responsive to them as they really are.

Understanding self-betrayal and self-victimization can soften our accusations of others, open us to acceptance of their efforts, and enable us to let go of our accusing attitudes and emotions. These benefits of thus opening ourselves to the truth about others will be discussed further.

CHAPTER 5

BEING FALSE TOGETHER

CONFLICTING STORIES

How do people afflicted with anguished, accusing thoughts and feelings get along with others? How do others react to them? The answer is that others, feeling accused, seldom respond gratefully, and as a result the self-betrayers' relationships become terribly entangled. This adds to the difficulties they experience in trying to escape from their negative thoughts and feelings.

Here is the general pattern in which self-betrayal turns our relationships into an emotional bondage from which we typically can see no escape.

1. We adopt accusing and self-excusing attitudes and feelings.

2. We think we can hide them, but we can't. Our real attitudes and feelings toward others come across to them. As Friedrich Nietzsche wrote: "We can lie with our lips, but we tell the truth with the face we make when we lie."

3. Feeling accused, others almost always take offense; they develop an accusing attitude and accusing feelings toward us.

4. Perceiving their response, we feel just as offended by them as they do by us. In our minds, this gives us proof that we're fully justified in blaming them.

5. Because we're so absorbed with our own feelings, we do not see what's going on. We do not see that instead of trying to hurt us, they feel mistreated and threatened.

In their response to us they are only trying to deal with
the judgmental person we have become. They are only
responding to the kind of person we're giving them to
respond to.

Here, then, is the overall picture of the interaction: *We* concentrate on *their* misdeeds in order to have proof that they are to
blame and not us. And *they* focus on *our* misdeeds for the same
sort of reason. Thus, we and they set in motion round upon round
of edgy and sometimes hostile interactions, in which each blames
the other and exonerates himself or herself. Self-betrayal invites
more self-betrayal, which invites more self-betrayal.

Glen's Story

The following story, which like the others in this book is true,
illustrates this pattern. It is drawn from the early married life of a
couple I'll call Glen and Becky. It comes in two versions, his and
hers. In neither version is the full story to be found, because each
person is enclosed in his or her own self-absorbed perception of
the events. When the two stories are brought together, some
astounding truths about relationships suddenly come to light—as
you will realize once we have read the two stories. The first version
is Glen's.

When Becky and I got married, I discovered she was just
about perfect. In fact, that was her one fault—her perfection. She was determined to do every "supposed to" she
had ever heard. She could not rest, enjoy life, and be easy
until every one of those "supposed to's" got done, and she
couldn't let her husband rest either. It was clear to me that
she would be more happy and less frustrated if she weren't
always preoccupied with her lengthy list of "supposed
to's."

The longest part of this list concerned Christmas and

the elaborate preparations required to make it perfect in every way. In Becky's mind, you could not give a gift unless you made it yourself . . . from scratch. To buy a gift was thoughtless. It didn't show you really cared. I cooperated with this policy before our brothers and sisters got married and we all started having children. But pretty soon there were dozens of presents to make. Initially, we would begin in October; later we started in September, then August—then even June! The black hole called Christmas was widening and swallowing up the entire year.

Nor could we buy Christmas cards like other people did. We had to make them—dress the kids up in shepherds' costumes, with the littlest one as baby Jesus, gather hay or straw for the manger, and take a picture for the card. I'm the fellow who scavenged the countryside around Providence, Rhode Island, every year looking for straw or hay in October. And once we got the card printed, we couldn't just sign it and send it. After all, we hadn't contacted all those people in a year. We had to write a letter on each card. Many nights I stayed up, my head bobbing sleepily over the desk, composing personal letters by my own hand to folks I could sometimes barely remember.

But what bothered me most was Becky's saying, "I'm the only one who cares about Christmas. If it weren't for me, we wouldn't do anything nice."

Then we started exchanging gifts with other families. Don't ask me what got into us. The other families would give a book or some jam or a box of cookies. We made raspberry yogurt, with raspberries we had grown ourselves in the summer and frozen, or granola loaded with chopped dried fruit, which we had also produced ourselves. (Berries, apricots, and prunes are supposed to taste different when they're homegrown.) And of course we couldn't just take the stuff to people's houses. We had to sing carols on the doorstep. In parts. That meant rehearsals. Some of our children have toured the world in choirs; some, nearly monotone, hate to sing. On the doorstep one child or another would get stepped on or pushed out of his or her turn to ring the bell, so there would be hassle up to the last second, and then we'd display our smiling lips to hide the hard, sidelong glances that kept everyone in line. It took many cold nights for our irascible little band to finish spreading Christmas cheer.

Don't get me wrong. There was nothing about any of this that wasn't first-class. But as we'd sit in the kitchen helping the children decorate the bottles or boxes for the food we would deliver, or glare at each other on somebody's doorstep, I would think that here we were, night after night, doing all the peripherals, the showy stuff, the trappings of Christmas, without any of the spirit of Christmas, which was what my wife said this was all for. We'd be exhausted and grumbling, I'd think of what this was costing me professionally, and Becky would complain that she was the only one who cared about Christmas. She'd say, "I feel like I'm dragging everyone through Christmas. If it wasn't for me, no one would ever get a present ready or even think about making Christmas nice." More than once I'd lie in bed, too tired and irritated to sleep, mentally composing a Pulitzer-prize-caliber short story entitled "The Woman Who Destroyed Christmas."

When Glen told this story to a group unfamiliar with the idea of self-betrayal, he received much sympathy, especially from the men. Many were quick to say what Glen and/or Becky should have done. "Glen should have put his foot down." "They should have negotiated a compromise—this much time on Christmas and no more." But once people learn about self-betrayal, they can see the self-absorption and self-justification in stories like Glen's. They can see the accusation in his way of nursing his victimhood. They know that the other side of the story must be very different.

Becky's Story

How would you have responded had you been Becky? What would it have been like living with a man who believed your aspirations for the family were ruining his life?

Several years after the Christmastime conflicts came to an end—we will learn later in this book how this happened—Glen asked Becky to write her recollections of them. For anyone who takes Glen's side when they hear his story, hers comes as a jolting revelation.

> When we were first married I had looked forward to building traditions that would hold our family together, and Christmas was the best opportunity to do that. Since the essence of Christmas was sharing something of oneself, making gifts was important, especially because in those days we didn't have much money. Because Glen did things like that before we were married, I had every reason to think he would share this commitment. But then I discovered that he was content to postpone what had to be done for Christmas. He didn't seem to want to put himself into it. He was clearly anxious to get the preparations over with; his work seemed to matter to him more than the family. He was willing to dash out at the last minute and buy things that weren't meaningful. That was the very opposite of the meaning of Christmas.
>
> It's not that I would have minded buying gifts, if they could have been picked out thoughtfully so they would be meaningful to the people we gave them to; I would have felt fine about that. But we couldn't afford nice gifts, so in order to give people presents that would show we really cared, we needed to make them. So here I was trying to

economize, and Glen was oblivious to that. He was willing to spend the money foolishly. It's really hard to try to create meaningful family experiences when the person who is supposed to be your partner is reluctant about the whole endeavor, and when he does participate he does so with obvious resentment. I could see the enthusiasm drain out of Glen whenever there was something about Christmas that needed to be done.

Well, I decided if I went ahead and got Christmas started early he would get into the spirit of the thing and want to be involved himself. But that didn't seem to work; the more I did, the more he was willing to let me do. The projects he was in charge of, like making the Christmas cards, would get postponed and in many cases not done at all. And when they were done I could see he resented the time it took. His heart just wasn't in it, that's all.

So you can see my predicament. In order to keep it all from being put off to the last minute, I would start talking about Christmas early, trying to get him involved in planning, but each year he seemed to want to do less, so I'd try even harder to start earlier to get the plans made so I'd have more time to do it myself, and more opportunity to try to get him interested and involved. And it also frustrated me because I really didn't want to be badgering him about what he was supposed to do, and I didn't want to be the heavy all the time, but it seemed that if I didn't pressure him he wouldn't get involved at all.

❧

COOPERATIVE CONFLICT

If you heard Glen and Becky tell their stories separately, you might think the two of them were scarcely living in the same world. How can two people experience the same events so differently? The answer to this question lies in the fact that the two stories complement one another; they are two halves of a single whole.

To see this, think first about their respective individual assessments of the problem. *What did Glen think the problem was?* That he and Becky didn't have enough time or energy to get everything done? That they hadn't gone into this Christmas thing with a sufficiently clear understanding? (Should they have entered into some sort of prenuptial agreement?)

Anyone who thinks this is how Glen thought of the problem won't have paid careful attention to his story. If in those early years you had asked Glen to identify the problem, he wouldn't have hesitated. He would have said: "Becky. Becky is the problem. I married a fanatic. She must have been born with an extra Christmas chromosome. Her relentless demands are making normal family life impossible."

Now ask yourself: How would Becky have answered the same question? *How would she have described the problem?* She wouldn't have hesitated either: "Glen's the problem. From the way he treated me and other people when we were dating, I expected someone completely different, someone more committed to our home life. He's not invested in our family projects. His mind is somewhere else half the time. He undermines everything. I don't think he has any Christmas spirit at all."

Glen thought Becky was the problem, and she thought he was the problem. Each blamed the other for the Christmas troubles between them.

Next question: *If Glen had had the power to make it happen, what would have been his ideal solution to the problem? In his fantasies, what did he wish for?*

Had you asked him this question at the time, he would have said his ideal solution was for Becky to change. Become reasonable. Relax her demands. And similarly for Becky: In her fantasies

Glen needed to change. Wake up to the needs of the family. Put his heart into the family projects.

The ideal solution for each of them was to have the other change.

But because these ideal solutions were based on blame, they could never have worked. To see why this must be so, let us ask this question: Did Glen and Becky ever try to implement their respective solutions? Did they ever try to get each other to change? You bet they did—occasionally by directly voicing their complaints, but more often by subtle innuendoes in what they said or by huffing and puffing about to show how burdened they felt. Each had his or her own style of conveying the message: "You are really making things difficult for me, and you need to stop!"

Did either of these two people appreciate the other's accusing efforts to get him or her to change? Did either ever say, "Oh, thank you very much for pointing out these shortcomings to me. Why did it take me so long to see that this is what you wanted? I'll put my heart into doing just what you suggest!" Was this the reaction?

Not on your life. Very few of us would have reacted this way. Instead we take offense when we are accused. We feel attacked. We dig in and defend ourselves. A six-year-old was causing a ruckus in the supermarket, pulling cans off the shelf, climbing in and out of the cart, and demanding candy. In exasperation her mother gripped the little girl by the shoulders and harshly told her, "Sit down!" "Okay," the daughter responded, "I'll be sitting down on the outside, but I'll be standing up on the inside!" As a wise person once said, "Criticism produces results 180 degrees opposite what was intended." Trying to "fix" the other person almost always backfires.

Since Glen couldn't have his ideal solution, how <u>did</u> he deal with his problem? He coped. He fought to maintain some balance and sanity in the family. In spite of the pressures, he strove valiantly to keep up at work. He said he distinctly recalls the sensation, when staying up one night to write personal letters on greeting cards, of carrying on "in a plucky spirit." That was the best way he could think of to deal with the difficulties he was sure Becky was causing.

In fact, if someone had told Glen at the time that Becky blamed all the Christmas problems on his refusal to throw greater effort into Christmas, he would not have denied it. He would have said, "Sure, I hold back—I have to, because of her excessive demands. It's the only way to put on the brakes. If I didn't we would have Christmas for breakfast, lunch, and dinner 365 days a year."

In Glen's mind, he had to hold back—otherwise Christmas would have taken over their lives!

And how did Becky try to solve her problem? She tried in every way she could think of to overcome or compensate for Glen's resistance so the family could enjoy memorable Christmases. "I would start talking about Christmas early, trying to . . . get Glen interested and involved." She coped by making plans for everything that might need doing so nothing would slip, and by following up with hints and suggestions designed to keep him on task. What else could she do with a partner who chronically dragged his feet?

Indeed, had someone told her Glen's opinion about the cause of all their Christmas difficulties, Becky wouldn't have denied that she pressured him. Remember her words: "I really didn't want to be badgering him about what he was supposed to do, but it seemed that if I didn't pressure him he wouldn't get involved at all." So what was the reason for keeping all that pressure on? Glen was holding back! That was why she pushed him so.

In her mind, she had to pressure him—otherwise he wouldn't do anything at all!

So while Glen was holding back because of Becky's pressures, Becky was pressuring him because he was holding back.

Glen's solution to the problem was the very problem Becky was trying to solve. And Becky's solution to the problem was the very problem Glen was trying to solve.

Glen's solution = Becky's problem

Becky's solution = Glen's problem

He said he hated her pressure—but his attitude and behavior created her need to pressure Glen; it was *her* solution to the family's problems. And she said she hated his holding back—but her attitude and behavior created his need to hold back; it was *his* solution to the family's problems.

Each of them struggled to protect the family from dangers he or she blamed on the other, dangers that in fact they both were helping to create.

Blame Provokes Blame

Glen feared that if he did not continue doing what he was doing, things would get even worse, and Becky feared the same. This is always the case with mutually accusing self-betrayers. Both are certain that what they are doing is necessary to keep the undesirable behavior of the other from getting completely out of hand. Both believe their accusations are restraining the undesirable behavior of the other and that therefore they are saving the situation. But in fact they are doing exactly the opposite!

This formula can be represented as a cycle in which each party's response feeds the other's, round and round. The cycle escalates over time. The more Becky pressured Glen, the more reason he had to insist that other projects besides Christmas needed his attention. And the more he did this, the more panicked she became about getting everything done in time for the holidays. In one way, this collaboration resembles a self-accelerating machine that automatically opens its throttle as it increases its speed. The faster it goes, the faster it makes itself go—until it breaks apart.

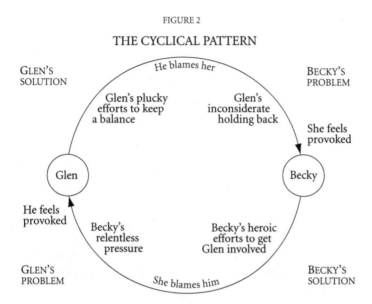

FIGURE 2

THE CYCLICAL PATTERN

Becky and Glen collaborated in each other's behavior. He was her accomplice, and she was his. Because of the dynamics of the cycle, a court of moral law would have convicted him as well as her for driving the family to extremes and would have convicted her as well as him for sabotaging the family projects. Neither of them acted by themselves. They helped each other do what they each said they hated.

To me, this cycle is utterly amazing. How could a circumstance be more curious or more potentially tragic? Here are two people in love with one another, speaking to each other without rancor, striving to do good as they see it, and yet, by every effort to make things better, actually making them worse. Each sought to save the family from the destructive influence of the other, and the more they did this the more the cycle escalated.

It was this cycle of mutual blame, not the number of Christmas projects, that endangered the family. By participating in this cycle, Glen and Becky polarized each other and poisoned the family atmosphere.

We have seen that our accusations give those we accuse good reason to do the very thing we are blaming them for. This fact has a most astounding implication: *Generally speaking, we share responsibility for the way we are treated.* If we want to know what impact we are having on others, we need only to examine their responses to us. I am not speaking about the treatment we receive from someone who appears in our life suddenly, out of the blue, like a criminal burglarizing our house or a tyrant who devastates our lives by oppressive edicts and armed force. I am talking about the treatment we get from people we live or work with day to day. In general, the more closely we are involved with someone, the more the principle applies. *To see ourselves, we need only to look at others' reaction to us.*

So it is our attitude and feeling toward others that gives them provocation and excuse for doing what we are blaming them for. This principle can be expressed in this brief maxim: *Seeing other people as the problem is the problem!*

A Name for the Pattern

In spite of the fact that nothing is more commonplace, we have no adequate word in our language for the cyclical pattern just described, just as we have no adequate word for getting stuck. What shall we call it?

Others have noticed aspects of the pattern and have invented names that seem to work. One of these names is *vicious circles.* Other names are *dance* and *spiral* and *games people play.* In some but certainly not all respects the pattern resembles *codependency.*

Psychiatrists sometimes have used the term *deviation-amplifying feedback*.

Like R. D. Laing and Howard Stein, I prefer the term *collusion* (although what they mean by this term differs significantly from what I mean—in their theories, for example, collusion does not grow out of self-betrayal). When used for this purpose, the word *collusion* is metaphorical. In the literal sense of *collusion*, the parties involved are perfectly aware of the mischief they are up to, perhaps communicating by secret signals. Though the individuals participating in the collusion pattern I have described have no such awareness, they appear to, and that's why I like the name *collusion*. They push each other's buttons so unerringly that they seem, like literal colluders, to be acting on a pre-arranged plan—as if they had agreed, "Look, you give me an excuse for my misbehavior by misbehaving toward me, and I'll do the same for you."

But of course they have no such plan; they do not aim deliberately to provoke each other. As we are about to see, it is the readiness of each to take offense that turns whatever the other does into a "direct hit" and the other person into an unerringly accurate offender.

∽

BLINDNESS OF HEART

You can see how Glen and Becky drove each other deeper into their defensive, self-worried positions. He saw himself as acting in self-defense, in response to her offensive behavior. *He could not see* that on her side, Becky believed that *she* was acting in self-defense and that it was Glen who was behaving offensively. *He could not see* that her motive wasn't to demean him, but to protect herself and the family.

His defensiveness and self-absorption imposed a limit upon his reality, which is represented by the edge of his box (see figure 3). How she felt, including her real aspirations and fears, lay beyond that limit.

And these same sorts of things can be said of Becky. Glen's defensiveness came across to her offensively and triggered her defensive reaction. And therefore *she could not see* that his motives were not to selfishly take care of his own needs and to fight against what she was trying to accomplish in the family. She could not empathize with him any better than he could with her. His hopes and feelings and fears lay beyond the limits of *her* box. Figure 3 represents all this.

FIGURE 3

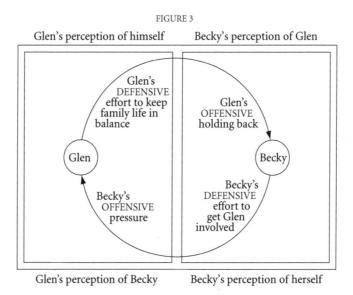

The boxes superimposed upon the circular diagram represent the limits and distortions of Becky's and Glen's understanding. The perceptions that lie within the walls of their respective boxes are misinterpretations of what lies beyond those walls. He sees her in terms of *his* self-absorbed worries and therefore has little sense of *her* worries. And the same is true of her.

We can see that what appears to be sheer selfishness, malice, or even abusiveness from the outside is on the inside deep insecurity, deep worry, and deep fear. The person who seems so offensive is in fact carrying on self-defensively, doing the best he or she can see to do in the situation. No wonder Becky and Glen felt at cross purposes and afflicted by each other!

The large box around the whole cyclical configuration indicates how completely Glen and Becky were tied to one another even while experiencing themselves as completely alienated from one another. This can be expressed in these words: *When we are in the larger box together, we are in our smaller boxes alone.*

In this book we will speak only of two-person collusions. In fact, almost all collusions involve many people. Often a number of such multiple-person collusions are linked together in chains. We will talk about such chains in chapter 13.

ᕤ

GIVING OTHERS
POWER TO CONTROL US

We need to learn a little more about colluders' ability to hit each other's buttons consistently and accurately, almost as if they took dead aim, knowing instinctively or by experience exactly how to get the other's goat.

"Why did you look at me like that?" one demands indignantly.

"Like what? I didn't look at you any particular way."

"Don't deny it. I know what it means when you look at me like that."

We now understand how one person can do such things to another without possessing any special skill at giving offense, and probably without even trying to provoke the offended. It can be done because *the offended one is already set to take offense—is on the alert for anything that might be interpreted as offensive—and actively takes offense whenever he or she can.*

Consider Becky in the Christmas story. She could hit Glen's buttons unerringly only because he was looking for anything that might validate his claim to be her victim. The general principle is this: *One person can* give *offense only if the other will* take *offense.* One person can insult, humiliate, intimidate, anger, bore, or provoke only if the other actively construes what he or she does as insulting, humiliating, intimidating, angering, boring, or provoking.

This observation has a surprising and frightening implication. When we think about how deftly and consistently one colluder like Becky can provoke another like Glen (and vice versa), we may be tempted to say that she exercises power over him. She keeps him upset by all her demands. And once we say the same sort of thing about Glen, we want to call their relationship *a power struggle.* But to describe the situation that way is misleading. It is far more accurate to say that *Glen put himself in Becky's power.* He *enabled* her offensiveness by his readiness to take offense at just about anything she did relating to Christmas. And on the other side, *she* put herself in *his* power and enabled *his* offensiveness in the same way.

Thus colluders only *appear* to control one another; in truth, they give control of themselves to one another, like people volunteering to play the part of puppets in a Punch and Judy show. *They individually use their agency, which is their power to act, not in controlling the other but in allowing themselves to be controlled!* They use their power to act to put themselves in one another's power! We use words like *touchy, thin-skinned,* and *hypersensitive* to describe such people. Sometimes I have thought of them as missile-seeking targets.

This is a pathetic picture of human relationships. Individuals scramble to control or dominate or manipulate one another in order to get what they think they want, when in reality they are giving themselves over to the others' control. Each is swept along as if in a whitewater flood by the offensiveness they ascribe to others. No one quite feels able to take responsibility for the direction of the group, whether it's a marriage, a family, a neighborly relationship, or a work team. The result is that tensions and even hatred escalate beyond what anyone intends or wishes, with each party certain of the malice and perversity of the others. Managers in one northwestern corporation that was riddled with collusions called this "the monster system." Another and most ugly word for it is *war.*

Thus do colluders lock themselves together in a single, complex control system wherein each gives power to the others. Their destinies are tied together more surely than with steel bands. The strength of these bands is to my mind one of the most astounding aspects of all human experience.

It also astounds me that people maintain the control system without deliberately trying to keep it going. None of them has a plan in mind to provoke the others so as to get proof of his or her innocence. It is enough that each of them feels victimized and just by feeling this way turns anything done by the others into a victimizing act. Together they conduct themselves like colonies of ants, who in their swarms go individually about their different duties without comprehending any overall colony strategy, but do so with an efficiency and coordination that could scarcely be improved upon if they *did* have an overall plan in mind. Colluders, too, swarm in their colonies without having in mind the circular and mutually reinforcing provocations they supply for one another, and yet they could not do it any better if they were being orchestrated by an invisible hand.

Each of us is bonded to other people in one way or another. In some cases these are bonds of love. In the case of colluders, they are bonds of suspicion, enmity, and fear. Colluders knot themselves together more and more tightly even as they individually feel further and further apart—misused, isolated, lonely, and alien. They're in bondage to the emotions by which they resent or fear or have contempt for one another. The bonds between them are bonds of anguish, not bonds of love.

CHAPTER 6

THE DARKNESS OF OUR EYES

Losing Our Way

Black Elk, the holy man of the Oglala Sioux, said, "It is in the darkness of their eyes that men lose their way." When we are stuck in a troubled emotional state, unable to see our way forward, we think it's because darkness shrouds our pathway. In reality, the darkness is in ourselves.

We can express and amplify Black Elk's point in the language we have been using in this book. This will enable us to review what we have just learned about collusion:

> As long as our feelings are accusing, whatever we do will smell of accusation.

> Others will detect little clues of tone and expression, revealing how we really feel, even when we take pains to pretend otherwise. And as we learned in the chapter on collusion, they're not likely to respond gratefully, but more likely to accuse us in return.

> And then *we, in turn,* will take offense, convinced by their accusing response to us that we were right to accuse them in the first place!

> Thus we will have lost our way—not because something evil has befallen us and deprived us of a clear view of the path that we should walk, but because of the evil toward others in our own hearts. "It is in the darkness of their eyes that men lose their way."

Now, if this darkness were outside of us instead of inside, our predicament would not be so terrible; we would not feel utterly helpless. But because the darkness is *within,* we can't see how to escape it. With every effort to find some way forward into light, we carry the darkness with us. It does not matter how generously or kindly or uprightly we try to act, we will do it accusingly. As the title of a Jon Kabat-Zinn book has it, "Wherever you go, there you are." We are like prisoners who try to escape by digging a hole in the wall of their cell and, crawling through it, find themselves in another cell. Self-betrayal and the self-deception and collusions that come with it are a kind of mental and emotional imprisonment.

Counterfeiting Goodness

We may not be prepared for all the implications of Black Elk's insight. Among other things, it means that *as long as our hearts are wrong, we can't do right.* Being I-It, we cannot act in an I-You way. Our actions can never be more than counterfeits of generosity, kindness, or consideration, for they will bear the taint of our impatience, resentment, suspicion, anxiety, fear, or whatever accusing thoughts and feelings we may have. In the hardened I-It condition, we are temporarily incapable of a completely caring response. The darkness in our eyes keeps us from seeing how such a response would be possible.

In a letter he sent to me, a young man named Ethan told of discovering that certain things he had done, which he thought of as acts of goodness, were in fact counterfeit. He was working, at age twenty-one, in a volunteer organization. This is part of what he wrote:

> I have only a few more months left of my work here. I have learned that I am here to love and not just to work. When I began I thought my purpose was to do the work, and everyone here thought me the hardest worker. It took me a long time to realize that this was an excuse.

Loving is much harder for me than work. With work you are satisfied right away with your efforts. When you come back to your quarters to sleep at night your body is all worn out. You know you have made a sacrifice. Until now I thought this was all there was to what I am supposed to be doing. I couldn't have been further from the truth. I have been given a personality through which I could love people, and I have not used it.

To put it bluntly, I had a kind of physical gratification in the exhaustion I felt from working hard, but I wasn't giving myself completely. And my joy was not full.

I remember my family took a trip to Scotland a few years back, when I was eighteen. I was the one who went to work two days before departure. I packed all the bags. I cleaned and packed the car and made sure everything was in order. I prepared meals when we were travelling. This work ethic served me well when I was in construction; I was the hardest worker and everyone told me so. Anyway, it was in Blackpool, on the way home, that I began to discover how inadequate my life plan was. Someone asked me to do one too many jobs, and I blew up. I had the perfect excuse. I had been doing all that work. I had the physical exhaustion that backed up my case. But I had not given all of myself; I had only worked. Because I did not love I did not know what joy is.

But I'm beginning to know that joy now.

Think of the various "kindly" things Ethan tried to do. If we speak of them superficially enough, so that we give no hint of his resentment, we can make them sound genuinely kind. We can point to the fact that he packed everyone's bag, cleaned and loaded the car, and prepared the meals. But even though he worked hard to get these things done, the "kindness" in them was counterfeit. The summons or prompting he had felt required him to do them in a truly considerate spirit, and this he did not do.

Fable

Speaking and acting according to our feelings is always the right thing to do.

Fact

If our feelings are not right, then expressing and acting upon them won't be right either.

We Fool Only Ourselves

It doesn't take much reflection to realize how warped the world is for those of us whose actions are morally counterfeit. We think we're doing what's best, all things considered, when we're not. We think others are treating us maliciously, or at least inconsiderately, when that may not be true. We think that their wrongdoing toward us will somehow make our conduct right. What should we call such irrationality? I call it *self-deception.*

But generally speaking, *other people are not taken in by our self-deceived, counterfeit actions.* Those who are not self-deceivingly stuck in their own accusing thoughts and feelings will see our public presentation of ourselves for what it is—an insecure, self-conscious, anxious striving to make a point about ourselves that is always a bit excessive, like bad acting. And even those who are deep in self-deception themselves will pick up on our accusing attitude and will interpret it in the worst possible light, as we learned when we studied collusion: They will tend to perceive it not as defensive but as offensive and will readily take offense

To illustrate the way others see through our counterfeit sincerity, consider the efforts of two colluding people to "communicate" about their differences. Glen (see chapter 5) says to Becky: "Let's talk about what we'll be doing for Christmas this year." His voice is as sweet and soft as he can make it. Does she think Glen has changed? Not likely. Despite the tone of his voice, his accusing and self-excusing purpose can be felt in his speech. Becky can sense it, so she thinks, "Here it comes. Another sneaky effort to get out of his responsibilities."

Becky says, "All right," as cordially as she can, trying to hide her deep suspicion. She has read recently that you can influence people most effectively when you listen before you speak. "What activities do you think we should plan?" she asks. But she's thinking, "Activities for the children, Glen, not for yourself." Does Glen think she's changed? Does he believe she's ready to compromise? No. He feels the edge in her voice; she cannot conceal it. "New tactics," he thinks, "same old strategy." And he braces himself for the demands he's sure are coming.

Thus "communication" solves nothing when it's mistrustful, and on self-betrayers' lips it is always mistrustful. In fact, it makes things worse; it collusively escalates the negative responses it is supposedly designed to stop. In truth, it cannot qualify as real communication at all; it's a different sort of act altogether. It might better be called "verbal sparring."

The same holds true of other counterfeits of goodness. They perpetuate collusion. Groveling for others' approval doesn't make them more accepting or appreciative. Adopting a certain body language to make others feel comfortable is quickly seen to be manipulative. Claiming one's rights in an accusing spirit may win lawsuits, but it will alienate most people.

Freud and his followers say that on a "conscious" level we do not comprehend why we act as we do, but "unconsciously" we know full well. But I believe we have no such unconscious self-knowledge; we possess no deep awareness of the truth. In fact, the truth concerning our self-betraying conduct is always out in the open for all to see, and to the degree that they're free of self-deception themselves, others perceive it. We are the ones who comprehend it least, because of our self-betrayals.

EVEN CONSCIENCE
GETS CORRUPTED

When we self-deceivingly counterfeit the considerate I-You responses required of us, the condition into which we have put ourselves can properly be called *moral blindness.* In this condition, we use words like *good* and *kind* and *upright* to describe behavior that merely appears to be good. Consequently, we are left with no words to describe genuine goodness, kindness, and uprightness. And when that happens we cannot tell the difference between the counterfeit and the genuine; we cannot avoid mistaking the counterfeit for the real thing. We become helpless to tell right from wrong anymore. This is what I mean by *moral blindness.*

How do we blind ourselves so? Think about how, when our hearts are open and sensitive, a prompting to treat someone considerately comes as a gentle invitation to do something we have nothing against doing and indeed welcome doing. It may invite us to comfort a child, help an elderly person onto the bus, cheer up a friend who is down, or assist a spouse with a Christmas project. I know how these promptings feel because I have felt them when my heart has been right. We jump forward willingly, even when what is required seems difficult physically or mentally or even financially. Such willingness expresses our innately considerate and generous nature. When our hearts are right, the obligation we feel to treat others generously comes to us as an opportunity.

But when we betray ourselves toward others and accuse them in our hearts, the way we experience the prompting changes in quality. Since we are sure others are mistreating us, going out of our way for them seems burdensome and even costly—and our now-perverted conscience backs us up. Thus does self-betrayal turn a potentially delightful opportunity to serve other human beings into a chore, a drudgery, a duty onerous to be borne. As we learned in chapter 3, in the I-You mode serving them may be hard, but in the I-It mode it is hard to bear.

You can see this by imagining yourself in the place of a self-betrayer—Jennifer, for example, whose story we read in chapter 3. You feel you ought to visit your hospitalized aunt. You decide to watch television rather than go right away—only the first part of the program, you tell yourself, and then you'll go. You get absorbed in the show, perhaps even more than if you had not needed an excuse for not going to the hospital. You may feel bothered by questions about what you're doing. Why haven't you jumped up from the couch, turned off the TV, grabbed your jacket, and started out the door? You think about not knowing your aunt very well. You remember how she seemed disinterested in you the last time you met. You worry about the awkwardness of trying to start a conversation with her. As you think these thoughts, the summons of your conscience persists: Visit your aunt!

But now that summons feels different. Why? Because you have been noticing, or inventing, negative qualities in your aunt you had not focused on before—qualities that might make it difficult to visit her and therefore give you an excuse if you didn't visit her. *And, therefore, what you now feel summoned to do is not to visit with a person who needs your company but to visit a person who in all likelihood will be disagreeable.* Earlier, you were almost looking forward to the visit, and now you feel pressured by your obviously absurd sense of duty to do something that will cost you a lot in terms of time and self-respect! Why, you ask yourself, should you sacrifice for someone who doesn't deserve it?

In no time at all you have so twisted things, so distorted your conscience, that the wrong thing to do has actually come to seem acceptable and perhaps even right. We can almost hear you (Jennifer) saying, "It's just not right for me to have to spend one of my precious evenings with a person who probably doesn't even want me to come and who certainly wouldn't do the same for me!"

By such rationalizing, our conscience can become so distorted that even learning about self-betrayal may not untwist it—I have even heard people say: "Well, I can see now that I've been betraying myself by not telling so-and-so what a jerk I think he is!" For such people, the right thing seems so costly—since it would be done for people they think are mistreating them—that they conclude it must be wrong.

So what you, in your imaginative role as Jennifer, would have accepted as right had you not betrayed yourself—visiting your hospitalized aunt—you have come to believe to be wrong. And what you would have thought wrong—staying home—you have come to think of as acceptable, maybe even right. Your self-betrayal and the accompanying accusation in your heart have corrupted your conscience. You can't see straight or think straight about your situation with your aunt anymore. In that regard you have become morally blind.

During the Christmas scenarios Glen, too, went through contortions that corrupted his conscience. The good he felt prompted to do became infused and infected with his accusing and resentful way of being. All the kindness he could muster got twisted up with his unkind feelings toward Becky. Consequently, treating her kindly became a hardship instead of a welcome opportunity. His grudging efforts to cooperate became an expression of his unkindness toward her instead of a genuine kindness. He even remembered thinking, "This is crazy" and "Giving our lives to these feverish and all-consuming projects just can't be right."

Similar things might be said about Becky. Her offense-taking had made her as morally blind as her husband.

In self-betrayal our moral sense or conscience becomes untrustworthy. In the darkness of our self-absorbed, suspicious thoughts and feelings, we cannot discern the way forward. We may think we know how to alleviate our troubled emotional condition, but we don't. Just how this happens—how we corrupt our conscience through our self-betrayals—we will examine in the next chapter, and there we will begin the discussion of what we can do to reverse the damage.

Fable
Conscience always tells us what's right, according to our own deepest values.

Fact
Like perceptions, memories, emotions, moods, impulses, and so on, conscience can become distorted, so as to support the lie we're living. We can make right seem wrong and wrong seem right.

SELF-JUSTIFYING STYLES

The varieties of moral counterfeiting seem endless, but here are a few examples:

> Conscientiousness, a good thing in a person whose heart is right, is, when counterfeited, what we call self-righteousness. Another version of it is perfectionism.

> Forthrightness when counterfeited is tactlessness or insensitivity.

> Humility counterfeited is self-disparagement.

> Standing up for one's rights, again a good thing if done with a considerate heart and for the right reason, becomes, when counterfeited, contentiousness.

Counterfeit consideration is the cloying behavior of the
"pleaser."

It will be helpful to describe just a few of these counterfeits,
which we will call *styles of self-betrayal.* Knowing the pitfalls makes
it easier to avoid them.

We might also call them *story lines,* for they are the various plot
patterns we invent in which we turn out to be exonerated or deserving in the way we have chosen to live. What we do may in fact be
counterfeit, but in our stories we appear morally courageous, or worthy of much better than we got, or unwilling to give in to opposition
or bad fortune, or in some other way fully excused or justified.

Some of these story lines emphasize our conscientiousness.
We think of ourselves as doing our duty *in spite of* how other
people are treating us. In other story lines we admit to falling short
of doing what we know we should, and we blame others for it. In
stories of both kinds, accusation and resentment play a central
part. We blame others either for making it hard for us to do our
duty or for keeping us from doing it.

In learning about these story lines, it helps to keep before us
some actual examples, such as those that follow.

Self-Assertiveness

Jennifer, the college student we just discussed, worked herself
into believing that visiting her aunt, who after all probably
wouldn't want to talk with her, would cost her too much personally. So she felt she was in danger of being taken advantage of and
therefore needed to look out for herself. "It's just not right for
me to have to spend one of my few nights off traveling across
town on the bus to see a person who probably doesn't even want
me to come," she said to herself. Thus she transformed the wrong
of neglecting her aunt into the counterfeit right of taking care of

herself. Self-assertiveness counterfeits our legitimate need and obligation to take proper care of ourselves.

Self-Righteousness, or Making Oneself a Martyr

Instead of staying home self-assertively, Jennifer could have gone ahead and visited her aunt in spite of the personal sacrifice it required. Precisely because of the hardship involved—remember, her thoughts and feelings focused on her aunt's criticisms of her and on the difficulties of taking the bus to the hospital—she could have silently congratulated herself for rising to her duty, in spite of all the obstacles. We call this style "self-righteousness." It consists of doing what's outwardly the right thing, but resentfully and grudgingly—and therefore proudly.

Self-righteousness can also be considered an instance of holding feelings inside ourselves rather than letting them out. Here is an example of that type of self-righteousness: Philip, one of my research associates, said he came home one night fantasizing about how loving he was going to be to his children.

> I planned, after an orderly dinner with no squabbling and no stern looks from me, to gather our two little children around the fireplace, read them a story, tuck them into bed, and tell them I loved them.
>
> My train was an hour late. When I finally got home, I went through the door determined to be cheerful and kind. But dinner wasn't on the table. Marsha wasn't even getting it ready. It was her turn to fix it, too. Was she waiting for *me* to do it?
>
> For a moment I felt I ought to help her out. But then I just got bitter. How could I be the kind of father I'm supposed to be in this kind of mess?
>
> I felt like letting out a bellow, but I didn't. I never do. I did what I always do. I hung up my coat (so there would

be at least one thing put away in the house) and went to work cleaning up the mess. First, I put the children in the tub and got them properly bathed. Then I did the dishes and put away clothes and vacuumed everywhere.

Marsha said, "Please, stop, will you?" I'm sure she felt humiliated to have me pitch in when she had obviously been wasting time. People who don't act responsibly are going to feel humiliated by people who do.

But I didn't say anything back. Maybe I should have given her "what for" or not helped her at all. But I wasn't going to stoop to her level. And I tried not to have an angry expression, even though it was hard. I'm above pouting and tantrums and that sort of thing.

It took till ten o'clock. When we went to bed, Marsha was still upset. After all these years I know her well enough to know that no matter how hard I had worked, she still wouldn't have appreciated it.

In some ways, Philip *appeared* to be doing what he felt he ought to do and did not seem to be a self-betrayer at all. He rolled up his sleeves and went to work. He didn't bellow, though he felt he had plenty of reason to do so, and he didn't storm out of the house in a huff. He was a man who felt he should do his part and work with his wife at home, and so he pitched in and he helped her. . . .

But not really. His was not the manner of a person who dives into the work because he's anxious to help, any more than was Ethan's cleaning the car, packing the lunches, and so on, for the family vacation. The primary point of Philip's conduct wasn't to rise to his duty and help, but *to prove* he was rising to his duty. He cleaned the house not because of Marsha but *in spite of* her. He made the effort *not for her but for himself.* So he cleaned the house without really being helpful—a counterfeit act, like Glen's participation in the Christmas projects and my "mature" and steely voiced answer to my son Matthew's question.

Childishness

You can also imagine Philip acting in a childish manner that is one of the opposites of self-righteousness. Picture him refusing to pitch in and help clean up the house and loudly criticizing Marsha besides. He doesn't hold his feelings in when he wants to bellow; he lets them out. He throws down his coat, stamps his feet, and yells, "Don't you know Thursday's my hardest day? I come home exhausted, hoping for a little peace, and this is what I get! What've you been doing since you got home? Watching TV? I take over when *you're* late, but when *I'm* late nothing gets done—even though it's not my fault the train was delayed!" (To keep this childish version of Philip distinct from the self-righteous one, I'll call him Philip II; we'll talk about an I-You version, Philip III, in the next chapter).

The differences between childishness and self-righteousness are all behavioral and outward, not attitudinal and inward. The thoughts and feelings from which these responses spring are nearly identical. Both versions of Philip feel victimized by what they see as their wives' inconsiderateness; they both live in a world transformed into a place that makes it hard to do the right thing. This inner similarity of the two might seem surprising, because the outward differences could scarcely be greater—the childish Philip rants, swears, and refuses to help, while the self-righteous one furiously vacuums the floors, broils the hamburgers, and scours the kitchen. But inwardly, in regard to their perception of the world and their feelings about it, they are very much alike. They differ in style, not in substance.

Thus self-betrayers' outward style should be considered a matter of insignificant detail. Indeed, a self-righteous person who becomes convinced she's "wound too tight" and needs to change will try to find some way to express her pent-up feelings and "let off steam"—and as a result only manages to act childishly. The outward details change, but the accusing attitude remains. Similarly, the childish person who realizes his anger is destroying his relationships will try to find a way to "control his emotions"— and if he does, he will only be acting self-righteously. Again, the details of his way of being change, but not its accusing, I-It essence.

Perfectionism

Perfectionism is a close cousin of self-righteousness. The difference seems to be that self-righteousness is arrogant, self-congratulating, dramatic, and usually interested in making sure everyone understands that "I'm doing my duty." Perfectionism, on the other hand, seems obsessed with the duty itself, whether or not people can see it being done. Perfectionists seem more obsessed with convincing themselves, rather than other people, of their worth.

Imagine a perfectionist person in Jennifer's place. Not only would she have immediately gone off to visit her hospitalized aunt, but she would have found other ways to convince herself of her worth, like bringing homemade snacks, brightening the hospital room with decorations, and following up with a note on a perfumed card. To those of us in a perfectionist mode, the world presents us with a barrage of "moral" demands, and we consider ourselves members of a moral militia marching bedraggled but brave to the cadence of "shoulds" and "oughts" that we alone can hear. We are desperately anxious to prove we are doing everything that might possibly be good to do, fearful we will not qualify as worthwhile if we pass up any chance to sacrifice ourselves. Hence we're perpetually exhausted. We're sure our health is slipping. It's hard for us to sleep. We feel we're getting old before our time. We're forever postponing opportunities to rest or play. Our conduct seems to pose the question: What more can possibly be expected of a human being?

Yet we are not at peace. Our massive conscientiousness is accompanied by an equally massive, though possibly denied, resentment. In our eyes, others seldom do their share. We've got to do it or it won't get done. When others volunteer to help us, we don't readily consent. "Oh, no, it's all right. I can manage it." And why don't we want their help? Because we so desperately seek approval, especially our own approval, that we cannot miss an opportunity to get it.

But a perfectionist's conscience cannot be satisfied. Meeting its demands does not put it to rest. This is simply because, fundamentally, perfectionists are interested not in *being* conscientious but in proving their conscientiousness, and this requires demanding more and more of themselves, unendingly.

This, incidentally, helps us understand what's wrong with one frequently heard excuse. People sometimes say, when they think about self-betrayal, "If I did everything that seemed right to do, I'd be so frenzied and weary I wouldn't have time for anything else. I can't put that kind of pressure on myself!" However, when we are not betraying ourselves we do *not* require more of ourselves than we can do. We may wish we could do two needed things at once, but we don't have any reason to beat ourselves up because we can't. We do that only if we're self-betrayers of the perfectionistic kind, having to prove we're doing all we can because our hearts are not at peace about ourselves.

∾

"I'M JUST NOT ANY GOOD"

We will need to consider one more style of excuse-making. It's given a section of its own because it requires a more thorough treatment than the others. It is generally more difficult to recognize as the living of a lie.

We've talked about three styles or story lines in which Jennifer might have carried out her self-betrayal regarding her aunt. In one, she visits her in the hospital proudly conscious of what it's costing her to do it. This we called *self-righteousness.* In another, she stretches herself beyond all reason to do everything imaginable for her aunt, fretting morning and night over whether she's done enough. This style we called *perfectionism.* In a third story line she stays at home, insisting it's not fair or right to have to pay such a price for someone who won't even appreciate the visit. We called this style *self-assertiveness.*

Besides these three story lines, there is available to her another, which we'll call *self-disparagement.* Jennifer might stay at home, castigating herself for failing to do what she should have done. Imagine her, brooding about what an unworthy person she must be not even to have the gumption to visit a relative who has fallen ill. She feels crummy. She remembers the many times she has disappointed herself this way. She thinks, "More proof that I'm just not one of those courageous, good people who does noble, admirable things for others."

It *looks like* she's admitting a truth about herself, but not so. Instead, she's putting forward an excuse. She doesn't do what she's supposed to do because, she claims, she's just no good. *Blaming oneself can work as an excuse just as well as blaming someone else.*

Like all self-betrayers' excuses, this excuse always includes an accusation of others, though more subtly. You can see this in the following story, in which Ardeth is sitting at the piano with her daughter Tiffany.

Ardeth: We pay Mrs. Simpson forty dollars a lesson, and
    you refuse to practice.

Tiffany: I *am* practicing!

Ardeth: You're more worried about what you're wearing than about doing the serious work Mrs. Simpson gives you. What good is it for us to make the sacrifice so you can have this good training when you won't make the time count?

Tiffany: You always say that. If you'd quit bugging me all the time, I could practice just fine.

Ardeth: It doesn't do any good to practice a piece incorrectly. You learn to play the wrong way, and then you have to waste a lot more time undoing the bad habits.

Tiffany: I know what I'm doing. You're not the one Mrs. Simpson shows how to do it.

Ardeth: You might as well take the group lesson from Miss Baker for fifteen dollars if you're going to practice it wrong.

Tiffany: If you're so worried about the money, why don't I just stop taking lessons?

Ardeth: Don't fly off the handle. When you get all upset, you can't concentrate on practicing.

Tiffany: I came in this morning and started practicing, and all you can think of is everything I'm doing wrong. I don't even want to play the piano. I could have gotten my blouse pressed in the time you've wasted hassling me for nothing.

Ardeth: You see, you're trying to get out of practicing just like all the other times. You see?

Tiffany: Okay. So I *don't* want to practice! So I *am* trying to get out of it by all my little tricks! I *am* only interested in what I'm going to wear to school so I can impress all the boys. I *don't* think that playing the piano is the most divine thing people can do. So now are you satisfied? I'm just exactly as rotten as you say I am!

Ardeth: That's all I'm going to take of this, Tiffany Ann
Thomas! I do everything I can to help you develop your
talents so you won't turn out to be a nothing, and this is
what I get. Get practicing, young lady, or you won't be
going out with your friends for a *month!*

Initially, Tiffany countered her mother's charges of poor dis-
cipline and neglect by contending she was practicing as well as she
could. Then suddenly she shifted, "confessing" to everything that
her mother had accused her of. "So now are you satisfied? I'm
exactly as rotten as you say I am!" By this stratagem, she robbed
her mother's criticisms of their force and gave herself a new and
different justification for what she was doing. This was a justification more difficult for Ardeth to deal with than Tiffany's previous
arguments. The excuse Tiffany had now was iron-clad: "I can't
help what I'm doing because *that's just the way I am!*"

In this mode of self-presentation the self-disparager *appears*
to confess to being completely at fault. She *appears* to accept as
true the "I am worthless" image. But this is not so much a forthright confession as a strategy for evading responsibility, an excuse
for not doing what needs to be done.

When we are caught up in self-betrayal, "admitting" we are
unworthy is just one more strategy in our repertoire. It gives us
just as good a justification for acting irresponsibly as the strategy
of condemning others. It is a powerful maneuver because claiming to be a victim of our make-up or nature is even harder to
refute than claiming to be a victim of others. (To call it mistaken
seems like telling terminally ill patients that they are exaggerating
their illness.)

The maneuver is powerful for another reason. We think that
we are being honest, that we are "admitting the truth at last." If we
were living a lie before, then surely, we think, we are telling the
truth now. Indeed, we can say that although we may not be the
wondrous individuals we have made ourselves out to be, we at

least are not being hypocrites anymore. We believe we have mustered up the courage to be honest with ourselves. But the truth is, we are taking up this position accusingly and self-victimizingly—and therefore with violence in our hearts. We make people feel guilty for not rescuing us, or for being successful themselves, and thus hold people hostage to our misery (recall Wally's unwillingness to sing in front of his friends, described in chapter 4).

We have all met breastbeaters who, convinced of their worthlessness, beat themselves up verbally and emotionally. Breastbeaters are not as purely self-condemning as they look. Theirs is really just another way of playing the victim and nurturing feelings of self-justification. Nietzsche wrote: "When we despise ourselves, we love the despiser in ourselves."

Thus Tiffany said to her mother: "I'm a spoiled and lazy kid wasting your money and trying to impress the boys. I'm just exactly as rotten as you say I am!" By this she blamed not only something inside herself she believed she wasn't responsible for, but her mother also. Tiffany is gaining again that delicious sense of self-justification that for a moment she thought she had almost lost. She wouldn't have admitted it, but she loved the self-despiser in herself.

We can imagine Tiffany play-acting this part just a bit, only half convincing herself of her victimhood. But in many other cases self-disparagers experience themselves rather thoroughly as worthless and unacceptable. They know first-hand—and they are right—that their suffering is real. They are *sure* of their worthlessness and unacceptability.

Ernie, one of our salesmen who works on straight commission, is constantly down on himself. He's one of those guys who talks himself out of making about half the calls he should be making. And he backs away from opportunities to close a sale.

It seems to me like he's on the verge of tears most of the time, because of the hopelessness of his situation, I guess. I've heard him say, "Nothing breaks my way" and "I can't seem to do anything right." He hates himself for all his failures and yet he keeps failing anyway.

He's said several times he'd like to quit because he's dragging all the rest of us down. One time when I was reviewing his monthly performance, he asked how I could stand to have a person like him around.

Self-condemning guilt like Ernie's can be thought of as self-betrayal on the "pay as you go" plan: *If as guilty people we feel terrible enough, then we have paid for the right to keep wallowing in our problems; we do not have to accept responsibility for them.* By seeing himself as no good, Ernie grabbed hold of a perfect excuse for not performing. He *could not* do any better than he did because he was convinced there was something wrong with him— and there was also something wrong with all those others whose example or competition or contempt or rejection of him put success beyond his reach.

Ernie's story raises an issue we should address here. Any one of the styles or story lines we've discussed can dominate a person's life so completely that it seems to define his or her personality and character. Ernie's particular self-disparagement seems at least as enclosing and final as any of the other story lines, even at their worst. Of him we want to exclaim, "That's just the way he *is!* It's not a matter of his choosing how he will be. So it's foolish to imagine him changing in any fundamental way."

That indeed is how he seems. But against this impression there's something hopeful to keep in mind, which springs from what we are learning about the origin of negative, afflicted attitudes and emotions. To the degree that these attitudes and emotions are accusing and self-excusing, we are responsible for them, and to that very degree we can stop indulging in them. For a lot of people the major question is *whether* we can escape them. But the *whether* question is settled: We *can* escape. The vital and imperative question is *how*. Even someone like Ernie can abandon his life story line and start afresh, like a writer who junks a novel she's been writing when she realizes she'll never be able to make it work.

೧৲

No Exit?

To the extent we have stricken ourselves with moral blindness and made ourselves unable to tell our counterfeit actions from genuine goodness, we have lost the opportunity to do what is genuinely good. That opportunity has disappeared from the world as we are experiencing it for one simple reason: Everything we can think of to do while in our darkened state will be no more genuine than the acts we're trying to stop doing. Our efforts to get ourselves unstuck only keep us stuck.

Think about Glen in the midst of his Christmas collusion with Becky, fending off her pressures, preoccupied with how he would get his responsibilities at the office completed, and imagining the chaos that would befall the family if they tried to implement all her plans for Christmas projects and activities. In that condition, he could not conceive of responding to her the way he had before the Christmas collusion began. He could not imagine, given the frustrated and accusing feelings in his heart, of delighting in her being, prizing her ideas, wholeheartedly seeking her happiness, wanting never to be out of her company, or welling up with a grateful and generous spirit toward her. He could not cherish her while judging and criticizing her. Becky as he knew her before she became so demanding, he could cherish—but not Becky the way she was now.

You can see Glen's moral blindness in this. The opportunity to do what would have been truly considerate, generous, and caring was hidden from him in the most effective manner possible—by his own self-worried, self-excusing attitude. That opportunity disappeared from the world as he perceived it. It had no place in the interpretation of Becky that he projected onto her. He could not have discerned that opportunity no matter how hard he scanned the situation in front of him. That's what it means to be "in the box"—to be reduced to moral blindness by the darkness of our eyes.

No wonder, then, that he thought his wrongdoing right, or at least excusable. For there lay before him only two main ways to respond to Becky, and both of them were accusing and self-excusing. He could refuse to do much to help her on the Christmas projects and believe he was standing up for what he thought was right. Or he could give in, sacrifice his work and the balance of family activities he kept talking about, and do everything she wanted. These were the possibilities as he saw them—submit, give in, and sacrifice, or stand up, assert himself, and defy. Both of these alternatives are accusing; neither is generous-spirited, kind, happy, or truly willing. Thus, *the boxed-in world we experience as*

FIGURE 4

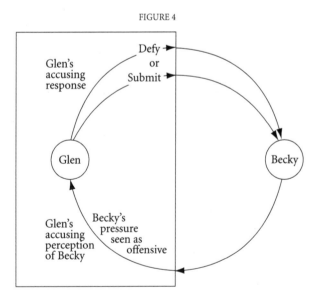

self-betrayers offers us opportunities to submit in humiliation or to stick up for ourselves defiantly, which are both self-absorbed actions, but it offers us no chance of simply doing the right thing without concern for ourselves.

What has just been described—the condition of moral blindness in which we cannot distinguish between doing the right thing and portraying ourselves (falsely) as doing the right thing—explains why we are stuck. We have no way to test our thoughts and feelings and actions to discover their dishonesty because we have lost touch with the honest thoughts and feelings and actions we would need to compare them to.

Our predicament is not unlike that of the victim of one of those detective-novel burglaries in which the priceless diamond tiara is replaced by a cubic zirconium imitation that looks just like it to the untrained eye. When the owner checks to make sure nothing has happened to her prized possession, she always receives reassurance that it is safe and sound, and she may therefore never discover her loss. In just this way, Glen (of the Christmas story) and Jennifer (refusing to visit her aunt) and Ethan (packing the family van and making the meals) all felt they knew all about what it meant to treat family members kindly. In observing themselves, they could see with their own eyes an individual trying his or her best to be kind in spite of a situation that made it hard. Yet all the while what they were doing was counterfeit and wrong, and what they were thinking and feeling was self-deceived and false.

We shall never get out of this predicament until we can chase the darkness from our eyes, see what's right without distortion, and do the right without counterfeiting it. This requires a change of heart. But how can we change our hearts when we can't even appreciate how much our hearts need changing?

Answering this question, at least in part, is the purpose of the next five chapters.

CHAPTER 7

THE LIGHT
BECKONS
ALWAYS

Attunement of Souls

We are constantly receiving signals from others that reveal something of their needs and hopes and fears. Martin Buber expressed this idea in these words: "Living means being addressed." We are called upon by others' unspoken requests, expressed in their faces and gestures and voices, to treat them with consideration and respect.

Recall the mother we read about in chapter 2 who felt she could not keep from criticizing her sloppy teenage daughter. Very likely the message that addressed her was not "Don't scold her; listen to her." More probably that message seemed to come from the girl herself: "Don't scold me, Mother; listen to me!" To be a person in a family or community is to pick up from others such gently expressed imperatives as these. As we observed in chapter 2, in large measure our humanity consists in our ability to sense and respect and respond to the humanity of others.

We should mark this point well. The part of our nature that is sensitive to the reality of others makes possible both our deepest sorrows and our deepest joys. It is by this capacity that we are able to attune ourselves one to another, soul to soul, and bond together in friendship, love, and loyalty, or else turn one another into enemies and bond ourselves to each other by suspicion and fear. The second, discordant bonding is the bondage of anxiety and strife and helplessness in which we self-betrayers get ourselves emotionally stuck. The first, resonant bonding is freedom from all that discord and suffocating self-worry.

One summer our family drove to our friend Bob Amott's

cabin on the Snake River in Idaho for our vacation. On the way we sang together for what seemed like hours: "Barges" and "Mrs. O'Leary" and the Jell-O commercial and a couple of dozen other rounds, faster and louder and more creatively with every mile that passed. Nobody got tired. What stopped our singing was some-one's saying, "Anybody remember the time when . . . ?" Invariably Matthew's recollections were the funniest because he could remember every detail of everything that had ever happened to him and could mimic all the people in the story. The windows were down because the station wagon wasn't air-conditioned, and all the children had their feet out to feel the breeze around their ankles and through their toes. I could tell that Susan had freed her mind of the lists of doings that preoccupied her at home, and I thought, "This is exactly how it's supposed to be."

What does it take to achieve such emotional intimacy? The fundamental ingredient is an awakening of each individual to the others and a willing effort to respond without any personal agenda in exactly the way that seems most right, considerate, and helpful. Susan had opened herself to a lively gratitude for the closeness we were all feeling for one another—even though, to her embarrass-ment, we had left the flowerbed by our front stairs still unplanted. I had tossed overboard my worries about the work deadline I would not meet, as if they were baggage too heavy for the trip. Andrea was not thinking about Cassie's having broken her water-color box that very morning; diffident and cautious though she was, she accepted and appreciated her rambunctious little sister without any reservation. And when Tim leaned his head on Emily's shoulder and later draped his legs across her lap—invasions of her space that had thrown her into a tizzy on other occasions—she did not find him the least bit annoying, but instead became his older and wiser sponsor and read him stories when the others slept. No one expressed appreciation out loud—indeed, I may have been the only one thinking how happy and perfect was this day—but for each of us the others mattered more than defending our individual rights and ensuring our personal comfort. The profound sense of connection we felt one to another that summer's day would not have been possible except for the capacity in each of us to sense one another's inward yearnings, fears, and love.

ᴄ᷍

CONSCIENCE AND THE TRUTH

What happens, then, when we fall into self-betrayal and ruin this attunement? What becomes of our connections with one another when we lodge ourselves obstinately within our individual boxes? Do we close ourselves off from such connections entirely? If so, what hope have we of emerging from the condition that Black Elk called "the darkness of our eyes"? To answer these questions we need to learn a little more about conscience and its relation to the signals that flow to us from other beings.

The Light That Comes from Others

In chapter 2, we spoke of the indications always available from others, guiding us in how we ought to treat them. If we are at all observant, we usually have a pretty good sense of other people's state of mind—for example, whether they are angry, distressed, or glad about their present situation—and this guides us quite well in how we should act toward them and what we ought to say. Tim's head snuggled on Emily's lap and the contentment on his face showed her quite clearly what she could do to please and reassure him. She needed no special training to understand how laying her arm across his chest and talking with him about the party at her friend's house would affect him; this was a know-how she had already acquired as part of living with others during her fourteen years of life.

We need some names for the signals that come to us from others without any special effort on their part. We might speak of receiving a prompting or summons, of sensing an imperative or obligation, of feeling called upon to respond in one way or another, of being given guidance. We might also speak of others' inviting our response. But for the purposes of the discussions to come, I want also to use another term, one that may at first seem a bit puzzling. I want to call the signals that flow to us from others *light*. It's a helpful name for these signals because it suggests that, like the physical light that illuminates the world for us, these signals show us the way forward.

Conscience May Change, but the Light Does Not

In chapter 6 we discussed corruption of conscience, and we need for just a moment to review what was said.

When Jennifer began to find faults in her aunt, to cover Jennifer's failure to visit her aunt in the hospital, she made that visit seem hard to make. Why should she put herself in the company of a person she knew was critical of her? What might have seemed to her an invitation and an opportunity now struck her as awkward and humiliating.

Once this deformity of soul had taken place—once the moral blindness had set in—Jennifer's conscience was thoroughly bamboozled. Whatever she did received her conscience's approval, for remember, she could no longer tell the difference between a counterfeit of goodness and the real thing. If she had made the visit, her conscience would have patted her on the back, because making that visit would have been a hard thing to do. When she failed to go, her conscience endorsed that too, for the same basic reason—because it would have been hard to do.

We can see from this example that by means of our conscience, which ought to protect us from self-deception, we are able to fabricate support for whatever lie we may be living!

What happens in such cases? How do we lose our sense of right and wrong? Isn't our conscience still active?

To answer those questions we must draw a clear distinction between the light, or the source of our understanding of right and wrong, and conscience. The light does not get snuffed out. It continues always to stream toward us from the faces and voices and gestures of others. "Living means being addressed." Precisely because the light originates not from within ourselves but from the inward life of others, nothing we do can staunch its flow. Our conscience, on the other hand, is part of us, one of our faculties or abilities. If we deceive ourselves, conscience is deceived also. The light does not change, but conscience does. And it changes by making the light seem different than it is. It distorts the truth about others.

Historically the word *conscience* was used to designate something different from our sense of right and wrong. Studies of the development of the word from its Latin beginnings (and also the development of its Greek counterpart, *suneidesis*) reveal that historically it meant nothing more than being conscious of ourselves, our responses, and our actions. It is, literally, the knowledge of ourselves that we share with ourselves. Think of it as partly a sort of self-monitoring by which we observe whether we are acting according to our sense of right and wrong and partly a talking to ourselves about how well we are doing. Thus, if we have done nothing wrong, we can say, truthfully, "My conscience is clear." If we have done wrong and admitted it to ourselves, we say, "I have something on my conscience."

It's this conscience, this self-understanding, that changes when we betray ourselves; it gives the light a distorted meaning that serves our self-justifying purposes, a meaning it does not have in and of itself. We should be warned that the adage, "Let your conscience be your guide!" is sound advice only when we haven't allowed our consciences to become corrupted. Sometimes it's better to say: "Let the truth (about others' needs, for example) be your guide!" Or, "Let the light be your guide."

Now, you may not want to use the word *conscience* as I have used it. You may prefer saving this word to describe the source of our understanding of right and wrong. Obviously, you can use the word that way if you like. All that matters here is that, however we choose to use the words involved, we avoid confusing the two elements we are talking about: (1) the reality of other creatures and of God that guides us in how we ought to respond to them, which I have been calling *light,* and (2) our inherent capacity, which I have been calling *conscience,* to monitor what we are doing. Light we do not control and cannot change; conscience we may misuse to twist our perception of the light and of how faithfully we are responding to it.

ᔆᕉ

A PERVERSE SENSITIVITY

We self-betrayers, then, do not lose touch with the light. In fact, we're intensely preoccupied with it—in its twisted form, of course. We stay vigilantly alert to others, on the lookout for evidence that will justify us. Almost always, this evidence against others is our distorted interpretation of the very signals that, if our hearts were not accusing, would reveal to us their needs. In the Christmas story, Glen took attentive note of every one of Becky's needs for help on Christmas projects. But he perceived them as pressure to ignore the rest of his responsibilities and throw himself recklessly into these projects. And for her part, Becky never failed to note well all of Glen's desperate efforts to get to work on time or relax with the children and took them to be further attempts on his part to get out of his Christmas responsibilities.

We might be tempted to call those who would do this sort of thing insensitive to others' feelings. After all, they seem to treat others as objects to be used or pushed out of the way. But on the contrary, they are *hyper*sensitive to one another, alert to every possible indication of inconsiderate or neglectful intent. That's why we think of them as insensitive—not because of inattentiveness but because of selfishness. Their keen attention to one another resembles that of a soldier on guard duty, alertly suspicious of everyone, whereas a true sensitivity would be more like the attention paid by a medic to a comrade's battlefield wounds. Our insensitivity as self-betrayers is best described not as attending to ourselves rather than to others, but rather as attending to others *for our sake* rather than *for their sake.*

The word *perverse* aptly expresses this self-absorbed hypersensitivity to others. *Versio* means to turn, and in earlier times *perversion* meant to turn away from the sacred or enlightening things toward something profane or degraded. More recently, the word has acquired the connotation of obstinacy or willful hardness, as when we say of people who refuse to admit something that's right in front of their eyes, "They're just being perverse." This word helpfully captures the fact that the guarded, suspicious, I-It attitude is not a way of being on its own, but a twisting, distorting, or misshaping of the natural, good, and graceful way of being that would be ours were we not caught up in self-betrayal.

I Am My "Box"

What we are learning in this chapter helps to clarify what was intended with the box metaphor introduced in chapter 2 and used in chapter 5 to represent important elements of collusion. The walls of the box don't surround us, like the walls of a room. They don't cut us off from other people. Instead, they're our distorted perceptions of people. It's best to think of the box as the self-absorbed, defensive way we become when we betray ourselves. We aren't isolated *within* the box. We *are* the box.

We might liken ourselves to a malfunctioning television set, picking up the signal but distorting it terribly. Or, to change the metaphor, we might think of ourselves as a lump of murky gelatin, as compared, say, to a perfectly clean pane of glass with no irregularities in it at all. Signals from others can and do penetrate, but they get warped and jumbled by the irregular texture through which they must pass.

We can represent this in the box model:

FIGURE 5

I AM MY BOX

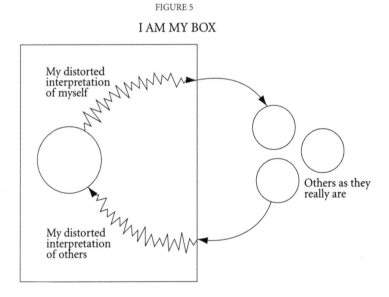

The point is that in self-betrayal, we *do* pay close attention to the people we harden ourselves against. But, as Leo Rosten is reputed to have said, "We see them not as *they are* but as *we are*."

This truth suggests that we must also use Buber's term *I-It* with care. We do not really regard other people as objects when we are in that mode of being. Instead, we regard them as subjects, able to act on their own and be impressed, intimidated, or otherwise manipulated by our self-displays. The way we sometimes treat people may bear superficial resemblance to the way we treat mere mannequins, but when we observe it closely we see that it differs profoundly. The story of the "intellectual" honors student from chapter 3 shows that even to marginalize or reject people requires recognizing and acknowledging something of their inward life and their ability to perceive and respond to us—in short, something of their humanity.

⁓

SAME REALITY, DIFFERENT INTERPRETATION

In this chapter we have discovered that the light that will dispel the darkness of our eyes is constantly available, pouring toward us in an uninterrupted stream. Upon this truth hangs our hope.

And we actively attend to and appropriate that light, but in a perverse way that turns it into darkness. We don't cut ourselves off from it; we vigilantly misconstrue it and simultaneously keep our attention away from the light that would flow to us from other, more positive relationships. Upon this truth hangs our despair.

It follows that what we need is not more light—not any additional understanding of right and wrong. Light is abundantly available. We have access to plenty of outside help. What we need is to receive the light straightforwardly and to respond as we feel directed.

Yielding to the light is deceptively simple. Remember Philip, the impatient husband in chapter 6? We considered him in both a self-righteous version, Philip I, and a childish one, Philip II. Imagine now a Philip III. Like the others, he comes home late, envisioning a quiet evening with the children, only to discover an awful mess that requires a few hours of clean-up. Like the other Philips, he feels that he ought to help his wife, Marsha, with the cleaning. But unlike them, he simply helps her. No resentment. No fanfare. No secret wish for a video camera on the wall to record his performance. It goes without saying that he would rather be doing something else less taxing and less disruptive to his plans. Or at least he would rather be doing something else if Marsha didn't need him. But she does need him, and so he prefers to help her. He savors no sense of superiority or triumph as he works beside her. Nor does it occur to him to blame her or anyone else, because he doesn't need to justify or excuse himself for anything.

Philip III cherishes exactly the same hopes for the evening and encounters exactly the same mess and confronts exactly the same wife and children as his self-righteous and childish counterparts. He is addressed by exactly the same light, offered the same guidance, placed under the same obligation. But he doesn't distort this light; he has no need to. Is it unrealistic to say that he sees Marsha as needing his help? Would it be going too far to say he's glad he's home to help and perhaps even wishes he had been able to get home earlier? Is he able to see exactly how things are with Marsha because he's not concerned about himself? Yes. He sees her clearly because he is not accusing her and distorting his understanding of her situation and feelings. Quite apart from the state of his physical surroundings, he lives in a blaze of light.

Conscience without Stress

People who chronically interpret others defensively and self-protectively think the Philip IIIs of the world are naïve and even stupid and in any case set up to be taken advantage of. They cannot believe a person could be better off seeing others compassionately and actually wanting to help where help is needed.

This is the moral skepticism of a corrupted conscience, which experiences doing right by others as a drudge, a sacrifice, a favoring of others' needs over one's own—or else a self-righteous project for "goody-goodies." As we have seen, doing the right thing is never an easy, natural, welcomed opportunity for a corrupted conscience.

But when we simply do what we think is right—when our conscience is clear—we have a wholly different experience of invitations to right and wrong. We may scarcely notice, or not notice at all, that something is being required of us. It doesn't strike us as hard to treat other people considerately because we have no reason to think those people don't deserve it. Our responses flow easily from us, without restraint, because we are simply allowing ourselves to be as we really are. The "promptings" that come to us don't have that burdensome, "ought to" feeling. They seem more like the invitations and opportunities they are than like demands.

This explains why, when we search our past for episodes of "doing right" or "doing our duty," we are unlikely to recall, under that label, the moral invitations we've experienced and obeyed. They didn't seem like calls to duty. When we became aware of others' needs, we made no fuss about doing what they required, because we weren't chalking up points for ourselves on a mental scoreboard. For that reason we don't remember them as times when we did anything remarkable. In contrast, the occasions we are most likely to remember are the times when we resisted doing the right thing and therefore found it difficult and admirable to do. Our sensing of right and wrong, of how we ought to respond to others, is like a current in which we float downstream: We seldom notice it until we try to swim against it.

This is one reason why it is mistaken to get discouraged when thinking about self-betrayal. We tend to call to mind only a portion of the evidence relating to our moral character—we remember the unworthy acts and not the worthy ones, because the latter were acts we took no notice of at the time. Very likely we have performed many worthy acts we did not notice at the time and consequently don't recall. We ought not to overlook the fact that we simply and straightway do much and perhaps most of what we feel we ought to do.

The following dialogue, which comes from Jim Robertson's fertile imagination, illustrates the flow and serenity of the life guided by the light. As you read this imagined interview, remember: two people can receive the same signals, same invitations, and same guidance, but interpret them differently.

> Host: Snow White, it's been claimed that you weren't the least bit miserable while you were living with those dwarfs. That's awfully hard to believe.
>
> Snow White: There wasn't anything to be miserable about.
>
> Host: You are a princess. Before you fell into that situation, you had all sorts of people waiting on you. And then suddenly you were forced to keep house and fix meals and wash clothes, not just for one man with the idea that a woman's place is to be stuck at home, but for *seven* of them!
>
> Snow White: They were very kind to me. I enjoyed getting the little place in order, as best I could.
>
> Host: In order to feel good about yourself, I suppose—keep up your self-esteem.
>
> Snow White: I don't think so. It's just because it needed cleaning.
>
> Host: You could have made them your servants. They adored you. You were more experienced and sophisticated than they.

Snow White: They worked hard all day in the mine. I didn't know anything about mining, but taking care of the house and the clothes and the meals was something I could do, so I did it.

Host: I hope you won't be offended if I tell you that this story reminds me of Patty Hearst. You made yourself the slave of seven grimy little miners way below your social class, and not one of them with an ounce of sex appeal as far as I can see. Perhaps you don't want to disclose what went on in that little nest, away from the rest of the world. I'm giving you an opportunity to tell it how it really was. (Pause.)

Host (continuing): Well, I can see you're not going to take this chance to set the record straight. Let's turn to our other guest, Cinderella, who like Snow White has also undergone a long period of deprivation and enforced labor. What I can't understand about you, Cinderella, is how you stood it when the others got to go out in society, to fancy balls in elegant gowns, and you couldn't.

Cindy: They didn't seem to enjoy themselves very much. I tried to cheer them up, but they seemed to like being unhappy. I think I love living a lot more than they do.

Host: But even after you got to go to a ball yourself, you were content to come back to work. Haven't you ever heard the famous saying, "How're you gonna keep them down on the farm, after they've seen Paree?" How could you ever be happy about your lot in life once you saw how the other half lives?

Cindy: I don't think a person's lot in life is a reason for her to be unhappy. My sisters do, and I feel sorry for them.

Host: What galls me is that your stepmother never got what was coming to her. If your story had been fiction instead of real life, you can be sure she would have!

Cindy: You want her to be punished? Oh, you didn't know her as I did. I can't imagine that anyone could have done anything to make her any more miserable than she was.

Host: Stop the cameras. We're not getting anywhere at all. This is one interview that won't get on the air. Nobody's fault, ladies. Some people just don't interview well.

༄

AN END TO SELF-BETRAYAL

We have seen that the light remains abundant and available throughout our emotional attacks upon others. What we need to do is stop distorting and turning away from it.

But how? How can we allow ourselves to receive and accept the truth about the other person or about ourselves straightforwardly, instead of using it for our own defensive purposes? What steps can we take to let our hearts be softened?

Certainly we can do it by ceasing to betray ourselves, for self-betrayal is the root cause of the grief we want to escape. But how can we stop self-betrayal if our best efforts to do right can only be counterfeits of the right?

An important clue can be found in Buber's invented word *I-You*. It is one word, not two. The *I* part can't be pried away from seeing the other as a *You*. *I am the way I see the other person.*

This suggests that we will be able to change ourselves in an indirect way, from I-It to I-You, if we can allow the other person to affect us differently. If that person can become a *You* for us, then, without deliberation, strategy, expertise, or willpower, we will become I-You people. Just allowing this to happen will reverse the transformation brought about by our self-betrayals. The truth about those we have accused, if we can only receive it without censorship, resistance, or distortion, will return us to the open and generous condition of our childhood. It will free us from the prison of our accusing, self-victimizing thoughts and feelings, for we will cease projecting a threatening interpretation onto others' and in that way we will escape our "box." We will become again the beings we really are when we aren't working hard to be another way.

I want to close this chapter with an illustration of this liberating transformation from an I-It to an I-You way of being. It's Glen's story of how his Christmas collusion with Becky came to an end.

One Christmas season Becky befriended a younger woman named Karen. (Her concern about others and her gift for friendliness has made Becky a surrogate mother to many people over the years.) Together they decided to make Christmas presents for certain neighborhood women in need. Two of those women were invalids, and a third served as an officer of an international charitable organization and had little time for herself. Becky and Karen planned to glue fine art prints to wood blocks with worn-looking edges and varnish them to look old. They thought a grouping of such prints would look handsome on a wall. They asked me to cut the blocks and scallop and burnish the edges.

About this time something happened that I cannot completely remember or reconstruct. Looking back, I can only suppose that Becky felt differently toward me from how she usually did as Christmas approached. I say this because *I* felt different. Some partial softening in her must have begun to soften me. I recall being very much in love and vowing to put my whole heart into anything Becky wanted me to do.

You need to understand something about this vow. It

contained no gritty determination, no resolve to suppress my wants in favor of Becky's. It was more like the marriage vow of a person buoyant with love—a vow without any reservation in it, spoken with the whole of myself. The resolve issued not from the will but from the heart. A fundamental change had already taken place in me. My whole desire that Christmas was to help this person, who was both my wife and my friend, achieve whatever she had set her heart upon.

So I prepared a dozen blocks as artfully as I could—a grouping of four for each recipient. This pleased Becky enormously, and her pleasure pleased me enormously. The results were so successful that Becky and Karen decided to make mounted print groupings for other women they knew, twenty of them, in fact—eighty blocks of wood in all, each with edges scalloped individually with my jigsaw and carefully burnt with matches. I did not resent doing this even for a moment. It was for Becky.

Of course the two women quickly ran out of prints to mount. It happened that from museums I had visited all around the world I had gathered a collection of just the sort of prints they needed—quality prints of works I especially enjoy. (Often the best reproduction of a piece can be obtained only from the museum that houses the original, so I could not realistically hope to replace my collection.) In my former frame of mind and heart the thought of varnishing any of these treasures would have struck me as desecration. But I was not in my former frame of mind. Or perhaps I should say, not as deeply in it as before—I have to admit that I noticed Karen's superb taste in picking out some of the best prints. Even so, it surprised me that I felt no pain at her choices. The project was for Becky's sake, and by comparison that collection did not matter very much. I was happy.

A day or two later, Karen appeared at our house with

two scraggly pieces of door casing, wanting to use my radial arm saw to make swords for her twin boys. I told her not to worry about making them; I would do it. I bought some fine hardwood and fashioned two neatly shaped and sanded and suitably blunted play swords—not really for Karen, but for Becky, because it was the sort of thing she loved to do for people.

Then came the time for producing the granola and the raspberry yogurt and the dried fruit balls for distribution to the neighborhood and our more far-flung acquaintances. Most uncharacteristically, I took the lead. I got everyone organized and cooperating in the project. We had a mountain or two of granola cooling on the kitchen counter and more in the oven. We were singing Christmas carols. It was still early in the evening—we had plenty of production potential still left in us—and out of the blue Becky said something that stunned me.

"Why don't we put all this stuff away and just sit around and enjoy being together?"

I said, "What?"

She went on. "It doesn't matter that much if we don't get all these gifts finished."

I looked right at her while trying to register the meaning of what she was saying. Then she added: "I'm worried about your work, Glen. Tomorrow you go to the office, and I'll finish this up myself."

I could hardly believe what I was hearing.

And that's what we did that Christmas. We worked on some projects, but not frenetically. We relaxed and enjoyed the season. I accomplished quite a bit at work. We did not get everything done, which did not bother Becky a bit. She was sublimely happy.

Though I have often reflected upon those happy days in that holiday season, I cannot remember or reconstruct the steps that led Becky and me to our change of heart. I recall only that one week I was chafing under her pressures to produce and "just knowing" her to be almost certifiably pathological, and the next finding her not only free of the fanaticism I had ascribed to her but on the contrary sensitive, solicitous, and spontaneous, and, as far as I was concerned, altogether free of fault.

How could I have been more mistaken? The truth was, she didn't care about Christmas any more than I did! How could a human being change so completely? Preoccupied as I was with this transformation in Becky, I did not appreciate right away how much the change in her was linked with an equally dramatic change in me. I looked at her through new eyes, felt for her from a new heart.

There's nothing mysterious about any of this: When we abandon our resentments, we no longer live in a resented world. Others become real to us. We have a sense of how they feel and what will please them. And pleasing them is what we desire to do, because we have put away our resentment. That's precisely what happened to both Glen and Becky, each responding with more sensitivity and care to the other's growing sensitivity and care.

In this mutual consideration, good feeling escalates as surely as ill feeling escalates in collusion. Each person discovers the fathomless and refreshing reality of the other. This makes acting considerately toward that person delightful and in that sense easy—and whatever it costs in time or means doesn't matter anymore.

But how can we get to this point? How can we do the sort of thing Glen and Becky did? Once we have so corrupted our understanding that we can't see our way forward, but find that everything we do only seems to make matters worse, how can we then open ourselves to the light that's available to us?

These are questions we will address in the next four chapters. We will consider several different but closely related approaches we might take, all of them having to do with yielding to the light or, in other words, to the truth about whomever we have been accusing. We are going to see that by doing this, we abandon whatever lie we may have been living. Wholeheartedly embracing the truth cannot coexist with living a lie.

CHAPTER 8

OPENING
OURSELVES TO
OTHERS

TOUCHED BY THE TRUTH

When someone we have been blaming becomes real to us, we change. We become a person who sees another person as real. We change from being accusing, guarded, and self-absorbed to being open, self-forgetful, and welcoming.

Of the various kinds of situation in which this change of heart takes place, and the various processes by which it takes place, I've chosen three to focus on in this chapter. *Each of these has to do with letting ourselves be affected by light coming from others, or, in other words, by the truth concerning what they are feeling.*

One situation that can occasion a change of heart occurs when the person who has been the object of our suspicion, fear, or resentment disarms us by the way he or she responds to us. Perhaps another family member does not take offense as we expect. Perhaps a friend obviously delights in seeing us again or goes out of her way to assist us. Perhaps a parent loves us without reserve. Such responses can soften even a cynical or spiteful heart, and there are people who affect and soften others daily simply by their constant and disarming compassion, love, or welcoming attitude. They may or may not express their feelings verbally (others, including children and animals, can keep us open to life and hopeful simply by their love or loyalty).

It is altogether too easy to minimize the salutary influences of such welcoming, I-You people upon the character of families, communities, and nations. I do not think this world would be tolerable for any of us without these people—and perhaps many of us can at one time or another be counted among them. When we have hardened and withdrawn into ourselves, as we all do at times, we desperately need to encounter other beings on a fairly regular basis whose regard for us or for others softens us again.

In the next chapter, we will meet several such people. For now I will offer a story so slight and simple that it might easily have gone unnoticed. I offer it not because it's singular, but because it isn't—because it represents uncounted numbers of nourishing acts that almost never get acknowledged, even at the time, even silently. Yet in spite of that, the small acts of kindness I *do* remember sprinkle my recollections of my life like mountain flowers in bloom.

When I first drove the southern California freeways in mad traffic many years ago, I was trying to get onto the San Diego Freeway heading south from an undersized on-ramp. A woman pulled past me on the left, into a position where she had good visibility and could pull in front of me and grab the next chance onto the freeway. But then, when the first break in the stream of cars came, she waved me on past her. That had been her intent all along, to help me into the traffic flow. I am still moved when I consider that fleeting act. I never saw her face, but strange as it may sound for me to say it, I loved her.

The second kind of situation in which we change by opening up to others differs from the first in obvious ways. Here, the person blamed suffers some stern adversity or tragedy that renders him or her helpless and thereby makes our various petty, self-absorbed concerns minuscule and shameful by comparison. The vulnerability of that person, struggling with his or her difficulties, melts our hearts. A story I heard from a crusty, old-line manufacturing engineer named Monte will show how this happens.

Monte's son, whom he considered irresponsible, called him one day to ask if he and his wife could stay with Monte for a few weeks. They had gotten behind in their rent and had been evicted. Monte agreed reluctantly, though he considered his daughter-in-law even more irresponsible than his son.

When the couple arrived in a rented moving truck, they revealed that they needed a car for a while, as theirs required a major repair. With even greater misgivings Monte again consented, and so they went off in his car to buy some things they needed. An hour or so later he got a call informing him that they had been in an accident. And his daughter-in-law was the one who had been driving! This threw Monte into an inward fit. He stomped around the house for the entire time it took the couple to bring the car back. (Though bashed, the car could be driven.)

When Monte heard them pull up in front of the house he told himself he could not go out to meet them with all his hostility "hanging out." So he collected himself as much as he could, tried to calm down, and put on the best, most considerate kind of smile a person is capable of when treated as he had been treated. It was in this condition, determined to act cordially, that Monte descended the stairs and walked out the front door toward the curb. He would listen to their side of the story, he told himself; he wouldn't raise his voice.

Monte was almost to the car before he could see his daughter-in-law, who was sitting in the driver's seat. Her head rested on the steering wheel, and she was sobbing. At that moment, he said, his heart melted.

What melted this man? He had, after all, done everything that lay within his power to act as considerately and generously as possible. What melted him was the sight of his daughter-in-law broken and contrite. This image punched through his shell of self-concern. It disrupted the certainty with which he had judged her. It threw him and the confidence with which he looked down on her into confusion.

Seeing another's helplessness and vulnerability can do this to us. To realize that behind an indifferent or hostile or arrogant façade another person is struggling just to claim a place in the world, a place she does not really believe she deserves—this blows our superior attitude to smithereens. All the willpower Monte could muster had failed to extinguish the accusation in his heart, but something about *her,* the very person he had been despising, rendered him unable to retain his hardness toward her any longer.

I have spoken as if Monte was humbled by the image of his daughter-in-law broken by adversity. This is only partly true. *The sight could humble him only because he allowed it to.* His own responsiveness was the critical factor. This is a universal truth. Scenes that some regard compassionately may not affect others at all, or at least not appear to affect them. Consider the images from the holocaust death camps that we watch in horror and tears in PBS documentaries. The Nazi personnel responsible observed those same scenes daily, in person, with what at least seems to have been utter indifference and in some cases satisfaction.

PLENTY THERE TO MELT OUR HEARTS

There is a third kind of situation in which the truth about another melts our hardness of heart. In this situation the person we are blaming, unlike Monte's daughter-in-law, may show no vulnerability at all. In fact he or she may even consider and treat us as an enemy. And if so, to open ourselves to them we may need to be confronted with the truth about their feelings and fears by some extraordinary, arresting event. We may even need to make some extraordinary effort to discover it.

The following story was told by a man, whom I'll call Hal, to a group in Minnesota that I was teaching. It recounts Hal's relationship with his son Robby, who as a young teenager had hardened himself toward his family. The story is an example of how someone who makes every effort to mask his vulnerability (in this case, Robby) can nevertheless melt a person's heart—provided, of course, that that person will allow it. In the story Hal told, the softening of heart also required one of those extraordinary events I mentioned. The event was Hal's finding a school essay written by Robby's older brother Tom. That essay disclosed to Hal things about Robby that Hal had not known. In recounting the experience, Hal actually read Tom's essay, a copy of which he had with him, to the group.

This was Hal's story.

Robby, our sixth child, was as lovable a little boy as I have ever met. Everyone who got to know him said the same. He couldn't say his *l*'s and *r*'s very well; when only three he climbed up on my bed with me, put his stubby little arm around my neck, and said "Daddy, when peopoe come on ow pwopoty, we want to say, Get off ow pwopoty. But then we wemembow it's weewee Jesus's pwopoty and so we say, Come on ow pwopoty."

Though exceptionally strong and competitive, Robby never learned to play baseball because baseball takes place in summer, and to get to practice he had to walk through neighborhoods where he would encounter animals, and he was incapable of failing to stop and spend as long as possible with an animal when the chance arose. He always retained at least one for a roommate, if not a dog or a cat, then a rabbit or a rat. And he feared nothing. When not more than eight he was walking down the street with me and saw three boys about nine or ten beating up on a younger boy. Without any hesitation Robby piled into that fray and pushed the bullies off.

Robby had taken for his hero his brother Tom, four

years older. He enjoyed what seemed an idyllic life, as happy as a boy can be imagined to be. But during his twelfth year something awful happened. A charismatic and troubled young man a year older than Robby had moved in on a neighboring street. He had organized a number of his peers into a gang that called itself "The Vandals." They became the prime juvenile concern of our local police department. Robby was popular and "cool," so it was not surprising when they began recruiting him. It did surprise me, though, that he succumbed. Almost overnight he turned angry and destructive. His new friends would come for him in the middle of the night, and he would slip out the window to join them. My wife, Karina, and I were heartsick. Why would he ever have taken up with such so-called friends when—as far as we could tell, anyway—his life had seemed so perfect?

I knew Robby's will to be so strong that any forcible restraint would only make him more determined. So I resolved to do everything I could to keep our relationship alive. After he would cause his nightly ruckus at the dinner table and storm downstairs, I would go down to his room and talk, sometimes for long periods, until he would finally open up and laugh with me a little. When he went out at night I got in the car to find him; I wanted him to know that I would always be out there looking for him, and soon he stopped going very often.

We sought for some way to reconnect him with animals, hoping that this might soften him again and draw him away from The Vandals. I hit on the idea of buying him a horse. But, knowing that Karina would rightly not approve of buying the worst-behaved child the most prized present, I conspired with Robby to buy Karina a horse. With the help of a dear friend, he learned to care for and handle it. I arranged for him to be invited to work on a ranch in Arizona; he quickly became so skillful and trustworthy that the owner allowed Robby alone, among a number of young men who worked there, to ride his thoroughbred horses. But when Robby came home for the school year, he took up with his old friends again.

I gave Robby all that was in my heart to give, as did Karina. In fact, I believed myself to be as loving as a parent can be toward such a child. But often I resented his inconsiderate ways and the disruptions they caused in the family. At those times I looked upon him as ruining, if not our lives, then at least our peace.

Just how far short I fell of appreciating the truth about Robby became clear on one spring evening in 1990. I discovered an essay displayed on my computer monitor when I went upstairs to my office. Robby's brother Tom had written it for an English class at the university. Only partway through my reading of it, Robby became fully real to me. I could understand from his perspective why everything had happened as it had. And my feelings for him changed as radically as my understanding. My hardness toward him disappeared. The circuit of love between us, though long disconnected, was reestablished, and my heart glowed with sorrow and joy.

Here is the essay I read that evening on the monitor screen.

"Cowboys and Indians is our favorite—we always play, just Robby and I. At first we are both mighty braves, but I soon become the Chief, and Robby my warrior. We play all day, then at night in the darkness where no one can see I say, 'I love you,' and he says it back. It is weird to say that to another boy, but I love Robby. Our dreams are like movies, to run away to the mountains, living like Indians with long hair.

"Tufts of hair fall onto the sheet hanging around my neck, one end of the hair frayed and split like a horse's mane, the other clean and sharp. Summer is the time for hair cutting. The old sheet that Mom had wrapped around my neck hangs on my body limp. I have no

muscles to fill it in. Clumps of hair fall onto my lap, forming a strange pattern on the stain positioned on the sheet.
I wet the bed sometimes. Robby and I have tried to avoid
this for four years now. No one else on the block has to
have a butch for summer, so why do we? Mom tried to cut
it alone but she couldn't catch us. She waited for Dad to
return from work. He plops me onto the high chair and
sits there to make sure I won't move. Robby cries also. He
could care less but he wants to be like me.

"Indian style, Robby sits on the floor, his face streaked
like a badly washed window, the tears cutting paths in the
summer dust of his face. He looks at me like a sad sheep
dog, his hair in his eyes. I am the Chief and he is my warrior. He would rather die than betray me. I have given in
and am having my head shaved, so he is also.

"The buzzing of the razor sounds like the background
noise of our old record player. Mom's hands feel steady as
I sit in the chair. Suddenly the buzzer stops. I hear the
snapping of the scissors. I'm surprised when I look at my
hair in the mirror. She's not going to buzz the whole thing.
I step down from the chair with grown-up hair. Robby
climbs onto the chair expecting the same haircut. He steps
down completely shorn, like a sheep who has lost his prize
wool. We are different for the first time and we both know
it. 'It doesn't matter,' I say, but it does.

"That summer I sit at the table and tell stories after
Robby goes to bed. I catch him looking and listening
through the spaces between the stairs. He wants to hear
my stories. But I have hair and he doesn't. None of my
other friends are buzzed that year either. On the fourth of
July, I leave with them and he follows me like a puppy. He
has always come with me before, so why not this time? I
guess he doesn't know what to do without me. 'Get out of
here,' I say. My friends all laugh. He keeps following. 'I'm
going to kick your butt if you don't leave.' He cries, tears

cutting paths in the dust of his cheeks again, and I run with my friends laughing and following me.

"That night I lie down with firecrackers ringing in my ears. The door opens a little and I see shiny cheeks and a fuzzy head poke through the opening. 'Sorry I followed you, Tom. Good night, I love you.' I don't say anything. The door closes. I turn on the radio so I won't have to think about him.

"I love Robby. We are still best friends. At family reunions we stick together. I hang out with Robby because we don't fit with our cousins. They come from another part of the country; they talk different. This year at the reunion Robby and I don't have any shorts so we take off our pants. Our tan bodies are bronze, accented by our bleached white 'Fruit of the Loom' briefs. We find a sprinkler with which we can spray the other kids at the park.

"We take turns drenching people. Suddenly I turn on Robby, spraying him until he's soaked. He doesn't say anything, just looks at me and wonders. I'm tired so he takes the sprinkler. He suddenly turns on me. The water hums as it sprays past my ear. He can drench me. He hesitates, then turns and sprays someone else. I want him to spray me back so I won't feel like such a jerk. I walk behind him, pulling down my 'Fruit of the Looms' as I go. 'Just for that,' I say, 'I am going to pee on your back.' He pleads no. I laugh. Yellow liquid splatters on his shoulder blades, steaming a little as it rolls down the trough made by his spine, down into the back of his shorts. He doesn't move. Christie, my little sister, sees. 'I'm telling,' she shouts. I run, with Robby running after because he doesn't want to be left alone.

"Dinner is not very good anyway. Salad and squash are all we eat in the summer because Mom says we are to grow what we eat. I just want to be excused. Dad looks up from his dinner at Mom and then at me. 'Did you pee on Robby today?' he asks. Without even looking away I say,

'No.' 'Did too!' Christie retorts. Looking at Robby, Dad asks if it's true. He doesn't even pause; he has already made up his mind. 'No, I was wet from the sprinkler,' he says.

"School comes again. Our hair grows longer. We are the same again, but not really—like an ice cream cone, if it starts to melt there is no way to make it look the same again no matter how you lick. I need money now. I steal from Dad. He never misses the money, and only Robby knows. He never tells. Soon he needs money, too. He's young and gets caught.

"Dad asks who took it. I say, 'I didn't.' 'No one is going anywhere until we find out who took it,' Dad says, trying to sound mean. I look at Robby. He has faith in me. 'Robby took it,' I say. It is silent—like when someone dies, no one knows what to say.

"The Chief has betrayed his warrior.

"It would be better if he had betrayed me. When a Chief betrays his warriors, they kill him.

"Robby just makes new friends.

"He doesn't follow me around anymore, though he would like to. He still says, 'Good night, I love you.' I only answer, 'Good night.' Once he says it twice, hoping to hear me say 'I love you' back. But I do not say it.

"I am his idol still. Anything I do, he does. What I wear, he wears. Mom even stops buying separate clothes for us. Although he never lets me know that he is copying me, he wants to be just like me. I have long hair to my shoulders in a ponytail. He wants one too. Mom says no. We are different, and we both know it.

"I leave home for several years, and when I return, my hair is short. His hair is longer than mine ever was. He hugs me, but he doesn't say 'I love you.' At night I wait for him to return from his date. When he arrives, I say, 'I love you'—twice. There is no answer. He doesn't say it, but I think my warrior loves me still."

That was Hal's story of how his heart opened to his angry son. What touched him so? Wasn't it simply Robby's humanity? Wasn't it Robby's gritty effort to steel himself against being hurt? Wasn't it Robby's anxious determination to cultivate and hang onto his new friends? In short, wasn't it the truth, understood and appreciated for the first time, about the boy's feelings and struggles?

Whether you call this Robby's humanity or the truth about Robby doesn't really matter. It shone like a light into Hal's inner darkness. It came as a gift, a gift that changed a discouraged and somewhat self-pitying man. It came—and we should remember this—from the boy Hal had considered the destroyer of the family's happiness. It was a gift Robby gave just by being.

In the realities around us there is plenty—plenty and to spare— that is able to soften and humble us and open our fearful, judgmental, hardened hearts. Whether those realities have that effect depends upon our opening ourselves to them.

∽

AN EXPERIMENT IN OPENNESS

The change in Hal, like the change in Monte, seems to have depended upon an unusual event. In Monte's case it was the sight of his daughter-in-law, sobbing; in Hal's, it was finding that essay. Though Monte braced himself and made preparations to control himself, he couldn't by an act of will break down his suspicion and anger. Similarly with Hal—though he had sought to serve and understand his boy, he hadn't managed to look upon him in that fundamentally different way that I have called a change of heart. Realizing this, we cannot restrain ourselves from asking this question: Must we wait for some unexpected, calamitous news about whomever we have been blaming before our hardness toward them can be broken? Isn't there anything we can do on our own, any initiative we can take, to set the process of change in motion?

We need to remind ourselves of a point made in connection with Monte's experience. What softened the hearts of both men was not merely learning new information. Information can affect us only to the extent that we allow it to. We know from the self-betrayal cases we have studied that we can accusingly and vigilantly collect every relevant scrap of information or insight available without experiencing any softening of our attitude. In order for the truth about a person to affect us, we must be receptive. We must have eyes to see.

This important fact should not discourage us at all. When we go in search of understanding, and do so sincerely, we put ourselves in a *receptive* posture toward the truth. This posture is different from being concerned only about justifying and defending ourselves. *In this new, searching posture we are acting upon a desire, even if only feebly formed, to be different. And we are doing it with a willingness, perhaps only slight, to use what we discover respectfully. Though our attitude may not yet be compassionate, it is crucially different from unbending accusation.* A crack has opened in our shell, and a little light has broken through. We have become able to entertain a possibility we had been rejecting and have given ourselves a genuine chance to be softened by truths we have yet to discover.

There are some fairly systematic ways to go about this search for the truth concerning the other person's inward reality. Each of them focuses in some particular way on reconsidering our judgments about that person.

Here is an example, which I am going to call *the reconsideration exercise.* The exercise is preceded by these instructions:

> Imagine you are living in a world that is different from this present world. *You* are different, in that you are taking no offense. No matter what others may be doing, you do

not feel they are hurting you psychologically or emotionally. You harbor no accusation within your heart. In this
imagined situation, yours is an I-You way of being. But
this is the only difference between your imagined world
and the present actual world. In your imagined world,
everyone else is exactly the same as they are right now.

Now from your imagined perspective, think of someone who has inconvenienced, irritated, or injured you in
some manner, or who is doing so now. Think about that
individual as long as you like—but if at all possible only
from within the I-You mode.

Then, when you feel ready, take a pen or pencil *and
write a description of that individual.*

Don't try to make that person seem better than she
(or he) really is; don't just tell all her good qualities and
ignore the bad. Instead, describe her accurately; describe
all her qualities—those you have up to now thought bad
as well as those you've thought good. Just be sure to
describe them, if you possibly can, from your new, unof-
fended point of view. If she's a self-betrayer, filled with
negative emotions, describe that. Tell the truth.

I do not require those who do this exercise to express publicly
what they write, though they may if they want to. I scrupulously
try to avoid invading their privacy. But I do invite them to share
any insights they may have gained from the experience. Some of
them feel frustrated—at least on the first try they cannot seem to
imagine themselves into a compassionate outlook and therefore
have nothing to say. But others come to what I consider a remarkable degree of self-understanding. Here are some examples of
insights I have heard expressed:

I discovered that what the other person is doing really
isn't being done to me. He's just lashing out to try to make
himself feel okay, and I just happen to be there.

❧

I was flooded with compassion. I feel feelings I didn't know I was capable of. His self-betrayal didn't offend me anymore, but I felt sorrow for him. I longed for him to change.

❧

It hurt me to think of all the things I have done to hurt him.

❧

By being offended I have added fuel to her offensive ways of acting. I have promoted her destruction of herself.

❧

I realized I have never been hurt. Only my pride—and that isn't me. For nineteen years I was in a relationship that I resented. And now I can see that in all that time only my pride was wounded, not me. My pride isn't me.

❧

Doing this exercise releases you from reacting. It sets you free.

❧

The irritability of her qualities is something to which I have been contributing.

❧

I realized I didn't really know him. He's just been someone who's irritated me for a long time, but I didn't know him.

❧

When we no longer need the other person to validate the lie we are living, she becomes real to us—a real person like ourselves with real feelings.

❧

The same features that can be described irritably can be described compassionately.

The woman who shared this last insight—I will call her Claudia—wanted to tell about the person she had in mind while doing the exercise. In the class, she did not say he was her husband, but I knew he was, for she had explained her worries to me when she called me about enrolling. After the class, she said:

> For twenty years I have seen this individual as cocky and demeaning in his manner. In my eyes he acted so superior I felt put down in his presence. Other people felt the same way, and that is no doubt why he had personality conflicts in his work. But as I did this exercise I suddenly saw all the same qualities that had offended me in a different light. I saw him as a little boy who was afraid of life and everyone around him. He hadn't changed, but I had. Where I had been heavy inside with self-pity, I now felt only love. And where he had seemed cocky, he now was only insecure and even afraid.

"I suddenly saw all the same qualities that had offended me in a different light." These were qualities of the very person that not long before she had accused of blighting her life. *What brought about this new understanding was not a change in him, but a change in her.* When he became more real to her, she herself became a more "real" person—more open and responsive and centered in another person outside herself.

After a break in a training course for business leaders, a handsome young man named André asked to share something. He had used the break time to call his wife, to tell her how he was going to be different.

"I wish I could be there," she said.

"It's not necessary," he replied.

"But then I could make some changes too."

"No, I am changing," he said, showing the depth of his understanding, "and that will be enough."

This man understood. He understood that by his change of heart he would put an end to all the difficulties he had been giving her to deal with. She would then be free to be the kind of person he had just rediscovered her to be. Reconsidering her, he could see how big a part he had played in any problems between them and that her part in them had depended heavily on his. What he said to her expressed his high regard for her and his belief in her.

In another class each person present wrote a personal collusion story. I asked them, "Who is responsible for a collusion?" Instantly and almost in unison they responded, "I am." This is the same deep wisdom André had expressed.

Over the course of more than twenty years I have watched many people change by engaging earnestly in this exercise. Taking up the sensitivities of an I-You person for the purpose of this exercise can bring about a change of heart. We enter into the realm of pondering, meditation, inward searching, or prayer, and by this means withdraw ourselves from distractions and addictive desires. I speak here of more than the cultivation of silence, stillness, and quietude, an art especially perfected in some Eastern religions. I speak of reconsidering, with a good and courageous heart, our self-absorbed judgments and proud attitudes.

Inside the Other Person's Box

Some of the people who can't quite get the full impact of the reconsideration exercise on first try—and most of those seem to get it if they try again, when they have more time—have less difficulty with an exercise that centers on an actual collusion in their lives. I simply invite the people present to write the story of a collusion cycle in which they have been involved.

Most people do the exercise by filling out a collusion diagram that looks like this:

FIGURE 6

COLLUSION DIAGRAM

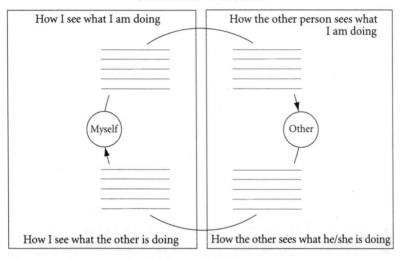

How I see what I am doing	How the other person sees what I am doing
Myself	Other
How I see what the other is doing	How the other sees what he/she is doing

Any of us can fill in our own side of the story with ease, since we will have gone over it in our minds many times. The challenge is to fill in the other person's side of the story, for it is acknowledging what he or she is feeling and experiencing that we have been refusing to do. Doing this part is vital. It liberates us from the falsity of our side of the story, for we cannot put ourselves in the other person's position and at the same time continue to accuse him or her. When we do put ourselves in the other's position, we in effect "break through the wall of our box," or, in other words, we give up projecting our accusing attitude onto that person and are suddenly able to see things straight. *Occupying the position of another person for even a few moments means admitting that he or she might not be guilty as charged, and with that admission, our previously inflexible accusation crumbles.* It always works out this way—the truth dispels the lie.

LISTENING TO A FACE

A California woman named Jenny told the following story in a course I was conducting; it illustrates what can happen when we open our hearts to the truth. These are her words:

> Erin doesn't care if her schoolwork is right and even cheats to get it done. Like any concerned mother I have taken charge of the situation and I make her do her homework, even if it takes her hours. She whines and complains, and I encourage her as cheerfully as is possible when a child is acting like that, but she keeps it up anyway. I get sterner until finally I start yelling at her.
>
> The trouble with Erin is especially frustrating because for years I have given her my best efforts. Our first daughter, Ashley, was the most beautiful and delightful and gracious child I have ever known. She lit up any room she entered. But she was killed on the way to kindergarten nearly ten years ago. Erin wasn't as naturally charming, and so, sensing the danger of the comparisons with Ashley I would inevitably make, I decided I would give her physical love—warm hugs—every day of her life. I have done that faithfully, but apparently to no avail.
>
> Well, because her work did not improve, her teacher recommended last week that she repeat the second grade. I was assigned to help Erin with her flash cards. She counts on her fingers or guesses or, I swear, gives the wrong answer when I'm sure she knows the right one. It is about as frustrating as anything I have ever done. I think, "Is she doing this on purpose? Why? I've been doing the right things to help her. She just refuses to cooperate!"
>
> I haven't just provided a home for her. I've played with her and helped her with her schoolwork and given her

physical love and then I've gotten kicked in the teeth. I don't know what more I can do.

In the third session of the class Jenny recounted a moment in which this story of her relationship with Erin underwent a profound revision. Jenny was able to perceive Erin differently—or I should say, truthfully. She experienced a change of heart. Later she recounted what happened in a letter, from which I quote.

The experiences in the class have helped me look at both Erin and myself differently. What I learned will be with me for the rest of my life.

I realized how much I had been a part of Erin's problems, how I was always harder on her than on the others. When we worked on the flash cards I was outwardly encouraging, but inwardly I mistrusted her, and she felt that message from me. I cried when I realized the price she had to pay for my inability to love her without reservation.

After I came to this realization, I was a different person when I was with Erin. One afternoon we went over her flash cards. I believe she sensed something different about me, because she missed only three out of some thirty cards, whereas before she would usually only get about three right. And to top it off she left the table with a smile instead of tears.

Things went fine for a couple of days, but I have learned that change doesn't happen overnight. Sunday was a real test day. Erin did everything imaginable to frustrate me. We try to make Sunday a family day, and she said, "I hate being with the family—I want to be with my friends." My normal response would have been, "Erin, don't talk that way. You're going to be with us today and we're going to have fun together!" But this time I pulled her up on my lap and looked at her, and I had this overwhelming feeling of love for her that just seemed to flow between us. I hugged her tightly and told her how much I love her.

I realized that for the very first time in eight years I was expressing true love for her. Previously I had hugged her, but the love didn't flow. This time the love just flowed. It was as if I was holding a new baby for the first time. Tears were streaming down and she looked at me and said, "Are you crying because you love me, Mommy?" I nodded. She whispered, "Mommy, I want to stay with you forever."

From where did the light come that dispelled the darkness of Jenny's eyes? Partly from Erin. It was as if there issued from Erin's face, and especially her eyes, a call to her mother: "I am struggling. I need you. I am hard toward you only because I am afraid of your hardness toward me. Please don't harden your heart against me. Don't close me out."

No doubt Jenny had often heard this call. But until the day she wrote about, she interpreted the call as Erin's whimpering or obstinacy. As long as Jenny remained resentful and anxious about her own place in the world, her eyes were darkened; she could not discern Erin's fears or hear her call.

I have been suggesting that, strange as it sounds, Jenny *heard* this call or summons when she *looked* at Erin, especially when she looked into Erin's eyes. This way of talking is suggested in the writings of Lithuanian writer Emmanuel Levinas. Jenny heard the summons when *she began to listen to Erin's face.*

In my own life I have found very helpful a slightly different way of describing experiences like Jenny's. Jenny changed when she gave up trying to push her influence upon Erin and instead let herself be influenced by Erin. It happened when she stopped trying to change her daughter so as to make her own life story turn out the way she had in mind, with herself as heroine at the center of it. Instead, *she let the unfolding story of her life be determined by her daughter's need.* She let Erin's need direct her responses. It was from that moment on, when Jenny stopped trying to have the relationship her own way, that Erin stopped insisting on having it *her* own way.

From the countenance of every individual, as we stand before him or her, comes the imperative, "Treat me as a person separate from yourself, but just as real—with hopes and needs of my own." Or, to use the words of the philosopher Immanuel Kant, "Treat me as an end and not as a means." If we will hearken to this summons and do as it dictates, we will change in our relation to those people, if change is needed. We will care for them and resonate with them. And this change will happen naturally, without our trying to make it happen.

CHAPTER 9

INFLUENCE

Influencing
and Being Influenced

We have learned that one of the ways we can change in our hearts, in our way of being, is by opening ourselves to others and allowing the truth about their feelings and needs to influence us. It means letting ourselves be taught *about* them, and letting them be our teachers. It is this that brings about a change in us. It restores us from the defensive and hardened posture we have adopted to our more natural, open, and responsive I-You way of being.

These thoughts prepare us for two important and somewhat surprising ideas that cannot be separated from one another. Here is the first of the two ideas:

Allowing ourselves to be influenced is not only the way we change; it is equally the way we can influence and help change others. By allowing ourselves to be changed by others' influence, we become different: far less defensive and accusing, and far more caring.

Then, having changed, we give them a different kind of person to respond to than before. And we do this without making any effort whatever to manipulate them into being the way we want them to be.

We influence them simply by letting them influence us!

It should go without saying that when I refer to others influencing us, I do not mean that we allow them to persuade us to compromise what we feel is right. When that happens, we are using them as much as they are using us—using their persuasiveness to excuse ourselves in our own wrongdoing. By speaking of others influencing us, I mean that we let them, or the truth about them, guide us in treating them in the right way.

When we let others influence us in this manner, we give them a different sort of person to respond to, and this response on our part is what influences them. It influences them partly by eliminating the reasons and excuses we have been giving them for seeing us accusingly. When they no longer have to worry about defending themselves, they have the "space" to decide how they will respond to our new response to them. And very often they will respond in kind. *There is no better means of promoting another person's change of heart than allowing our own heart to be changed.*

We discovered this in analyzing Jenny's story of her relationship with Erin. It was when Jenny became a truly loving, I-You person, by allowing herself to be touched by Erin's struggles, that she suddenly gave Erin a mother to respond to who wasn't self-absorbed and accusing, a mother who did not judge or seek to manipulate her. Then, at last, Erin could respond unguardedly to her mother's influence.

Another example of influencing by being influenced is found in this story of a mother who had been trying to tell her six-year-old daughter not to try to clean the bathtub after her bath because of the mess she would invariably create.

> I had told her many times not to clean the dirty ring as the water was going out, because she always used too much soap, but that's just what she tried to do on this occasion. And sure enough, she once again used a great deal of soap. Suds were everywhere, even flowing over onto the floor, and she was struggling in vain to control them.
>
> My usual habit is to start criticizing immediately: "Look what you've done now. You've used too much soap!

Now I'm going to have to spend twenty minutes getting this mess cleaned up!" And then she carries on about how it isn't her fault and cries like I'm being an ogre, which really makes me mad.

But this time I didn't follow my habit. I said warmly, "You've tried to clean the bathtub. I really appreciate that."

And you know what she said? She said, "Yeah, Mom, but I used too much soap."

Our Influence Comes Back to Us

Now we are ready for the second of the two ideas.

When others undergo a change of heart (whether or not it happens in response to a change in us), *they* can influence *us* and help *us* change. For, as a result of their change, *they* give *us* a different sort of person to respond to.

By allowing ourselves to be touched or affected by this change in them, we are influenced to sustain our own change of heart or to allow it to be deepened.

Thus, by letting others influence us in the first place, we may influence them to influence us even more positively than before—and this can reinforce our change of heart.

You will remember Claudia from the previous chapter—the woman who thought her husband was cocky and contemptuous. When she stopped taking offense, she suddenly saw him in a new light, as insecure and afraid. After this event Claudia went to find him—he was living in a separate apartment at the time—and asked him if they might go for a drive. He consented. She expressed nothing about her altered feelings, but he sensed something different. As she listened he talked openly and freely throughout their entire ride together. This was unheard of in their previous relationship. In fact, one of her complaints had been that he was not willing to talk.

That change in her husband reopened her eyes to the man she had fallen in love with almost thirty years before. And predictably, this reawakening in her touched him further. Within a few days they were back together; when I heard from them several years later, they were still doing well.

So the change in us that comes from opening ourselves to others' influence invites responses from them that can reinforce our change. Our gift calls forth gifts from others; we get what we give, measured exactly. In supplying others an occasion to respond differently, we often find that in return they make it easier to be even more open and generous with them.

This self-reinforcing cycle, as you can see, is the positive counterpart of collusion. It is the dynamic aspect of what we have called *the bonds of love*.

Like many other crucially significant matters in human experience, this positive cycle lacks a name. So we must invent one, as we did with *collusion*. We will call the cycle *a considerate relationship*, signifying a reciprocal willingness on the part of two or more people to be open to and affected by one another. This will become an important concept in our further discussions of what we can do to escape troubled emotions and attitudes. Sometimes I will speak of *one person being considerate of another*, meaning that he or she is being influenced by the truth about this other person. And sometimes I will speak of *a considerate relationship*, meaning that *all* the parties involved are responding to one another in a considerate way and are thus being positively influenced by one another.

The discussions that follow in this chapter will sometimes seem to focus more on our influence on others and sometimes on their influence on us. Either way, what is said will apply to all of us; we should put ourselves in *both* positions. The reason for this we have learned already. *When we allow ourselves to be influenced, we influence, and those we influence—those who allow us to influence them—become an even greater influence on us.* Generally speaking, when we play one of these roles, we play the other.

∾

WAIVING OUR DEMAND FOR JUSTICE

Think about the enormous contrast between the "before" picture of our collusive relationships and the "after" picture, when we have changed and have become considerate. Before the change, we communicate the message, "You deserve whatever treatment you are getting from me. Justice is going to be done, and that means you must suffer." But after we change, we no longer demand that they pay the last farthing before we will let them off the hook for what they have done to us. We excuse them from having to pay because we no longer think they owe us anything. We drop all our charges against them. For their sakes we happily sacrifice all bitter satisfaction, all retribution, all demand for repayment, all vengeance. And we do all this without regret or second thoughts.

This sacrifice of retribution is not just an attitude of love, it is an *act* of love. We make the sacrifice because it is the right thing to do for them, not because we want them to do something for us.

> A man named Peter once visited me who had acquired a list of points I had written about self-betrayal and collusion. He said that the night before, he and his wife had stayed up late going over the troubles in their relationship, each acknowledging to the other where he or she had been in the wrong. "A spirit of love settled upon us," he said, "that we have not felt for many years."
>
> Then, he said, something equally memorable happened the next morning, the morning of his visit to me.

Seven-year-old Penny bounded into the kitchen and said, "Hey, something's different here. What's different?" Soon after that Billy, age ten, appeared and, as always, started tormenting his little sister. "On other days I would have become irritated and impatient and probably thumped him on the head, and I started to feel that way again. But I looked at Billy and felt the same love for him as I had for my wife the night before. I just looked at him and said, 'Billy, we aren't going to do that anymore.' And he stopped and then he put his arms around me and buried his head in my chest and wept."

This sacrifice of retribution I am calling love clears a space in which others can let down their guard and be emotionally truthful with themselves.

I met a man once who had taught himself to live by this principle, which he formulated in a couplet. Adapted to the terminology of this book, the couplet can be expressed this way:

When we criticize people, their consciences console them.
When we love them, their consciences indict them.

"One Person I Can Never Love"

Bruce is a broker in a Seattle firm. During a class I was teaching, he seemed a ready student. After the second session, he stopped me and said: "I believe I know where you are headed in these classes, and I agree with the direction. But I just want to put you on notice here and now that there's one person I can never love, and no one else in my circumstance could love him either." I listened without trying to persuade him otherwise.

Bruce had sold his very nice home to the individual he referred to in our conversation. The sale contract called for him to leave the major appliances—stove, freezer, refrigerator, and so on. But the buyer's wife informed Bruce one day that because she and her husband had their own appliances, he could remove these from the house. So he did. The buyer was furious. Then the buyer discovered that the air conditioning didn't work properly, and that there was a small hole cut in the living room carpet for an electrical socket that had been covered by a lamp when the buyer had looked at the home. After he had made an intensive inspection, the buyer found many other things wrong as well. He drew up a list involving many thousands of dollars.

Bruce felt he was being treated as if he were a criminal and was being accused, in an exceptionally nasty manner, of fraud. The appliance problem wasn't his fault; the air conditioning had worked the day he left; he hadn't meant to keep the floor socket a secret, and so forth. Both parties insisted it wasn't just a question of money; it was a matter of principle. "All I care about is seeing justice done," Bruce said. What the other guy was trying to get away with just wasn't right. Bruce stewed about it when he woke in the mornings, any minute during the day when his mind wasn't otherwise occupied, and all through the evenings. He even woke up in the night to fret and lay his plans.

They arranged to sue each other. Depositions were to be taken on a designated day between the second and third sessions of our class. But the ideas we had been studying in the class began to erode Bruce's determination to take vengeance. Somewhere during the night before the scheduled meeting, his heart changed. Suddenly the most important thing in his life was not to revenge himself upon his adversary but to do what was right. So he called him on the telephone.

"Whaddya want?" the buyer asked rudely.

"I was hoping we could avoid an all-out conflict and

be friends." The buyer was resistant, but reluctantly agreed to a meeting.

When they got together, the buyer asked again, "Whaddya want?" just as belligerently as before. Bruce picked up the list of items in dispute. Starting with the first item, he said what he thought was right. For example, he said he understood that any buyer would be upset upon discovering that something he had purchased was taken away, and he, Bruce, apologized—not only for removing the appliances but even more for having bad feelings toward the buyer. For each item he either offered to bear the expense or said he didn't believe it was his responsibility. His offers to pay for various things weren't the sort one makes hoping the other person will object and say, "Oh, it's okay, never mind." He really did want to do what was right.

When Bruce finished, the buyer sat silent, his eyes wet. Finally he said, "All my life people have been trying to take advantage of me. You are the first friend I ever had." Then for the next two hours he told Bruce his life story, including things he said he had never breathed to anyone else. When they were ready to part, Bruce tallied up what he owed and began writing a check. The buyer said, "That doesn't matter to me anymore."

"No," said Bruce, "I need to make it right."

"Well, then," the new friend said, "give me a hundred dollars and forget about it."

When Bruce asked for the meeting, there was, of course, no guarantee that the buyer would allow his heart to be softened rather than hardened. Nor were there any such assurances about the boy who spoke rudely to his sister, the girl cleaning the bathtub, or Claudia's difficult husband. But what amazes me is how often people do respond well—how often reconciliation follows a showing forth of love. Hard indeed are those who will not be touched by someone else's sacrifice of retribution.

$$\sim$$

THE INFLUENCE
OF LIVING TRUTHFULLY

Let us say that we *live truthfully* when we let the truth about others, including their needs and hopes and fears, guide the way we treat them. Living truthfully toward them is nothing more or less than being considerate of them and letting ourselves be influenced by the truth about them.

We have seen what happens when someone treats us truthfully. They give us no reason to be defensive and find fault with them. They grant us space to react truthfully to their truthfulness. Their considerateness toward us invites us to be considerate of them. They influence us by letting us influence them.

This brings us to a new idea. Others can have just as powerful an influence on us by treating someone else, some third party, truthfully and considerately. We call this *setting an example.* How can another person's good example inspire us so?

I want to suggest three closely related reasons.

First, an exemplary person shows us the truth about others by the way he or she responds to them. The following story illustrates this.

I once attended the annual social of an organization which I served as a consultant. I took note of the way the company officers tended to mix only with one another, and the managers and supervisors also kept company only with themselves. That meant the workers and interns also talked only with each other, mainly in departmental

groups. Then I noticed the second-ranking company officer approaching a man standing alone—a man who
worked in the company motor pool. The officer introduced himself, and they talked for a bit. The officer then
introduced this man to several other people, and I could
hear him telling something he knew about each of them.
A woman came by, a receptionist, also apparently by herself. The officer called her by name and said, "These
people need to meet you!" And he told them about her, in
detail. He delighted in these people—anyone watching
could tell that welcoming them was as far from an admin-
istrative chore as it could be. And of course they were
radiant.

At the same time, another event was transpiring, as
important as these. *I, the onlooker, was beholding, through
his eyes, something of the intrinsic significance of each of
these people.* He had demonstrated the inner richness of
each one, a richness to which others present, caught up in
their own agenda, were unattuned. I felt attracted to these
people to whom he was attracted and was ashamed that I
had frittered away a lot of the evening pursuing my own
conversational agenda. Through this good man's responsiveness to the truth of other people, I began to respond
to it as well.

Here is a second reason a good example inspires us in our
treatment of others. Exemplary people show us that opening ourselves to others is not to be feared, but on the contrary releases us
from the bondage of our fears. My story of the company officer at
the annual social illustrates this point. Indeed, no small part of
what drew me out of my bog of self-involvement was the fearless-
ness and freedom with which he threw himself into his engage-
ment with the people around him.

Finally, I offer a third reason for the power of example. Insofar
as we respond to another's example, we are in a considerate,

truthful relationship with our exemplar. My relationship as observer with that officer quickly opened me to him and to those with whom he was open. Though I may have carried myself through the early part of the evening in I-It oblivion, I became I-You in my newly formed relationship with him and, through him, with the others. This silent relationship with him lifted me out of my I-It condition. The petty, self-absorbed concerns I had brought to the party shrank to nothing: I became caught up in something beyond myself.

Holy Ground

When I met him, Eli was a bright and driving engineer in a large, technology-intensive company. Because of some of the things he had done in his specialty, he had been made chief of a section, with a broad span of authority and power. But if the company culture had been tolerant of complaints from people claiming they were treated badly, Eli would surely never have been given significant management responsibility. He was mean, vindictive, and even abusive, understandably mistrusted by most and hated by many. His marriage had become seriously troubled. The casualties on all sides of his life had grown so great that it began to be clear, even to his results-focused superiors, that they had a pathological case to deal with and needed to terminate him—though they had not yet done so.

In a setting at which I was present, Eli underwent a dramatic change. It was the occasion when Robby's father, Hal, told the story recounted in chapter 8. After Hal finished reading the essay written by Robby's brother, Tom, Hal said something else. His additional statement will help us understand why this story affected Eli so much.

Hal said, "I found out about what happened between Robby and Tom only a few years ago, when Robby was eighteen. Before that, I often looked upon him as a destructive force in our family.

But when I learned the truth, my heart broke for Robby. I wept for a very long time. I had been thinking about him only in terms of myself. He was the one who had the terrible burden to carry. I never treated him the same again."

A few hours after Hal had told his story, Eli had something to say. Holding back tears the best he could, he told of his childhood as a boy of Native American blood, being reared by an alcoholic father. He recalled accompanying his mother many times to the hospital emergency room to be treated for broken bones or severe lacerations inflicted by his father. When Eli was not yet fourteen, his father came home drunk one day and began to beat Eli's mother. Eli got a gun, loaded it, and went after his father. But his father heard him, got in his truck, and took off; he was just out of range when Eli got out to the street. Not long after that, Eli left home for good, with a heart as hard as he could possibly harden it.

Now, he said, after hearing the story of Robby, another boy who had hardened his heart at an early age, he began to think of how life had been for his own alcoholic father. He thought of the abuses his father had endured as a Native American. Eli said that in all of this angry man's life, he had never had the experience of being respected or of respecting himself. Eli thought of his own mental abuse of his father. He had been more an enemy than a son. And he thought of how he himself had treated most other people and the burden this had put upon them. It was wrong. *He* was wrong. He wanted never to be that way again.

Eli's immediate boss was present when Eli told his story. It took the boss's energetic persuasion to get the company's executive team to give Eli another chance; they couldn't believe a person like Eli could change fundamentally. But they agreed on condition that a two-day session be held with all his work group to see if they could come to a tolerable working arrangement together. Early in that session a man stood up, a man known in the company for his religious zeal. Like many others, he had been deeply offended by Eli's cruelty. He intimated, at least to my ear, that what he was about to say represented others' feelings as well. Then he said: "We have all been raped. We are being asked to forgive the rapist. And the rapist is sitting right here with us."

Eli did not respond defensively. He freely confessed how he had treated people, particularly the people in that room, and he apologized sincerely and pledged that he would never be that way again. Perhaps some accepted the apology; most skeptically agreed to wait and see.

Many are the stories that could be shared of what happened after that. The difference in Eli made a difference in everyone with whom he worked. For example, after working with Eli for the next six months or so, one of the union leaders, who herself had a reputation for being hard as nails, volunteered in a meeting: "I have acted at least as badly toward you as you have toward me, but until you changed I never could see it."

Many others responded similarly. Perhaps most significantly, some months after Eli's change, the man who had set his heart against Eli and called him a rapist was with Eli in a meeting in which everyone was sitting in a circle. This man indicated he had something to say. He stood up, walked across the circle, and stopped in front of Eli. Then he took off his shoes, and knelt. "I have been hiding my sins under the cloak of my religion," he said. "I am taking off my shoes because this is holy ground."

The relationship of that man to Eli turned from negative to positive, from collusion to consideration. Before, he was a man bitterly attentive to Eli's negative attitude toward both him and others; after, he was a man softened by Eli's truthful, considerate way with him, and perhaps even more by Eli's truthful, considerate way with others. He related to the truth about others *through* Eli and thereby became truthful himself, just as Eli had related to the truth about others through Hal. So truthful indeed did this man become that he could freely confess his own piously I-It ways and leave them behind him.

It is possible, as we have seen, to relate truthfully to someone who isn't being truthful—witness the stories of Jenny and Erin and Hal and Robby. But for most of us, most of the time, it is far easier when that person *is* being truthful. *We most effectively influence one another to change by letting ourselves be changed.* Then we invite them into a considerate rather than a collusory relationship.

~

Love Is Not Manipulative

Once we hear a story like Peter's, Bruce's, or Eli's, we may well be assailed by an almost irresistible temptation. We may think we can influence someone by deliberately mimicking the exemplary person's behavior. This seldom if ever works. We saw why in chapter 8. When we manipulate in this manner, we aren't primarily responding to the need of another but are pursuing the goal of getting them to change. There's an accusation embedded in this effort; the message is, "You're inadequate; you need to shape up." Thus our motivation is not pure, and that makes what we do a counterfeit of caring.

This helps us appreciate the paradoxical, or at least ironic, quality of influence. If we try to influence others for our own sake and not strictly for theirs, our efforts will probably backfire. Those we seek to change will detect our intent. It is simply futile to try to change another if we do so in a critical spirit, even a mild one. Generally speaking, we influence others most profoundly when we do not seek to change them at all, but simply go about straight-forwardly doing the right and loving thing.

We have already encountered several stories in which the contrast is clear between an apparently well-intentioned but self-absorbed and self-canceling effort to get another person to change and the power of a loving attitude. Jenny's and Erin's story is one of them; so is the story of Bruce and the buyer of his home. But none of them makes the point quite as forcefully as the following story-within-a-story.

I was speaking at a convention honoring a number of people for outstanding contributions to education. In my speech I told a story given to me by a friend whom I will call Marcel. This is what he told me:

My next-door neighbor, a man of about forty, was dying of emphysema. Though the doctors were alarmed, the man could not stop smoking. He smoked 180 cigarettes a day "and loved every one of them." He did everything he could have done to force or trap himself so that cigarettes would not be available. But he could not force himself to stop rationalizing. Always, when hard up against his cravings, he would talk himself out of his resolution to withdraw from his habit.

One evening, as the situation grew desperate, I went to the sick man's home. I said, "I have decided that if you are going to stop smoking, there has got to be something in your life that you can't rationalize away when the temptation gets too great. I've come here tonight to tell you what it is. As long as you are continuing to smoke, I am not going to eat. When you stop smoking, I will start eating again."

"But you can't do that. I won't let you."

"But don't you see? You can't stop me. So I am going to go now. And I hope you remember that I won't be eating as long as you are smoking."

I left, completely peaceful within, and I remained peaceful for two days. But as the third day of abstinence approached, I began to wonder whether I would ever eat again. I lost faith. Imperceptibly, my fasting changed from being something I was doing for my friend to an effort to try to force him to stop smoking. There is a profound difference between these two actions. I could not have failed in the first act, no matter what might have happened, but when I began to get involved in the second act I started to despair. For a while the essential ingredient was missing. I had to struggle to stop worrying about myself and regain the peace I had enjoyed.

At night after the third day, the sick man's wife appeared at my living-room door with a large cream pie. My heart sank: I feared my friend had ignored or forgotten or refused to believe what I had told him. But his wife told me to call him, and when I did he happily announced, "It's all right, you can eat the pie."

After I finished my speech at the convention, one of the honorees, a woman, came up and said, "That story was very inspirational. My children don't help at home as they should. For example, on Sunday, after I have worked hard to prepare a great meal, they take off to do their own thing. I have to chase and badger them to get them to help clean up, and by the time I get one rounded up the others are gone. I think I will tell them that as long as they won't do their part, I won't eat."

It won't surprise you to learn of the telephone report I got from this woman a week later. "It just doesn't work with my kids," she said. "I went without putting anything on my plate while they ate. When they asked me why I wasn't taking any food, I told them, 'As long as you aren't going to help me clean up the kitchen on Sunday, I'm not going to be eating.' And do you know what they said? 'You're sure going to be hungry, Mom.' And 'Maybe you'd better change your mind.' And 'Hey, this way you can lose a lot of weight.' And they were laughing when they said it!"

Of course, this woman could not have missed the point of Marcel's story more completely. It was not *what* he did that made his act influential. It was *how* he did it, or in other words, the attitude with which he did it. Indeed, I suspect that if he had encountered his sick friend on the day when he was more self-concerned than caring, he would have come across differently and might possibly even have discouraged his friend from trying to quit smoking.

❧

LOVE IS A POWER

We learned in chapter 5 that when we attempt to exercise power or control over someone else, we cannot avoid giving that person the very same power or control over us. In the world of human affairs, the will to dominate, even for apparently good reasons, nullifies itself. "Every force," says the Tao te Ching, "calls forth a counter-force."

But love is a power unmitigated. It allows others their freedom. Most ironically, it "compels" them to use that freedom. They *must* respond one way or the other to our love. They must either accept and yield to this love, which is the truth about us, or resist it. If they yield, they do what our love has invited them to do, which is to love us in return. If they resist, they refuse that invitation and find a way to think of us as their enemy.

I want to illustrate this power with a story given to me by Jane Birch:

While I was attending a Christian college, two friends of mine, Carrie and Mark, asked me to join them in playing a joke on several of Mark's friends, all of whom attended the same college. Mark had invited his friends out for an evening of fun. As part of the activities, he planned to drive his friends down the street where Carrie's family lived and pretend to have car trouble in front of their home. He would then go up to Carrie's house and ask to call a tow truck. Carrie's mother was to invite the whole group into the house to wait. Carrie and I were to be waiting inside, she as a member of the family and I as her friend.

The plan was that once everyone was inside the house, little things would begin to happen to gradually make Mark's friends feel slightly uncomfortable. Mark started it off by knocking over and breaking an expensive-looking vase in the hall and then excusing himself by saying it was an "ugly old thing anyway." Carrie and I posed as sophisticated, intellectual atheists who were studying psychology at a rival university.

Everything proceeded as planned, vase and all. After we sat down, supposedly to wait for the tow truck, Carrie and I began to make sarcastic comments about the hokey lifestyle of students at the Christian college. We asked Mark's friends if they would agree that Christians, in general, were fairly naïve and narrow-minded. We weren't rude, just sarcastic and witty, and therefore much more believable than I imagined we would be.

Although it was a setup, to Mark's friends it was all too real. They obviously didn't approve of us or our lifestyle, but as guests in the home, they couldn't just walk away. Instead, they gave each other "What have we gotten ourselves into?" looks. Occasionally one of them would try to "help" us understand more about their Christian beliefs, but their help didn't seem genuine. The weak smiles on their faces couldn't disguise the disgust in their eyes.

There was one exception. One of the girls in the group, Elizabeth, stuck out like a bright light on a dark night. She was sincerely appreciative of the family's hospitality—not in a showy but in a soft way. When the vase shattered on the hallway floor and the others stood around looking embarrassed, Elizabeth immediately went looking for a broom to clean it up. Though she hadn't broken it, she was the first to apologize. I was immediately taken by her sincerity and could hardly keep from telling her that it really was just a joke.

I was also amazed at her reaction to the two "intellectuals." While the others were embarrassed and exasperated, Elizabeth radiated a warmth that was absolutely compelling. It became terribly difficult to keep pretending when she was so respectful of everything we said. She listened attentively and tried her best to answer our questions, even when they were rude.

As I observed Elizabeth, I knew she was genuine. I was overcome with emotion. I felt accepted, even treasured, by this total stranger. If I had actually been a nonbeliever, none of the other members of the group would have given me any reason to change my mind about Christians. But Elizabeth did. She was different, and I felt different being with her. She seemed to have no thought or concern for herself; her whole attention was focused on the rest of us.

In subsequent days Carrie and I talked about what happened that night. She had exactly the same impressions as I did. For a long time I couldn't get Elizabeth off my mind. One day I ran into her in the arts building on the college campus. The moment she looked at me her face lit up, and that warm feeling I had felt before came back. "Here," I thought to myself, "is an authentic person." She seemed to have absolutely no concern for herself and therefore was able to be wholly concerned about me. She made me feel that I could say anything in her presence without offending her in the least. I felt accepted and cared for. Although I did not know her, I loved her for who I felt I was when I was with her. That was the last time I saw her, but not the last time I thought about her and the light I felt in her presence.

From contemplating this experience I have learned several things that are very important to me.

First, the "self" is a great burden. *Constant concern about the self is bondage. Self-forgetfulness is freedom.*

Second, *the person I could be is very, very different from the person I am now, and becoming that person is worth any sacrifice.*

And third, *there are people in whose presence I begin to be that person, and what they give me then is better than any worldly gift.*

In chapter 8 we spoke of the ways we can allow ourselves to be touched and positively affected by the inward reality of others, as revealed in the tone and manner of what they do and say. In this chapter, we called this *allowing ourselves to be influenced.* Then we found that being thus influenced by the truth about others is the best and most effective way to influence them, and if they open themselves to that influence, they in return work a deepening and enriching influence upon us.

Thus do bonds of love flow through us like the waters of life, circularly. We respond to others' enriching response to us and thus enrich them. What we give we get back, and more besides, when others put themselves into the circulation of good feeling and mutual respect. The remarkable Danish author Søren Kierkegaard coined a phrase for this sort of thing (though he used it in a slightly different way): *Like for Like.* How we are for others is how others are for us.

CHAPTER 10

THE TRUTH DISPELS THE LIE

"MIGHT I BE IN THE WRONG?"

Calling a change of heart "a healing" captures something important about it. Like the body's healing, it's not something we make happen. And it's not something that happens *to* us, either. We might describe it best with terms like *recovery* and *return* and *coming to ourselves*. Healing comes about naturally, when the causes of disease have been removed. It is a self-mending or recuperation that brings a natural return of our being to its proper condition.

This means the healing of the soul cannot be forced. We can try very hard for a very long time to think better of an enemy and yet fail.

But does it follow that we can't do something to put ourselves in a better position for it to happen? No, it doesn't. There's much we can do. For example, in chapter 8 I reported on a "reconsideration exercise" in which we make ourselves available to be affected by others and do so by thinking about them from an imagined I-You point of view. Effort and willpower cannot by themselves cause our heart to change, but that doesn't mean that we can't put ourselves in an optimal position for that change to happen.

A responsible step in loosening the grip of any lie we might be living is to ask ourselves, solemnly and seriously, this momentous question: "Might I be in the wrong?"

What gives this question its power? The answer can be stated very simply: Just to ask the question seriously, even without answering it, is already to undergo a change of attitude. A feeling of humility comes over us. Our focus shifts from the faults of others to the difficulties they may be suffering because of us. Our certainty of their guilt and our innocence is shaken.

To admit our errors or weaknesses in this fashion can bring us liberation and strength. It will seem ironic to say this, for facing up to the truth is usually what we most fear to do. Nevertheless, it's true. There is much transforming power in frankly acknowledging the truth about our own wrongdoing.

One of my associates, whom I'll call Alan, shared this story:

> Not long ago I was given a wallet for Father's Day. It was not the sort of wallet I would have wanted. My wife, Shirley, picked it out for me. I understand now to what lengths she went to find just the right wallet, but when I opened the box and looked into it, all I saw was a not-what-I-would-have-wanted wallet. Nevertheless, I was too considerate to hurt Shirley's feelings, or at least this is what I was thinking about myself at the time. So I said, "Oh, thank you. I like this wallet very much."
>
> She was looking right at me and she said right away, "You don't like it."
>
> "Oh, yes I do. Why, look at the nice white stitching on the edge. And all the plastic windows where I can put my credit cards."
>
> "You don't like it. I can tell."
>
> The situation was embarrassing me. My cheeks were getting red. I shoved the wallet in the box in the manner of a man whose gratitude has been rudely rejected.

Alan resented being given the wallet; to him it felt as though Shirley was setting him up for humiliation in front of his friends. He did not express this resentment childishly. Instead he did the "right thing"—or, to speak more accurately, counterfeited the right thing—by acting politely and thanking her. But she could tell that his heart wasn't in it. As we discovered in chapter 6, there's all the difference in the world between genuinely treasuring a gift and trying to show that you're treasuring it. So he responded to getting caught by taking offense and angrily shoving the wallet back in the box.

His story continues:

Shirley went into the kitchen. I began to think about what had happened. It came to me that in a certain very subtle way I had been putting on airs. I had been concerned about what my associates would think when I pulled such a wallet out of my pocket. I realized I had refused to see the wallet for what it really was—an expression of her care for me and a manifestation of considerable effort on her part.

Whereas I had been embarrassed and irritated before, I now felt sorry. What sorrowed me was not exactly the particular words I had said. Given what I was feeling about the whole affair, it was about the best thing I could say. I was sorry because of having those feelings. I realized I had actually been thinking that my wife was forcing something upon me that would embarrass me in front of my friends. And now it seemed incredible to me that I could have resented an act of genuine kindness.

I felt I ought to tell her forthrightly what I was feeling, and I did. By her look I could tell she forgave me without any reservation.

When Alan looked honestly at himself, he saw a man different from the considerate and grateful person he had been trying to present to Shirley. He saw a man annoyed and resentful and therefore far from considerate and grateful. The way he had been acting was not the truth. Contrary to what he wanted to believe, he had not been victimized by this woman who had worked hard to please him. He had victimized her.

The Astounding Act of Yielding to the Truth

We can spell out the things that happened within Alan when he truthfully admitted the wrong he had done. Listed below are some of them. Keep in mind as you read that they happened not in sequence, but all at once. In fact, it's most helpful to look upon them as just one event. The various points that follow are different aspects of that event.

First, Alan saw his fault.

Second, that meant he no longer thought of Shirley as the problem.

Third, his resentment of her evaporated. His accusing, victimized feelings were gone.

Fourth, he no longer felt helpless to deal with the problem he thought Shirley was causing him, because he no longer thought there was such a problem! What he had supposed to be the issue— her failure to appreciate and respect his taste—wasn't the real issue after all, only the apparent one. The real issue was his absorption in himself, which is the inevitable product of self-betrayal.

Fifth, he was able to see Shirley truthfully and to appreciate her feelings and needs. And when that happened, he told me, he felt flooded with feeling for her. "Suddenly," he said, "she took on the look of a woman who is loved." When he acknowledged the truth to himself, stopped nursing his identity as the Wounded-but-Valiant One, and let go of finding fault with his wife, she changed. His image of her untwisted itself. He saw her as she really was—and loved her.

Sixth, the opportunity to do the right thing reappeared in the world, whereas it had not been there before. At that moment, the right thing was to confess forthrightly to her what he had done. If he had tried to do this without first undergoing a change of heart, he would have done it for the wrong reason; his confession would have been counterfeit.

Seventh, he found himself at last able to influence her positively. She sensed his truthfulness and his sorrow and frankly forgave him.

In this list we can see the seven aspects of a change of heart that results from yielding to the truth.

Truth and Compassion

All of the elements listed above occur in the following story. I met the author, Cynthia, in one of my classes.

My husband, Shawn, and I are both writers. We have a baby. Shawn insists that I keep the house clean, prepare the meals, stay well-dressed and appealing, and, most of all, keep the baby absolutely quiet during his writing hours. I write during the baby's afternoon nap if I can, but usually late at night and early in the morning.

If there is any noise from the baby, Shawn is not patient. He bitingly asks whether I understand the importance of what he is writing for his career and our future. Until recently tears would well up in my eyes in response to this harshness. Sometimes I would protest that he had no right to speak rudely to me. A quarrel would ensue. But more often I would suffer this sharpness silently and bitterly. I could not understand why I had to suffer when I had done nothing wrong.

One morning I left the bedroom door ajar and the baby toddled out. She was scattering some of Shawn's pages when he saw her. He began to yell at me. I could feel the spray in my face. I began to burn with resentment and to search my mind for some way to respond in kind. But all of a sudden I thought, "It's a lie. What I am doing right now is a lie." I was doing the same thing I was imputing to him! My rage just melted. I was filled with compassion toward Shawn for the first time in a long time. In fact, all I could think of in that moment was how I could help my husband.

As part of her self-betrayer's lie, Cynthia perceived Shawn as a person hurting her feelings. Then, when the truthful self-confession came—"What I am doing right now is a lie"—she no longer believed that. She could see that her resentment and pain, which had come to an end, had been *her* doing. She now understood that he had not been hurting her at all. The only person to whom he was doing damage was himself. She saw a man making himself miserable, as part of an effort to feel justified in his anger toward his wife. He had been hurting himself, not her.

With the recognition of that truth came compassion and concern, which is what we would expect in a person who sees another person hurting himself. Cynthia's heart went out to Shawn. The same thing happens to any of us who acknowledge the truth as straightforwardly as she did. *The emotion we experience in the presence of the truth is love.*

We can give whatever name we want to Alan's fault—blaming Shirley when he was the one doing wrong, putting her on the defensive, thinking only of himself. Whatever we call it, the very instant that he acknowledged this fault, it no longer existed! Amazing! *By seeing and freely admitting our fault, we are rid of it!* We have only to confess to ourselves the truth about the wrong we have done and, by that very confession, we cease to do it. Why? Because when we are in self-betrayal, we are living a lie, and a lie cannot coexist with a full and free acknowledgment of the truth.

What we have just described is a man's change of heart toward his wife. Though not a full change in his way of being—that takes time, experience, and faithfulness—it can rightfully be called a good beginning. At that time, in that situation, Alan started to become a different man.

Counterfeit Honesty

Some people think they can admit to doing wrong and still keep doing it. But an admission that doesn't bring with it a softening of heart is a dishonest admission. What such people call "telling the truth" is a sort of intellectual game in which they rehearse to themselves some of the facts about what is happening while still hanging on to accusing, self-excusing emotions. Remember from chapter 2 that a self-betrayer can be right about the facts of a situation without letting go of the accusing emotion, which is the biggest lie of all. Genuine admission of the truth must be done emotionally as well as mentally, for we can lie while sticking strictly to the facts because the facts can't cause us to do wrong or take offense. Honesty through and through requires giving up the accusing feelings that go with our accusing thoughts.

You can test this for yourself. Recall the feelings you had on some occasion when you "told yourself the truth" intellectually but not emotionally. (For instance, suppose someone pointed out that you treated a certain person unfairly and you responded, "Yeah, yeah, I know I'm wrong"—without allowing yourself to feel the least bit bad about it.) Compare whatever feelings you would have had on such an occasion with feelings when you confessed the truth with your whole being. You will find the difference striking. In the former case, none of the seven aspects of a change of heart came about. In the latter, they all occurred. Together with your sorrow, you felt relieved and even joyful because at last the lie had been put behind you.

We must take great care that we don't block our exit from the box by counterfeiting an admission of the truth.

∾

FEAR OF WHAT WILL SAVE US

When we are stuck in accusing thoughts and feelings, we are usually reluctant to face the truth because we fear that it will condemn us. The truth frankly acknowledged will turn out to be heaven, but in prospect it looks more like hell. In this you will recognize the mirror image of what we learned from C. S. Lewis's allegory, which is that we cling to the tormented condition of vengeance, spite, and criticism that deserves to be called hell—thinking that our vindictive attitude somehow points the way to a solution of our problems.

We learned in the preceding section that when we confess that we have been wrong—not just on an isolated point of argument but in the way we have lived our lives—we no longer feel a need to blame others and to defend ourselves against them. We become free of the accusing, anguished thoughts and feelings with which we have afflicted ourselves, free to let ourselves be touched by others' concerns and aspirations and joys, and free to stop worrying about protecting or polishing our self-image.

So it is blame that we must let go of. *Blame is the lie by which we convince ourselves that we are victims. It is the lie that robs us of our serenity, our generosity, our confidence, and our delight in life.*

A woman I will call Virginia shared this account:

> A few months ago I was at dinner with my husband and three other couples. About the time dessert arrived, my husband turned and rebuked me for interrupting him. I reacted as if struck in the face, growing pale and rigid with shock and shame. Our dinner friends to a person witnessed the same thing: My husband had been an aggressive jerk, and I had been victimized by him. One friend was so upset by the incident that, when he saw me a few days later, he said he hoped I would seriously consider leaving my husband.
>
> My friend's reaction was even more disturbing than the incident itself. His words reflected back to me a portrait of a helpless woman abused by her man. I struggled for days with this awful picture. Then, without warning, something strange happened. In a moment of epiphany, the perception I had of myself as victim shattered like a

curtain of glass. With absolute clarity I saw that my "victimization" wasn't the result of something done to me, that instead it was willfully self-created. I even remembered the crossroad of choice on the night of the dinner: My husband made his remark, and I first felt wrongly accused and furious. Then I thought, just at the periphery of my consciousness: "You say *I* hurt *you?!* Well, honey, watch *this!*" And I launched into my act.

The scariest part of all was how skillful I had become at creating this image in the eyes of observers. If you had been there, you probably would have agreed that my husband was the beast and I was the innocent party. And, what is even trickier, until I saw this "victim form," I couldn't have stopped myself for love or money, because I "knew" that it was *real,* that I was *right,* that I was being mistreated.

The revelation stunned me. It had never occurred to me to see myself as a victim. My mother, now *she* was a victim. She had sacrificed her career ambitions to her family and to the cultural pressures of the day. And it was my mother who exerted control by saying that I or my father couldn't do this or that because it would hurt or scare her too much. I never acted like *that!* I was a strong, outspoken, liberated, self-sufficient, successful professional woman. I *couldn't* be a victim.

And then a realization slowly emerged from the shadows of my psyche. I had merely created a *style* that was different from my mother's, a style that I and my friends found acceptable. The mechanism itself, though, was identical.

My new vision proved itself right away. Once I began to act and perceive from outside the victim form, it had an astonishing effect on my marriage. If I did not become the victim, lo and behold, I no longer viewed my husband as the oppressor. In fact, his actions and intentions looked so different to me, it was as if I had placed a gargoyle's mask over his face, which I had now finally removed. Moreover, I saw in terrifying relief the damaging effect of my victim routine on him. In any fight, no matter how mutually pre-cipitated, my husband came out the bad guy. And because we are both melodramatic by nature, much of this was played out in public. So, over a period of time, many of our friends had begun to view me as the Good Wife Who Puts Up With It All and him as the Bully.

And here's the thing: Since I chose to step out of this pattern of mine, except for the occasional squabble, my husband and I have stopped fighting altogether, a circum-stance friendly observers might have thought as likely as hell freezing over. So who had been most in control of this situation, which had become so devastating to our mar-riage and to each of us personally? Who, indeed, had been victimizing whom?

As long as I could identify my husband as the monster—the one who prevented accomplishment, hap-piness, peace, creativity, etc.—then I never had to face the part of myself that actually prevented those things. As long as I could assign blame, I never had to face the monster in me and take responsibility for my own life and fate.

When I first saw this I became desperately depressed. I assumed that if I couldn't blame that which was outside myself, then *I* must be to blame.

And then the final piece of the puzzle appeared: *Blame itself was the monster*—a monster with which self-responsibility could not coexist.

So at last I faced that monster. And once faced, as monsters always do, it shrank and shrank until it was a tiny, squeaking little thing.

"Blame itself was the monster." Or more accurately, *the act of blaming*. For it's the act of blaming that "can't co-exist with self-responsibility"—or with freedom from inner agitation and strained relationships. Abandon the practice of blaming, and we see the fear melt away that we have associated with being honest about ourselves and taking the full measure of responsibility for our emotional and spiritual condition.

The blamer's lie is a work of darkness, and it disappears in the light of truth.

༺

FURTHER ALONG THAN WE MIGHT SUPPOSE

We have studied the power of sincerely and seriously asking ourselves the question, "Might I be in the wrong?" This leads us to another question: How can we bring ourselves to the point of asking *that* question with the required sincerity and seriousness?

The answer may surprise you: Anyone who asks the second question sincerely has already asked the first question sincerely. If we honestly wonder how to be honest with ourselves, we have already shifted toward an honest attitude. *Any* degree of doubt about whether we are right shows at least the beginnings of an earnest desire to reconsider our ways. Such honest concern lets a little light enter our minds, and in that light we can begin to see differently what we have been doing.

Recall Glen, the man who resisted the pressures of his wife, Becky, to throw himself into their annual Christmas projects. He found himself feeling trapped. He could, he felt, submit like a mindless slave to all her demands, giving up the possibility of getting somewhere in his career and doing other enjoyable things with the children, or else he could stand up for himself and draw the line. From his point of view, she was forcing him to choose. And as long as he kept himself boxed into this accusing interpretation of her, these were his only options.

But imagine the following turn of events. Glen asks himself the momentous question, "Might I be in the wrong?" Here is how his inner conversation with himself might unfold: "This is no way to be in a marriage," he says to himself. "I've been resisting Becky and critical of her for nearly half a year every year. What would it really cost me to put my heart into the projects she plans? Why am I acting as if I would self-destruct if I willingly did what she wanted me to do? And why am I so defensive ? Why do I work so hard to insist upon my own way?

In asking himself such questions, Glen is escaping the trap. He is not reacting in either of the ways he had thought were his only choices. He is not submitting abjectly to Becky, and he is not defying her. Instead he is looking honestly at himself. This opens him to possibilities for responding to Becky that were not available a moment before.

What possibilities? Think about this. By considering that *he* may have been in the wrong, Glen reconsiders his wife. "After all," he realizes, "she's only trying her best to make our life together good. Her hopes and dreams are for the children. That's what all her projects are about. What would it be like to have to battle your spouse in order to get good things done?"

Now Glen is no longer convinced that Becky is the cause of all their problems. He's able to see her in the same truthful light that revealed to him so much about himself. And seeing her differently, his feelings toward her change. They become more considerate. The possibility of treating her in a genuinely kind and helpful way is reappearing in his world. He's letting light into his soul.

How profoundly fascinating it is to realize that the way forward is simply to consider whether we might be in the wrong!

This realization distills for us a significant truth about what I've called *a change of heart*. We do not make progress in our way of being by working hard to make events go our way, using all our wit and skill to outmaneuver or overpower others to make them bend to our will. We get nowhere by forcing onto them our plan for making ourselves happy. But good things do start to happen as soon as we open ourselves to the light or truth that flows to us from others, so that it may write itself upon our souls.

With the material of this section in mind, you may need to reassess what you have been thinking about yourself. You may have been asking yourself, "How can I reconsider my ways when I'm barreling ahead in the strife of events, guarding myself against my enemies and trying to be successful?" But precisely because you are asking yourself that question, you already have the answer. You are already reconsidering your ways. You are already responding to light that previously you may not have been open to receive. You don't need to find out how to get started on the path of self-honesty; you're already on it. You may still have a distance to go, but you're on it. You will confuse yourself if you think you need to look elsewhere for the right path when you're walking along it already.

⌒∾

RELATIONSHIPS
THAT MAKE US BETTER

In reading so far, you may have been befuddled by a question that has often puzzled me. When we're "in the box," seeing others resentfully and distorting the signals that come from them, how can we suddenly perceive them truthfully and compassionately? All the clues available to us distort our image of them. We have discussed some of the means by which our false interpretations can be broken down. In this section and the next chapter we will learn about other resources that can help us do this.

Some of the most significant of those resources are those other beings—people, animals, even plants to some extent, and God— in relation to whom we are or can become more considerate. Our relationship with them is not collusive. These are examples of such relationships:

> Relationships in which we and the others involved are considerate of one another.

> Relationships with beings who are examples for us, whether we know them personally or not.

> Relationships with someone inconsiderate of or oblivious to us, toward whom we are considerate because of our understanding of and service to them.

In each of these kinds of relationships we are different in our way of being—less accusing, defensive, and petty—than we are in collusive relationships, and more open and caring. These non-collusive relationships give us especially good opportunities to yield ourselves to the truth and to become truthful individuals. They give us leverage to break our collusions and heal our relationships with our colluders.

The following seems to me to be the principle that should guide our effort to be honest, open, and understanding, and bring an end to our collusions:

> We can cultivate relationships in which we become more considerate.

> Then, when we return to our old collusions, we can bring our more considerate way of being with us, and be less vulnerable to old offenses and provocations.

We can think of cultivating such relationships as a peaceable way to invite a "transforming intervention" from others into our present way of being. We can also think of it as a peaceable way to bring a potentially transforming intervention into the lives of our former colluders. They have no choice but to react to the change in us, and the chances are good that they will respond in kind.

Let me illustrate the way we can invite others' transforming interventions into our present way of being:

> Paul, a teenager I know, found himself under a great deal of pressure to smoke marijuana. He was with a group of schoolmates whose acceptance he wanted, traveling in a van with them through a neighboring town. When they pressed him to smoke the drug, a round of rationalizations began to develop in his brain. But then he thought about his family, about how much he admired his parents and their kindness to him, and about a younger brother and two sisters who looked up to him. The pressure from the others was getting unfriendly. At a stoplight he jumped out the back door of the van and walked seven or eight miles home.

How Paul behaved in relation to those boys—or in other words, his insecure, approval-seeking way of being—disposed him to accept the drugs he was offered. *But this was not the only relationship in his life.* He had ties to others—his family members—in relation to whom he wasn't so self-absorbed. He could awaken himself to and reconnect considerably with them by turning away, in his imagination, from the immediate situation. That mental act drew him back into a more assured, less anxious way of being. *That is what enabled him, with a suddenness that otherwise would be incomprehensible, to reverse his response to his peers—almost as if, in that decisive moment, he had been transformed into a different sort of person.* He responded to those boys not as one bonded primarily to them, but as one bonded primarily to his family.

Remember Jenny and her "difficult" nine-year-old daughter, Erin (chapter 8)? When Jenny participated in a class with people who were looking at their lives honestly, she changed. In her relationship with them, she became a different sort of person than she was in relation to Erin. In this different setting, her sense of herself no longer depended on whether her little Erin showed well in public settings. Having withdrawn from being insecurely wrapped up in herself, she could now see her own small-mindedness for what it was, and she could appreciate in a measure Erin's valiant struggles to forge her own place in the family. The transformation that occurred in Jenny as she related to others in the class carried over into her relationship with Erin and transformed it also.

Perhaps we ought to pause a moment to put a frame around the truth we have just considered, because of the key role it can play in helping us to come to ourselves in honesty and be liberated from the attitudinal and emotional lies we often live.

> *Our understanding of right and wrong has power to take hold of us because it is rooted in truthful, living relationships with others.*

Thus Paul, the teenager, fleeing the situation in which he might have taken drugs, was not moved to action by some remembered rule, though that might have been part of it. He was moved by a living connection with certain people who made the rule matter to him. In his case, his considerate relationship with his family members instilled in him a lively sense of what he ought to do.

∾

WHO ARE THESE BEINGS
TO WHOM WE OWE SO MUCH?

Who are these others whose relationships with us can be so empowering? They are beings seen or unseen, factual or fictional, living or dead. They have perhaps respected us, believed in us, possibly counseled us. Perhaps we have served them when they needed us. We might know them personally or might have only read or heard about them—for instance, a parent who died when we were young, or a noble figure we have encountered in literature. Possibly they are not adult or even human; little children and animals can show us how to love. They might not even be visible to us. Socrates, one of the wisest of our race, said that from his childhood he received guidance from a "spirit" that warned him whenever he was about to do wrong. And many in the Judeo-Christian tradition speak similarly of a personal, spiritual influence that silently speaks in a "still, small voice."

Whoever these other beings might be, we are not defensive or mean-spirited in our relationship with them but are bonded to them in some form of idealism and love. With them, we are more straightforward, free of self-deception, and whole. The secret of their impact might lie in the understanding they extend to us, or in their example of putting the truth or uprightness or love first in their lives. It might even lie in the need they have for us to serve them. The point is that, with them, we are most ourselves, most aligned with the light that beckons us to follow an upright course, most absorbed in what really matters rather than in ourselves. Through our bond with them we find ourselves coming, like them, into a proper relation to truth and right, and we feel within ourselves a stirring spirit of respect, caring, and gratitude.

More about Example and the Truth

Consider again the matter of example. Jenny hugging her daughter with genuine love, the mother thanking her daughter for cleaning the bathtub, the broker trying to make things right with the man who was suing him, the woman who helped me get onto the freeway—these individuals had an influence on another person not just by their love, though that was part of it. They did it also by their example.

Think about what happens when others undergo a change of

heart in response to a change in us. They do not become our admirers or disciples—if they did, they would only vary the style in which they are colluding with us. No, *independently of us* they become devoted to the truth and capable of the generosity and love that the truth always awakens. Think about Robby's father, Hal: Part of what melted his resentment was Tom's courageous honesty in seeing how he had wounded his little brother.

This happened, too, with the man who hated Eli. Despite the attacks he suffered, Eli firmly kept to his resolve never to return to his violent ways. Over time, this example humbled Eli's enemies. It became clear that Eli was not just putting on a show. He did not call his persecutors rapists. His fidelity to the truth could not be called counterfeit. Observing this reverence for the truth, his erstwhile enemies were drawn to it themselves. Seeing Eli's courage in embracing the truth, they were emboldened to embrace it too. His example enabled them to recognize the violence in their own hearts.

I have frequently observed the profound influence of personal example in classes and seminars sponsored by the Arbinger Institute, the group that shares the concepts discussed in this book. Such seminars are designed to help individuals, families, and organizations bring about the kind of transformation in their way of being that I have been describing. The way this teaching unfolds matters. For example, the teacher takes care never to give any advice, for advice too often invites collusion. Why? Because some individuals resent having others take over their judgment and tell them how to direct their lives, even if the advice-givers are billed as experts. Others willingly turn responsibility for themselves over to such "experts" and do all they're told in a manner that counterfeits trying to do better.

So in these classes we do not analyze people's stories or tell them what to do. Instead we share true stories of self-betrayal, collusion, and the like, and invite people to write stories of their own—from any source. (Sometimes we mention that a story drawn from observation or experience is always better than a fictional one. It's quite impossible to make up stories as bizarre as what happens in real life.) Participants may share their stories if they wish, though they need not do so; we avoid invading anybody's privacy.

What happens in such a setting? For the large majority of people, hearing others' stories enables them to see their own experiences in a new, truthful light. They realize—usually instantaneously—that a story another has told is their *own* story, only with different details. This realization seems to sneak past their defenses. There is something almost irresistible about another person's facing and honoring the truth, without fanfare of any kind, but with courage and clarity and assurance. The other participants feel invited, even emboldened, to stand unflinching before the truth themselves.

By opening ourselves even a little to the remarkable spectacle of other people reconsidering their lives, we begin to reconsider our own.

Drawing on the Sources

Like love, the light or guidance or truth that influences us exists only in living form, not in principles or rules or expectations or advice, however widely circulated. (Even when we're influenced by reading books, an author is speaking to us, bringing to mind some of our personal relationships or inducting us into new relationships.) Through our relationships with exemplary people, through our own example, and, as I believe, through God's influence, that light spreads its moral illumination over our world. In most cases we have little or no awareness of where it is coming from, yet it guides our responses constantly and subtly haunts us for our misdeeds, calling us to reexamine our ways. It blesses us particularly if we have been carrying on in distress or strife, for when others intrude into our lives with their love or example, they make us wonder whether it's really necessary to live in such an anxious, suspicious, and guarded way. Those who have never had such relationships stand less chance of experiencing a change of heart.

My friends at the Anasazi Foundation, who run a remarkably successful wilderness experience for troubled youth, say that teenagers who as children were deprived of considerate relationships are less likely to turn from their troubled ways than those with some strong early-life bonding to family or other caretakers who lived by lofty values. The Anasazi folks have encountered a number of notable exceptions, but this rule holds enough of the time to remind us that although the influence of considerate beings from our past may not be apparent, it can nonetheless play a crucial role.

We need not be passive regarding these empowering relationships. We can spend time and effort actively cultivating them. (Of course this does not mean that we neglect our present partners in collusion, especially our family and others who need us. The very point of drawing emotional strength from relationships in which we are more considerate is to grow in our ability to turn the people we see as enemies into friends.) In our social activities, in our imagination, in reading, in meditation, or in prayer, we can concentrate on these empowering relationships and thus become more whole, serene, self-forgetful, and confident. We can draw our primary sense of who we are from such relationships. We can then reenter our collusive relationships, or enter potentially collusive relationships, better equipped to welcome others and treat them generously. We will have no reason to resort to an I-It way of being. The more we actively engage ourselves in bonds of love, the less susceptible we will be to getting ourselves stuck in anguished bonds of collusion.

CHAPTER 11

DOING THE RIGHT THING

The Right Thing
for the Right Reason

To stop betraying ourselves is obviously the most direct way out of the emotional and psychological messes that self-betrayal creates. By ceasing self-betrayal we abandon our reasons for accusing others in our hearts. And when accusation ceases, we are able to see others as they really are and to love them.

But ceasing to do wrong requires more than merely abstaining from certain actions, though that is essential. It also requires doing right. If we don't take positive steps to do right when we feel we should, we instantly plunge back into the emotionally dark business of wrongdoing. *Not doing right when we know what's right is doing wrong.*

And, in fact, one of the best strategies for escaping the emotional troubles we've been talking about in this book is simply *to do what we honestly perceive to be the right thing to do.*

But how is this possible? Haven't we been saying that, when we're living in an I-It mode, we can at best produce actions that counterfeit the good things we should be doing? How then can we self-betrayers *ever* do something that's genuinely good?

The story I'm about to share came from a middle-level information technology manager named Benson. Up to the time when the story unfolds, he had only two interests in life—his work and playing his drums in a band that performed three or four nights a week. New software strategies filled his head whenever he wasn't mending, polishing, or playing his drums. Virtually absent from his life experience was any concern about the needs and interests

of other people. Yet, as his story shows, he did something genuinely good. The fact that someone who had been self-absorbed
for a lifetime could act according to his deepest sense of what was
right supports my contention that each of us is capable of this,
even if we start out not wanting to.

> We've had a major project to network our systems to our
> vendors on one end and our outlets on the other. Our
> profits have been slipping and this would help us meet our
> projections. The whole company was depending on us.
> We'd turn out the heroes or the goats.
>
> But we run into all kinds of problems. Then Eric, our
> smartest software guy, can't stay past 5:00 for two nights
> in a row because his boy had a birthday, first, which I
> thought was pretty lame, and then his wife has to go into
> the hospital. Nuts! By now I'm pretty crabby because I'd
> missed a lot of sleep with no end in sight.
>
> That was Wednesday. Friday the band had lined up
> one of its best ever gigs and I could see me missing it. Next
> day we aren't making any progress and Eric gets a call say-
> ing his wife is worse. He's got to go and I hear him calling
> around to see if he can drop his kids off at people's houses.
> When he goes out he's embarrassed and says he'll come in
> as early as he can, but he'll have to pick up his kids and
> feed them and see how his wife is doing. As far as I'm con-
> cerned my gig's completely out the window.
>
> About 7:30 I catch a few minutes' sleep and when I
> wake up, I can see just as clear as day how ugly I've been
> to Eric. He needed someone to help, not someone to beat
> him up. I drive to the hospital and say, "Look, the last
> thing you need is to worry about anything besides your
> family. I'll take care of the project till you can come in."
>
> Next day I'm dragging and discouraged but I think, *I
> bet Eric's got more troubles.* So I go back to the hospital and
> sure enough, it looks like his wife might not make it. Even

though it's Friday I say to him, "I'll help you. I'll pick up your kids after school and take care of them." When I say this a powerful feeling I've never felt before comes on me and I have to control myself. He's pretty emotional too and says I'm the only person who has really wanted to help him. He tells me about how his wife has been sick for years and all his troubles.

While he's talking it's like he morphs into a different person right before my eyes, from someone letting me down into someone who really matters to me, and taking care of his troubles gets bigger and more important to me than the project at work and even the gig that I'd looked forward to so much. It was like I could see his soul, like all of a sudden I had something really important to be doing with my life.

Clearly, what Benson did wasn't a counterfeit kind of goodness. We know this from the change that took place in his attitude. Though prior to his kind actions he had been thoroughly self-absorbed, he came to an awareness of the right thing to do and did it.

How did he do it? How could he do a genuinely good thing when Philip I, self-righteously cleaning the house, could only produce a counterfeit? And Glen, with his plucky Christmas industriousness, could only produce a counterfeit? And I, "trying my best" to react maturely when Matthew was making demands of me, could only produce a counterfeit?

There are two answers to these questions, two significant differences between Benson and the three men I mentioned. First, though initially he could not act out of love for his colleague because he did not yet love him, he nevertheless *could* do something that wasn't self-absorbed. He could do the right thing simply because it was right—because that was how he felt he ought to act.

And that is precisely what he did. He had been upset with Eric. Then, after his nap, he felt bad about it. He realized he had been in the wrong. This is the second way he differed from Philip I, Glen, and me; he said to himself, "I can see how ugly I've been to Eric. He needed someone to help, not someone to beat him up." This self-honesty enabled him to appreciate Eric's plight and then want to help. At this point he had not yet experienced that surge of feeling and respect that came later, so these could not have motivated him to the degree that they did later on. Primarily, he went to the hospital the first time just because it was right.

Much of this chapter will be devoted to the important role played by the two things Benson did that enabled him to escape the box—he did the right thing because it was right, and he honestly confessed that up to that point he had been doing wrong. We will discuss these two factors in that order.

Integrity Leads to Love

Though doing right because it's right may not immediately give rise to respect and love, as it did in Benson's case, the chances are that respect and love will come if we persist—even in hard cases.

By doing right because it is right, we divest ourselves of the reasons we have had for finding fault and thus open ourselves to be affected by the truth about others—to see them as they are, to understand *their* worried and anxious interpretation of what is happening. As they thus become more real and important to us, we become more concerned for them and are able at last to do the right thing not just because it's right, but also out of love.

This was Benson's experience exactly. He started out irritated with Eric. He got a little rest and then in one of those stunning acts of self-honesty of which we all are capable he admitted to himself that he had not been kind to Eric. So he did what he felt he ought to do to help him. Then the following day, even though tired, he went further and visited the hospital again. It was then that he opened himself up to be influenced by another being's inner reality, and respect and love awakened in him.

Notice that *when we're thus awakened to the reality of another soul, our desires and our duty toward others come together;* we delight in serving them as we feel we should. Benson's story serves as a testament to that fact. From his initial I-It point of view, he couldn't imagine how this could be—he thought nothing could be less interesting or exciting, or more disruptive and annoying. But that's because *he couldn't comprehend love while he remained self-absorbed.* He could not imagine what advantage he could find in merely doing what love dictates, whereas when his heart changed it became a matter of utmost urgency.

ᗡᐧ

A STEP WE CAN TAKE

I want to illustrate the power of doing the right thing because it is right with a story that differs from Benson's in a crucial and very instructive respect. Awareness of another's soul and the respect and love that attend it do not take the author of the story by surprise, as they did Benson. The author longed for that love, but in spite of a great deal of effort found it very difficult to attain. Yet in the end his persistence paid off.

As part of the work of the Arbinger Institute, several individuals were preparing to teach some of the materials presented in this book. They were struggling to bring to their teaching the right kind of heart. Like most of us, they had assumed that teaching means adopting the role, the posture, the social position, and the mask of the teacher. This kept them from being real to, and reaching the hearts of, their students. Like many people in every walk of life—administrators, performers, counselors, artists, and parents—they couldn't quite forget themselves. Given a chance to teach their students, they could manage only to teach their subject.

One of these teachers, Doug, seemed unable to shed his particular burden of self-concern. For several years prior to the time of this story he had been struggling through an unreconciled conflict with a colleague. He had tried for years to resolve their differences, doing thoughtful things for the man, apologizing for misunderstandings, holding himself back for fear of offending—all to no avail. "Still there remained between us a tension," he wrote, "a binding yet repelling force that affected not only both of us but our families."

Coincidentally, Doug at this time was preparing to relocate to another state. He knew he would not have other opportunities to make reconciliation with his colleague. Yet try as he might, he could not discover where he had been at fault—how could he rectify a wrong he could not identify?

On the day before his move, Doug took his last possible opportunity, still not knowing what he ought to do. Here in his own words is what happened:

> I had intended to go over to this man's house between meetings, but was detained. Suddenly I saw this man walk across the parking lot to his car. I cut short the conversation I was in and almost ran after him. When I caught up with him I put my hand on his shoulder from behind, turned him around, entwined our forearms, then pulled him close to me. When you pounce on someone like that it usually means that you have something important to say. But what was I supposed to say? I still wasn't sure what my offense was.
>
> It was not until the very moment I looked directly and deeply into this man's eyes for the first time in years that I

could see my sin. At that moment I no longer saw him. I saw myself reflected! Where there had been no words to say, I found myself asking this good man for his forgiveness. "Why?" he asked. I heard myself reply, "Because I have loved you less. That is my sin: I have loved you less." Tears filled our eyes as I told him then that I loved him. He knew that I loved him. Whatever else I said after that really didn't matter much. After we parted I glanced back once to see him still standing where I had left him, his head down, and his shoulders gently rolling with his sobs.

Doug had striven for reconciliation for years. Though he had done all he could think of to do, his heart hadn't changed. It wasn't because he had made all that effort in order to please his vanity or to justify himself. He had made the effort because he knew his heart was not yet right toward his colleague; he could not stand to think he was offending him, even inadvertently, without trying to do something about it.

We do not control the timing of a change of heart. We make ourselves available for it by faithfully doing the right things for the right reasons; that much *does* lie within our control. But just when and how a change of heart will come we cannot force. *It's like physical healing: our spirits, like our bodies, seem to know how to heal themselves when the obstacles to healing are removed.* Our part—the part in which deliberation, planning, willpower, and persistence play their roles—consists of removing the obstacles.

Thus when Doug's change of heart finally came, it was partly because of his efforts over a long period of time. Imagine how different his experience in the parking lot would have been if he had kept a stiff and judgmental distance from that man all those years (and indeed it's doubtful that he would have gone out there at all)!

Lifted Out of Ourselves

The practical implications of this are obvious. We have learned in this book that, stuck in an unwanted I-It way of being, we cannot see how to change to the I-You way of being *directly.* Nevertheless, we can always do so *indirectly.* We can always, as a first step, do what seems right because, for us, it *is* right. And we can persist in doing it because it is right. And this is all we *can* do deliberately; it lies within our power.

But this much is enough. It lifts us out of self-absorption. It removes our defensiveness. It puts us in the mode of yielding to the truth—specifically the truth about ourselves and about what is right. And in this mode, we are available to be touched and softened by the truth about others.

Problems with Self-Improvement Goals

It is helpful to compare doing the right thing for the right reason with the idea of self-improvement, which can be found in one form or another almost everywhere in our culture. A product of that culture, I, too, have taken my turn being captivated by this idea. Discontented with myself at the age of twenty, I carefully listed every significant rule of conduct I could think of or could find in the books I respected. I told myself that if I could strictly abide by each one of them without exception, I might be able to rid myself of what I did not like in myself. It seemed my only chance. I smile now at my naiveté, but in those years I was desperate. I could not see anything else I could do.

Yet even then I knew deep down that my strategy wouldn't work. It was my motives that troubled me. If my motives stayed the same, wouldn't all my scrupulous rule-keeping amount to just so much hypocrisy? It couldn't really allay my self-doubt and bring me peace. What was I to do? *It seemed that my method for getting my heart right wouldn't work until my heart was right!* I hadn't sufficiently grasped the principle of simply doing the right thing for the right reason, in the faith that this would break the stranglehold of pride and selfishness.

Many self-improvement projects suffer from this same confusion. We set out to "re-invent" or "re-engineer" or "make over" ourselves personally. This requires imagining the kind of person we want to be and taking that image as our goal. Then we guide our efforts by that visualized image. Since we're trying to change from the unacceptable, self-absorbed condition we are in, our motives spring from that condition, and there's the rub. Being self-absorbed, we pay minimal attention to others' hopes and needs except when they serve to advance our self-improvement. This is true even if we say we're doing it to help them. Everything we do to obtain the goal embroils us ever more deeply in being the way we don't want to be.

Sometimes advice-givers acknowledge the need for a change of heart by cautioning that their instructions need to be carried out wholeheartedly and sincerely. They add the notion of a changed heart almost as if it were a worthwhile afterthought and not difficult to implement. They assume that it's the easy part when in fact it's the hardest part of all. In spite of the fact that our success in following their advice hinges upon the quality of our intent, they rarely offer us any effective suggestions for attaining the necessary change of heart.

SELF-HONESTY'S ROLE
IN DOING WHAT'S RIGHT

We are ready to look at the second factor that enabled Benson and Doug to do the right thing in a genuine rather than a counterfeit way. When they asked themselves what the right thing to do might be, they had to do so sincerely. How were they able to give up their self-absorption enough to attain this sincerity? Why wasn't the self-questioning just one more episode in their ongoing series of self-deceptions?

In asking himself what the decent thing to do might be, Benson *simultaneously* wondered whether he might be in the wrong. This kind of self-honesty must be present if, starting in a self-absorbed condition, we are to discern what is right to do. *If we do not suspect ourselves of having been wrong, our search for what is right won't be completely sincere.* Sincerely asked, the question, "What is right to do?" *includes* the question, "Might I be in the wrong?" With either of these questions we ask the other; we pull ourselves up short and start over.

This is the key: Even in *asking* this question, *if* we ask it sincerely, we begin to change in our way of being; we begin to become the kind of person capable of doing the right thing without counterfeiting it. For putting this question to ourselves sincerely means we are *already* troubled and wondering about ourselves. The initial act of self-honesty has already taken place.

How Can We Tell What's Right?

What has just been said might make it all sound too easy. If we're caught up in self-betrayal, our sense of what's true or right is hopelessly mixed with other, often competing, feelings. Doug no doubt felt insecure about approaching that man again. He might have remained annoyed with him for making a reconciliation so hard to achieve, and discouraged that the tension between them had gone so long unresolved. How, in such a confusion of feelings, does a person discern which feelings to trust and to be guided by?

Keep in mind as you think about this issue how very easy it is to be misled. When our hearts are hardened we also have false feelings about what's right and wrong. You will recall Jennifer, staying home from visiting her aunt in the hospital and finding so much fault with the woman that she actually *felt* it would be wrong to make the visit. Self-betrayers have feelings, often very strong feelings, and they get into trouble by trusting them.

Discerning the Feelings We Can Trust

A woman named Brenda came to see me about the hard feelings that had long been developing between herself and her husband. She told several stories of his slovenliness, his rudeness, and his anger. I listened. She bombarded me with a list of reasons why she ought to leave him. I listened. She told me what would happen if she failed to take this action. Then she asked if it was okay for her to do it.

I said, "You know the answer."

The room fell silent. I would not have disrupted that silence for anything. Brenda was going over in her mind all her arguments for leaving her husband. She hadn't found these arguments totally convincing; had she done so she wouldn't have doubted herself enough to come to see me in the first place. Her eyes reminded me of a person waiting at the edge of a momentous and frightening decision, but not yet ready to make it.

The silence persisted for a very long time, perhaps fifteen minutes. I waited. Finally she spoke and said: "I'm a pathetic person, aren't I?"

What had been the pattern of Brenda's inner conversation during all that time? Of course, I have no way of knowing the answer for sure, but from what she said later I suspect the inner argument went something like this:

"But he never shows me respect."

Silence. "Maybe that's not completely fair. I've criti-
cized him pretty harshly right from the beginning."

"No, nothing excuses the hurt. Bad habits I can stand.
But when he knows how he hurts me, then it's on purpose!"

More silence, and then: "On the other hand, *I've*
known how hurt *he* has been, and I *still* go ahead and cut
him down."

"Yes, but . . ."

"Why do I want to nail him to the wall, anyway? My
mother said I keep forgetting all the good times and
remember only the hard times, and that's true. Why do I
just emphasize the bad? Am I just looking for an excuse
not to try harder?"

In the silence of that room and without needing to defend
herself against any other person, Brenda allowed herself to *look at*
herself, and she saw a woman filled with accusations. She could
feel them inhibiting the spirit of life in her. *There was a difference
between (1) her accusing, self-excusing feelings and (2) the discomfort she felt when she observed herself having and defending those
feelings. And she could discern this difference.*

That's the key. To have feelings that are essentially dishonest (and
by that is meant any of the accusing, self-excusing emotions or attitudes we have been talking about) is one thing. It's quite another to
observe ourselves having these feelings and to see how we are afflicting others with them. Whereas in the first case we are being dishonest, in the second we are honest about our dishonesty; as we
learned in chapter 10, the honesty drives the dishonesty out. Between
the dishonest and the honest state of mind there is a world of difference, and, like Brenda, we can all discern that difference.

How it went with Brenda is how it goes with many. I was
teaching a group of managers in a traditional industry. They lived
to drink and gamble on big athletic events, they treated one

another callously, and they never showed sympathetic feelings, which meant that they pretended to be unaffected by anyone else's need. At the end of the teaching day, one of them, Jimmy, a craggy stub of a man of sixty who looked seventy-five, dropped his head in his hands, said something about his wife that, though muffled, was very appreciative, and wept. "This is the first time," he said, "I have ever been out of the box."

Can you imagine a life of abrasive and irresponsible attitudes suddenly challenged when their author, in a solitary moment, acknowledges his sense that it has always been false? It calls to mind that lone, unprotected Chinese revolutionary standing in the path of a tank in Tiananmen Square. To me, Jimmy showed that kind of courage. He sided with the truth. Such a profoundly private and personal decision is the beginning of an awakened life.

Brenda's and Jimmy's examples answer the question, "Can we trust our feelings?" The answer is: It depends on what kind of feelings they are. If they are feelings that come when we are yielding to the truth, we can trust them; if not, they will lead us astray.

The Buck Absolutely Stops with Us

How, then, can we tell whether we are caught up in dishonest feelings or proceeding honestly? What yardstick do we use to make certain we are not making a mistake?

The answer is, there is no yardstick. No handy tape measure or scale or barometer exists by which to assess the difference. No jury of public opinion can help us decide. No panel of experts knows any more than we do. Yet the difference between counterfeit and genuine is plain, as plain as bright daylight or the darkness of a moonless night. We not only can't rely on anything external to tell the difference, but we don't need to. This is something that human beings are simply able to do.

You might think, "Sensing what's right must certainly be a

defective and unreliable procedure then. No wonder people so often disagree about right and wrong!" This thought would be mistaken. What's defective is not our capacity to discern whether we're doing right or wrong, but our ability to formulate rules for doing it. Keep in mind that we can't formulate rules for doing many of the utterly simple things we do daily, like raising our arm, making our vocal cords work, and remembering a name. The reason is their simplicity. Rules are for the complex things we do by means of doing simple things for which there can be no rules. It would be foolish to question a capacity we exercise consistently just because we can't put how we do it into words.

Therefore I am prepared to say: When it comes to discerning when we are being taken in by falsified feelings of what's right and what's wrong, we are completely, utterly on our own. No yardstick or procedure can help us. *The only thing that can save us from being hoodwinked by our own dishonesty is our own honesty.* The buck stops right there.

Growing in Confidence

Most interestingly, the more vigilant we are in seeking the right thing to do and the more faithfully we do it, the more unerring becomes our sensitivity to the self-insistence of false feelings, and the more acute our distaste for them becomes. We grow in our courage to renounce them and follow our heart instead. Thus we become more able to discern our own spiritual distress and to protect ourselves from self-deception.

After twenty years of marriage, a woman whom I'm going to call Rachael was jolted to learn that her husband had been having an affair for quite some time. He had had a history of that sort of thing before their marriage, but had tried hard to put it behind him. "I can see so clearly that he tried to change everything except his heart," she wrote. She had long since recognized his fear of emotional intimacy and had sorrowed for him over that. Her story exemplifies complete honesty of soul. She said:

> One day in a heap of tears I decided that I still had a life and that I would not spend it being bitter and poisoning the lives of our children with venom about their father. I felt really rather wonderful after I made that decision. People now tell me they are amazed at my attitude, but I feel that it is not amazing. I just want to live a clean life, and poison does not allow growth.
>
> In the last week I have had two bitter divorced women call me up and offer a shoulder to cry on. Interestingly enough, neither of them heard me when I declined (graciously) their offers. They both are certain that I am seething with anger—because they are. In their eyes I belong to a club of women who need to "let it all out." Both of them offered to cry with me, talk with me when I need to talk, and ultimately have me participate in fanning the fire of "I-have-been-wounded-and-I-will-never-let-anyone-forget-it." When I told them how I feel—that my husband is ill, weak, and suffering and that I hurt for him—they tell me that I am really denying my anger and that this anger is justified. They don't hear me when I say that I want life, not death that I would carry around in my heart forever.

This woman had developed her discernment of the light and her confidence in it through a number of hard experiences. When very difficult trials befell her, she was ready; she knew which feelings to trust. Thus she was able to see through invitations to collusion that otherwise would have been very seductive and to spare herself a great deal of sorrow.

We use the word *character* to name a person's constancy over time in straightforwardly doing what honestly seems to be right. We can grow in this constancy, and it is our choice alone to decide whether or not we will. And we do so by quietly accepting and doing the right thing in the present moment—and then in the next moment, and after that in the next, and so on without end.

∼

THE CHOICE POINT

Behind all this discussion about what we can do to facilitate our own change of heart stands this simple question:

> Since we cannot bring about a change of heart in ourselves *directly,* what *can* we do directly that will *indirectly* bring about a change of heart?

The answer is this: *Even if we find ourselves unable to do the right thing with concern, compassion, or love, we can nevertheless do it because it is right.* The choice to do this comes at that point at which we decide between right and wrong. It comes as we decide whether to do as we feel it would be right to do toward another. Trying to intervene in the ongoing flow of our lives at other points doesn't work.

Sometimes individuals come to me reporting that they decided to do the right thing, no matter what, for a set period of time—a half a day, perhaps, or a day or a week. Their plan was to do it without quibbling or hesitating or counting the cost, but just to do whatever they felt was right to do. These grand experiments almost invariably turn out the same way, no matter who attempts them. Suddenly the world seems to become an easier place to live in. Other people begin to lose their edginess and become more cooperative. Being around them starts to be a more delightful and fulfilling experience. Ability to concentrate increases, because the need for self-worry diminishes. Setbacks don't seem so devastating.

Such are the consequences of doing what's right simply because it is right, even for a short period of time.

I believe it crucial to understand that, *to the extent that we're stuck in negative thoughts and feelings, we always get the choice point wrong.* This does not mean that we make the wrong choice. It means that we choose between the wrong set of alternatives. We *think* the alternatives to be various ways of acting or behaving— whether, for example, to speak out or keep silent, submit docilely or assert ourselves, punish or indulge, do our duty or refuse, and so on. *But if our hearts are not right, it doesn't matter which of these alternatives we choose*—they are at best pretenses of confidence or happiness, and at worst hypocritical, a counterfeit of uprightness.

Some of us may think we have another alternative available, especially if our emotional life becomes so hard to bear that we ache for a change of heart. In desperation we try to change our feelings or at least control them. And we discover we can't. We try to exert our willpower to stop being angry, envious, critical, bored, snappish, or defensive. The more we try, the more impossible the task seems.

So the choice that can change our hearts is not a choice of either our behavior *or* our feelings. The first does not affect our way of being and the second, which tries to affect our way of being, is impossible. Both of these strategies try to intervene at a point in our experience where we cannot intervene—where our efforts, however determined, can make no difference.

The choice point comes elsewhere. It comes when we decide whether or not to yield to the truth about ourselves, about others, or about what's required of us and be guided by it in our actions.

"In Case of Doubt, Abstain"—Completely

We need to explore further the matter of trying to control our feelings or attitudes. People whose negative attitudes, emotions, or moods cause extreme disruption in their lives tend to resort to self-control just because it seems the only thing to do. But the more they try, the more helpless they feel. They seem to be addicted emotionally. The matter of the choice point becomes particularly urgent for them. The following story will help us understand why:

> Julian had become very despondent over always being down on the people closest to him—his family and his co-workers, primarily. He was particularly judgmental of anyone who received some opportunity or recognition he wanted for himself. Though he despised himself for his constant criticisms of people, he couldn't seem to make himself stop. "This has all but ruined my family," he told me.
>
> What complicated the situation was that he said he had been trying to do thoughtful things for the people he judged most harshly, but it didn't help much. I seldom give advice, but in this case I felt a small suggestion might give him the leverage he needed. "You've got to impose abstinence upon yourself," I said. "You can't allow yourself to entertain even the suggestion of a critical thought. You can't tolerate thinking about another person's fault. The instant a critical thought even starts to appear, turn away in your mind. Don't go there. St. Augustine, who was a person experienced in turning away from temptations, said, 'In case of doubt, abstain.' That must become your watchword."
>
> "But people do have faults. That's reality."
>
> "True. And what are *your* faults?"
>
> "I'm always critical. But I feel helpless to stop."
>
> "You're saying: 'This is a fault of mine, *but not really*. It's *really other people's* fault, because they *make me* critical.'"
>
> "Are you saying I'm just making up an excuse?"
>
> "I didn't say it, you did."

"What would I need an excuse for?"

"What do you think?"

Julian became very, very thoughtful. "For not being truly kind to people," he said.

This might look like a logical deduction, as if he were concluding it from what he and I had said. I am convinced it wasn't. Our conversation up to that point only got him to the point of looking at himself and attending to what he already knew.

I said, "So as long as your critical feelings continue, you can't really believe you're responsible for them, right?"

"Yeah, that's right."

"Is that true even when you are trying to battle against those feelings?"

He pondered a while and then said, "I think I get it! Even when I'm trying my best to control them, I'm still hanging on to them! I'm using them for an excuse for not being really kind."

"So what's the best strategy? Having the feelings and battling against them, or . . . "

"The best strategy has got to be to not let myself get started on the feelings in the first place!"

"Julian, the point at which you can control your feelings is not when you are trying to deal with them. Then it's too late. *The point at which you control them is when you choose not to have them at all.* That is the choice point."

At this point Julian had become pretty excited. "What you mean is, I've got a chance to stop being critical and judgmental and sarcastic if I *just stop.* I can't let these feelings or thoughts get anywhere near me. I don't have a chance if I have the unkind feelings and *then* try to stop them!"

Perhaps seven months later Julian reported in, with a much brighter countenance. "It was very hard at first. But I worked at it until I could make myself do it. I just turned away when a critical thought started coming my way. I didn't drag myself away, like I was making a big sacrifice. That had been my old strategy, and it didn't work. Instead, I turned away quite lightheartedly. It got easier and easier to think about other people affectionately and appreciate them.

"But if I cheated in my abstinence program I would get fuzzy and confused in my brain and couldn't keep focused on what is important to me. I wouldn't be able to remember all the pain my 'addiction' had caused me. So I'd get swept off my course.

"I stayed on course by being very strict with myself, until I was pretty well free of this demon. But I have to keep on my guard because it would be pretty easy for me to slide back again."

Julian's abstinence strategy goes hand in hand with trying to do the right thing. In fact, it enables a person who has been doing the right thing in a counterfeit way to finally do it genuinely. *It might be best to think of abstinence and doing right as inseparable. Doing right is the way we abstain and the abstaining is the way we do right.* The emphasis on abstinence doesn't always seem to be all that necessary. It's useful when we experience our accusing, self-excusing emotions as addictive.

The strategy Julian employed can work just as decisively for other "addicted" patterns of feeling and conduct. It works for anger. It works for self-pity. It works for gossip. It works for laziness. It works for self-disparagement. It works for pouting and sarcasm and temper tantrums. I have even seen it work for gambling and sexual fantasies. It works for all the patterns of self-indulgence that linger after the heart first undergoes a change.

It could be a very productive exercise to take the habit that most heavily enchains you and go through Julian's abstinence program, putting your particular "addiction" in place of his chronic and apparently uncontrollable fault-finding. The approach he took can serve as either a primary or a supplementary strategy for dealing with and diminishing any emotional addiction, even though it seems to us embedded in our nature. "In case of doubt, abstain."

◦◡

WHEN THE RIGHT
THING BECOMES EASY

There's a special quality about the experience of doing right when we do it for the right reasons, and more especially when we do it out of love. We don't feel that we are having to exert our will or to insist on having our own way. That doesn't mean we aren't active and energetic; it means we don't feel any sort of emotional stress. We aren't having to submit to something we don't want to do, for we *do* want to do it, and because we want to do it, it doesn't feel like a sacrifice. Nor are we worried about what people might think, or whether we will get any advantage from what we're doing, or whether we might be wasting our time. We throw ourselves into the activity, whatever it might be, and feel easy and free in doing so. What we feel called upon to do may be hard, but not hard to bear. For we are allowing ourselves to be mastered and guided by our sense of right and wrong, and consequently we have great confidence that what we are doing is acceptable and worthwhile. We have no need to cover or justify or explain ourselves.

When she was my student, Laura Barksdale wrote this as part of an assigned paper. She entitled it "On Being One":

I was teaching part-time in the alternative high school. It's a school for kids who are struggling personally. They taught me about *being one*.

I had made a tool to help me explain self-betrayal. I

made it of four opaque, colored, plastic sheets stapled over a photograph of a human face. As the sheets were lowered over the photo one at a time, we could see the face less and less clearly. When the fourth was added, not even the faintest outline of the face could be discerned. My point was that by self-betrayal we so discolor our world that we see others dimly or not at all. One of my students pointed out that the plastic sheets reflected images the way a darkened mirror would. "Isn't it interesting," he said, "that when we get deep enough into doing what's wrong, all we can see is our own self?"

I thought later, if all I can see is myself, something is wrong. This is a red flag, a warning, like physical pain—a warning that I can no longer understand others or feel at one with them.

As I recall the times I have experienced that oneness, I can remember no awareness of myself. About two weeks ago I was taking a walk with two children, Daniel and Kristi, ages eight and twelve. We walked into the fields on the outskirts of the city. The day was perfect. Daniel said you could smell autumn. We all gathered up the large milkweed pods and scattered their contents into the air, creating a slow-motion snowstorm of floating seeds. The sun was large and yellow, and the children's hair, blown slightly by the air currents that carried the drifting seeds, was silhouetted against it. We spent a long time in the fields, talking and wandering. As I look back, still able to feel that day, it doesn't come to me how good "I" felt. I was not concentrating on myself.

Another time I called my mother on the phone. She asked what I wanted for my birthday. I told her I'd like her to paint me something. She said, "Okay, I'll paint the house next week." She rolled off the most beautiful laugh I've ever heard. Usually I have taken offense when she has toyed with me. But this time there was no "I" to do that.

My face formed a smile I could not refuse. It was a richly compelling moment, filled with feeling and love.

One either focuses on the "I" or sees others through it, never both simultaneously. If I'm absorbed in myself I'm not being one with others. If I'm seeing through myself— if I use myself to see—I'm in the midst of a day like the one I spent with Daniel and Kristi. Either I'm preoccupied with myself or I allow myself to simply be myself. I have either the disease or the cure.

Since chapter 7 we have been speaking of awakening to the truth. We have called it a change of our way of being, of our negative emotions and attitudes, and of our heart. You might think that such a wholesale transformation would be the ultimate objective. It isn't. It's only Step One. For having awakened, or reawakened, to the truth, we must ask ourselves, What now? How do we live the life upon which we are newly embarked? How do we maintain this welcoming, accepting outlook on everything? What kind of obstacles will we encounter? How do we stay on course? How shall we measure our progress?

The answers to these questions are not obvious, nor is putting them into practice easy. We will turn to these issues in the final three chapters.

CHAPTER 12

WHAT COMES AFTER A CHANGE OF HEART?

SUSTAINING THE CHANGE

In every era and culture, people have sought for and obtained the awakening we have been talking about. For some this change of mind and heart has come by way of quiet insight, or many successive insights, while others have experienced it as a cleansing and refreshing conversion to a new way of life. Many have written of it or made it the centerpiece of their religious or communal life, celebrating and memorializing it. It feels like a gift, and indeed it is a gift. None of us can produce it by our own deliberate effort.

But even at its most profound, the change of mind and heart amounts only to a beginning. We do not, we cannot, become considerate, self-forgetful, and generous beings in a moment. Following the initial softening experience we must re-enter our daily lives, there to encounter again all the same situations and people who have upset us in the past. We will find ourselves challenged, accused, and taken advantage of, just as we did before our change of heart. We will discover new manifestations of the weaknesses we thought we had overcome. We may relapse into old patterns and then become discouraged. For those who are earnest about their emotional and spiritual well-being, the issue becomes Can I sustain, under fire, my new vision of things? Can I learn to right myself when I bend or fall backwards?

In general, to maintain ourselves in our renewed condition we must continue in that same self-honesty, openness, and upright conduct that got us there in the first place. To the extent that we do this, our experiences will instruct us. Because we will interpret them differently, the same sort of encounters and circumstances that formerly reinforced our negative attitudes and emotions will instead reveal to us the truth about others and about ourselves. Our teacher will be the testing that life unfailingly arranges for us, augmented perhaps by considerate individuals who enter or re-enter our lives. "When the student is ready, the teacher will come." We will grow in experience, judgment, and wisdom. We will develop strength and assurance sufficient to keep us on our course.

In this chapter we will focus on certain dangers we may encounter in our quest to stay on course and how we might respond to them. Unfortunately, there is insufficient space in this book to treat other aspects of life highly relevant to this quest, such as adversity, sacrifice, service, work, and gratitude, all of which contribute to our maturity and refinement.

Not Progress but Stillness

Some of us who are seeking to maintain ourselves in our new, more open way of being get tripped up by our anxiety to measure our progress. We want to know how we're doing. But worrying too much about such things means we're probably still too self-absorbed to maintain whatever change of heart we may have experienced. Such worrying is not the sort of thing that people do when they are preoccupied with enjoying or assisting other people or accomplishing their work or delighting in learning or friendships or nature. Fixating on our personal progress makes what really matters go out of focus.

We can call to mind our discussion of self-improvement goals in chapter 11. There's nothing wrong with goals so long as we don't pursue them to prove we're something that we're not. But turning the maintenance of a change of heart into a project with measurable steps of achievement usually requires a pretty heavy focus on oneself. This produces only a counterfeit of change.

Preoccupation with personal progress in such matters usually indicates that we are not making much progress.

What, then, do we focus on when living in a self-forgetful and generous way, if not a goal? Part of the answer is this. We do not think of ourselves as "a force on the move" toward some important objective. Instead, we feel still, inwardly still.

Ask yourself, Who is the person I really need to be? A being who can come into existence only by determined, gritty effort? I think on reflection you will answer, No, the person I need to be is who I am already—or more accurately, who I will be if I cease trying to display myself as worthy and acceptable and thus make myself into a grotesque distortion of who I really am. If this is how you answer, you like many others intuitively agree that we become most ourselves, without distortion, when we relax our frantic effort to justify ourselves and allow ourselves simply to be still— which means, of course, renouncing the self-betraying way of life.

Still is just the right way to be.

You rise in the morning to go about your day. You remember a friend who has troubles. You don't quibble with yourself about whether to call her; you don't write a reminder on your Palm Pilot or in your planner to make the call tomorrow. You just call. Simple.

Your friend is appreciative. Even over the phone there's a warmth between the two of you that you don't recognize till later. But you laugh. You feel an easiness during the conversation, brief though it is, that nudges open the portals of the day. The way forward seems more warmly lit and inviting than usual.

Your spouse isn't up yet. You leave an encouraging note and a chocolate you brought home from work for just this purpose. Easy. There is no "do gooder" feeling about any of this.

At work, you talk with people about the interests you share. Word comes down that the project you've put your heart into for many months might be canceled. Others in your office wring their hands. The engines of speculation start churning out analyses of malice or mischief on higher levels. Past grievances are resurrected and amplified. Somehow, you don't feel flustered. Your inner stillness can't be touched by this. One way or the other, everything will work out.

Shall we call this stillness *progress?* I think not. You have made no progress, because there is no progress to be made. *Being fully human, fully who you are, is not an achievement. It's more like a homecoming.*

One teacher whose approach resonates with what I have been speaking of in this book told me, "Not one of my students who I think is doing well says, 'I am becoming better.' On the contrary, they struggle on with challenges that are much like those they struggled with before. But more and more frequently they have the sense of coming to themselves, and more continuously. An increasing portion of the time, they feel peaceful. But they don't notice it much. They're too caught up in whatever they're doing and the people they're doing it with and the people they're doing it for."

❧

RELAPSING

Being overly concerned about our personal progress is just one of the ways we can slip back into self-absorption. Before we look at some others, we will do well to study briefly some general features about relapses. We will focus on three of them.

First, *once we begin to slip, we tend to slip a lot.*

All the old suspiciousness, defensiveness, and insecurity return, the way drunkenness almost inevitably follows an alcoholic's decision to take only one drink. I'll illustrate this with the story, introduced in chapter 1, of a woman burdened with the behavior of the other members of her family.

> Though exceptionally competent, Victoria sabotaged her own management career by her determination always to get things done "the right way"—which meant Victoria's way. This tendency had just about ruined her family as well. "What a shock it was to me to wake up one day and realize why Ron (my husband) and my children appreciate nothing that I do for them, and I do a lot. Whatever our family activity, like working in the yard, going on trips, or deciding what clothes the children should buy, it always has to be done my way. 'My way or the highway'—that's me. Here I am, forty-eight years old, always thinking I know best and always needing to run the show and always blind and deaf where other people are concerned. Forty-eight years old and never realized any of this before!"
>
> Victoria's fifteen-year-old son, Rusty, had been doing very poorly in school and staying out long past the legal curfew. "He'd walk in and I'd start right away getting after him and telling him how to get his life straightened out." But with her change of heart, that stopped. Then one day he came home and she listened. Like the drummer, Benson, she discovered she really wanted to hear what he had to say. To her further amazement, he started staying at home more often. Some days he and she would talk for an hour or more. After several weeks of this he came home one day to ask if there was anything he could do to help her. She could scarcely believe it.
>
> These developments raised her hopes. "He's turning around," she thought. Not surprisingly but disastrously, she decided to do her part to help him along. She called the school to make sure he could still pass the term's classes if he applied himself. And when she saw Rusty again she carefully worked the subject into the conversation so she could encourage him, yet knowing she might

be treading on dangerous ground. After a few minutes, he left while she was still talking and didn't return until the next day.

Specters of all her old troubles arose in her mind. Angry feelings returned, especially against Ron for not making the boy toe the line. Then it dawned on her that she might have caused this new problem by returning to her controlling ways. She decided to make an extra effort. "I told myself I shouldn't get on Rusty's case; I reminded myself how effective it had been when I just listened. I even made a vow not to criticize or give him suggestions when he came back. But then when he walked into the house again all the old warning words just came spewing out as if I had no control of my mouth. I spent a sleepless night wondering why I would want to wreck everything, just when it was becoming so good."

Victoria's relapse swept her back into the I-It way with the same swiftness that her change of heart had swept her out of it. That's the first point I want to make: the slope is steep. Start to slide, and it's easy to find yourself all the way back at the bottom.

Second, *it is our old patterns of response, our old tendencies and habits, that we fall back into.*

What Victoria did to alienate Rusty again was the same sort of thing she had done before, apparently to prove to herself how much she was sacrificing to help her boy succeed. She had developed this style over a lifetime, and with her first relapse into self-betrayal she returned to it.

Third, *after undergoing a change of heart, it is ours to decide whether and to what extent we will indulge again in our old habits of accusation and self-justification.*

The change of heart does not obliterate our susceptibility to fall back into these patterns, and we activate that susceptibility if we begin to betray ourselves again. A relapse can be a minimal and instructive thing, indeed, part of a normal process of our growth, or else it can plunge us into a condition even worse than before our change of heart. We determine by our response which it will be. That response, which is actually many responses over the course of years, must be counted as important to our well-being as our initial change of heart. Think of it as the continuing decision whether to sustain that change.

◠

WHEN OTHERS DON'T RESPOND AS WE EXPECT

When those around us don't understand and appreciate the change we've made, but keep on in their old ways or worse, how will we react?

Typically we will be able to sustain our openness to them for a while. We can see that they mean to cause no harm but are only acting defensively.

But it is deceptively easy to take offense again and start to slip back into our old thoughts and feelings. We find ourselves having to pick up after the same people again or tolerate their boisterousness or because of them miss out on something we had anticipated. We get a little fussed. We can see so clearly how they are betraying themselves and misusing others. Why can't they see it?

Still, we try to buck up. But it gets discouraging, we tell ourselves, to always have to adjust or compensate for someone else's shortfall. We have caught a glimpse of what it might mean to live in peace and mutual consideration, and we want this for others' sake as well as for ours. This seems to have been Victoria's pitfall.

So then, after trying hard for a while to accommodate other people, we begin to wonder why they don't get it—why they don't come around to our way of thinking, why they have to be so obtuse (as obtuse as we were for so many years!). Very likely we will then start pressing them to change, and of course they will not take this very well. Outright impatience may follow, and everything we have gained will be lost.

We have forgotten the collusive role we have played in their response to us. Before our change of heart we supplied them with provocations and excuses for taking offense, for suspecting our motives, and for reacting to us accusingly. In effect, we "trained" them to respond this way. Yet, in spite of that, we unreasonably expect them to pick up on our change of heart, jump for joy, and quickly submit to a change of heart themselves!

Some do, of course. They detect the change in us right away and are softened by it. But others suspect we have only adopted a different strategy for getting our own way. These react to what they have believed about us in the past, reflecting back to us not what we are or desire to be now but what we have been. For example, if we no longer feel comfortable spending time doing what they like to do, they may think us "holier than thou."

And even if they eventually allow their hearts to soften toward us, they may escalate their offensive behavior for a time, as if trying to break us down or test us to see if the kindness we are showing them is genuine. This shouldn't surprise us. It is not any easier for them to be touched and softened than it was for us; they too must give up long-entrenched self-betrayals.

It is a key sign of danger when we expect that others should change in response to *our* change. This signals a lapse on our part, back into self-absorption. Why so? Because the moment we begin to feel that we need others to change before we can be free of our troubled, afflicting thoughts and feelings, we have either lost the joy we felt when we experienced our change of heart or else we never experienced that change at all. We're back in our self-absorbed condition or we never got out of it. Anyone free of that condition enjoys an emotional freedom that no external circumstance can destroy—including the reactions of other people.

Some of us succumb to a different danger when we start to slip. We use the new vocabulary, with which we now describe our past errors, to accuse others and decontaminate ourselves. If reading this book has led you to new realizations, you will very likely start to see self-betrayal, rationalization, accusing emotion, and collusion everywhere. You might then indulge in a feeling of superiority. You might use the weaknesses you perceive in others as evidence against them. Because you are paying the most careful attention to these matters of self-betrayal and self-deception, you're confident you can't be in the wrong. ("How *could* I be self-deceived?" you ask yourself incredulously. "*I'm* a keen-eyed member of the self-betrayal police!") Without realizing what is happening, you will have gotten yourself back in the same dark condition as before, not in spite of your new vocabulary but, ironically, with its help!

One man who had been particularly accusing of his wife encountered the material of this book in a class he took and made it a point to search me out. "I saw her in everything that was said. That class proved I have been right all along." Hearing things like this, I cringe.

When we are locked into self-betrayal, our capacity to take any situation whatever and twist it in our favor knows no limit. And our new vocabulary of self-betrayal and collusion enables us to do this more cleverly than ever. An instructional psychology professor heard me lecture on these subjects, marched home, put a stern finger in his wife's face, and announced, "I'm not going to collude with you any more!"

Many are the occasions over the years when, near the beginning of some class I have been conducting, someone says, "I wish my spouse were here; he (or she) really needs this!"

The general principle behind these danger signs: *When we find ourselves preoccupied with fixing others, we can know that we have either lost our softness of heart and generosity of spirit, or else we never regained it.*

∾

PRIDE USUALLY HAS SOMETHING TO DO WITH IT

Our relapses are often connected with pride, which is self-absorption differently described. After having gained a foretaste of a sweeter kind of life—a life in which we've treated others more considerately and had them respond more considerately to us—we might begin to congratulate ourselves a little. That's pride. Or, as we saw in the preceding section, we might become impatient with others if they don't respond considerately. That's pride, too, because we feel superior. Or we might think that because our feelings are less troubled and we're doing better with people, it's safe to indulge some of our former self-absorbed desires. We think we're not vulnerable anymore to our former selfishness and hardness toward others. This too is a case of pride.

Learning how and why this happens can help us both avoid slippages and recover from them.

The following illustration comes from a man I'll call Richard. His experience with the material of this book had affected his life deeply, so much so that he spent a good deal of time sharing it with other people. From my contacts with him I can attest that he does not exaggerate in describing an idyllic time during which troubling desires and impulses temporarily disappeared.

> Once I went for three and a half months without ever being rude to my wife and children. I could walk into a room where my children were quarreling and my wife was

tearing her hair out, and I wouldn't have to fight down any sense of inconvenience or irritation. I was simply able to handle the situation. I seemed to be able to soothe hurt feelings and break up squabbles very easily.

I could tell it was coming to an end when I started keeping track. One day, about three months into it, I thought, "Hey, the last time I felt any irritation at all was way back at Christmas, and here it is March. I'm really onto something here. I'm going to have to keep this up." That was a sure sign that the end was near.

About two weeks later I was upstairs in the bedroom, reading an important book related to my efforts to share with people my newfound way of life. My wife, Joanne, was downstairs doing the dishes. My daughters were in the bathtub. Kevin, my son, who was three years old or so at the time, had been bathed and was in his pajamas and was ready for bed. Suddenly I heard a lot of squealing and laughter coming from the bathroom. Kevin had returned to the bathroom in his pajamas and the girls were pouring water on him. Everybody was having a great time. Kevin wanted to climb into the tub with his pajamas on.

I heard all this commotion, but I kept reading. About ten minutes later the squeals of laughter turned to cries of discomfort. Kevin was soaking wet and starting to get cold. The girls didn't know when to stop. If it was fun to pour water on his head once, then it was going to be fun a thousand times. I felt for a moment that I ought to go check, but then I thought, "What's Joanne doing? She's downstairs in the kitchen, and I'm reading an important book. What's the matter with her? Can't she tell something's wrong? Why doesn't she take care of this?"

I started to feel irritated and then got mad. Right then and there the three and a half months came to an end. Everyone in the bathtub was crying. I went storming into the bathroom and yelled, "Kevin, get out of this room. You should know better than to come in here when your sisters are taking a bath!" Then I told the girls to get out of the bathtub. "Get your nightgowns on and clean up this bathroom and go to bed!"

Sadie, who was about two, looked up at me and said, "No!" I knew how to handle that! I picked her up by one arm and whapped her bottom and said, "Now do it!" She started bawling and ran off. The girls hurried to get their pajamas on and I took care of Kevin. All the while I was thinking about my wife, "She never even came upstairs. She's still down there doing the dishes." After I put Kevin into bed I gave the girls their orders: "Now get into your beds and be sure to say your prayers!"

It was at around 6:30. I slammed the door and stormed down the hall. When I opened up my book again and stared at the pages, all I could see clearly was that I had just blown everything.

Richard delayed jumping up to take care of the bathroom rumpus and, sure enough, he again began to feel swamped by many of his old feelings and habits of response. How interesting! A man lapses into self-betrayal and immediately his insecurities and self-absorption return. And pride returns with them. Why?

As soon as he hesitated to do as he felt he should, Richard thought about the importance of the book he was reading (a book, after all, that helps people become more healthy emotionally and get along better!) and of his need to take time to read it. Perhaps he sensed the significant role he might play in people's lives, teaching them the things he was studying. He was also aware of his calm effectiveness with his family of late and of doing more than his part at home and of the respect that was owed him for that. So the fracas his children were causing in the bathtub disrupted the Important Man Doing His Important Work! We might think his pride came first and kept him from doing what he sensed was right. No, the moment at which he betrayed himself was the choice point; if it hadn't been for this self-betrayal, he would not have begun to worry about his image and insist on his own importance.

Reflect for a moment about the connection between self-betrayal and pride. In self-betrayal, we inevitably seek to impress—if not others, then at least ourselves—because *there is simply no way to display ourselves as worthy and acceptable, except by means of producing evidence of at least deserving such emblems. We cannot do it just by being who we are. We have got to make a show of ourselves, to bolster up a fantasy image of ourselves, and this requires having something to show—some evidence of how worthwhile we are.* In a self-betraying condition, *how we present ourselves* unavoidably becomes the focus of our concern, and we mistakenly confuse it with *how we really are.*

We can use just about anything as evidence of our acceptability or importance, or at least as evidence that we deserve to be accepted and important. For example, we can use our appearance, manners, or hard work (think of Ethan loading the car and preparing the family meals). Or our knowledge or possessions (the college man in chapter 4). Or our prowess or talents, social position, or style of leadership (Jenny's approach to parenting and Eli's unwillingness to suffer fools kindly). Richard's chosen emblems of acceptability and importance were the type of book he was reading and the work he was doing and also what these implied about him—the kind of person he was, his sense of presiding over his household with a sovereign calm, and his swift, deft dispensation of justice when trouble arose.

"The Bigger Box"

Attachment to such evidence, which is pride, may keep us from looking honestly at ourselves in the first place, but often it doesn't. At that stage, before we have experienced a change of heart, we tend in our introspective moments to focus on how we have treated others, rather than on the fact that we are insecurely worried about our image. But the moment we start to slip after having experienced such a change, pride often becomes the main issue. We are concerned with what there is about our character, rather than merely about our actions, that keeps us from staying on course. We wonder, for instance, why possessions or power or property or reputation mean more to us than doing the right thing. Our failure to maintain our gains has shifted our concern from the kinds of things we have *done* to the kinds of people we *are*.

Think about Victoria, the woman who fell back into her controlling ways when her son Rusty started to show some progress with his problems. Her change of heart came when she realized how insensitive she had been in several specific relationships within her own family. But after her relapse, she examined herself even more thoroughly. And she could see how controlled she was by her attachment to her self-image as omnicompetent and unappreciated. Previously, she had tended to question her feelings and actions toward particular people. "Why don't I listen to Rusty more?" But now, with the relapse, she questioned the complex life-concerns out of which these feelings and actions seemed to spring. "Why am I this way?" she asked herself. "Why do I always have to be right?" In other words, "Why am I so proud that I have to make sure every success is my success? Why can't I ever let other people be the ones who are in the right and get the credit?"

We can never completely put an end to any localized collusion as long as pride remains. One reason is that it indicates that we haven't yet abandoned all our self-betraying ways. But further, as Richard's story shows, pride sets us up for further self-betrayal. Richard's pride made him hypersensitive, ready to be offended by almost anything done by the very people from whom he had taken no offense for three and a half months. The children's rowdiness and his wife's insensitivity to his wants showed a disrespect for his image of himself as the Important Man Doing His Important Work, and this he could not tolerate. (These things would have amounted to nothing at all had he been more concerned about his family than about himself.) The matter of pride must be considered especially relevant to relapse because pride makes further offense-taking inevitable.

For this reason we may call the larger framework of pride, with its attachment to self-image, "the bigger box." When our person-to-person collusions lock us into little boxes, we are anxious to secure evidence of our justifiability and acceptability—evidence which our subculture will recognize. Hence the term "bigger box" aptly describes the pride with which we cling to this evidence. .

Merely patching up our localized, strained relationships only takes us out of a little box, not the bigger box in which it is encased. Escaping our immediate cell, we're still locked up in the larger prison. If we crave the promise that attends an initial change of heart, we must be prepared to deal with the issue of self-image, or pride. As long as we stay true to the light and do not slip, the issue will not raise itself. But few of us never slip. Therefore it will be helpful to address the issue of safeguarding our change of heart from the corrosive effects of pride.

∾

SAFEGUARDING OUR CHANGE OF HEART

The moment we betray ourselves after experiencing a change of heart, we become insecure again and find ourselves once more hungering for acceptance and approval. In that condition we are liable to minimize others' interests in favor of maintaining our self-image. This puts us on the slippery slope into full-scale relapse.

The very first appearance of this self-absorbed need for approval ought to be taken as a warning that the draft we are about to drink is poisonous. As with the first appearance of a violent emotion or attitude, it helps immeasurably to act quickly. We may need to stand sentry against these intrusions as long as we live, but the stricter we are with ourselves, the less agitating and invasive our proud impulses will become.

We touched earlier upon the role of deliberate action, effort, and determination—in short, willpower—in attaining a change of heart. At this point we need to say something about its role in maintaining that change. We have already learned that although no amount of effort can cause our heart to soften to the truth or keep it soft, effort can prepare us to be softened. It is equally true that effort can play an indispensable role in aborting a relapse.

Happily, Richard's story of relapse ended with this kind of effort.

> I went downstairs, knowing what had happened and what it was going to take to make it right. When I talked to my wife I said, "You know what I've got to do?" And she said, "Yes, I know." So I went back upstairs and into the bedroom. We have a rule in our house with the children that when you fight with each other you have to go to your room together and stay there until you can hug and kiss and say, "I'm sorry" and "I love you." You have to be able to forgive each other first. Then you can come out of your room.
>
> So there were my daughters, all crying in their beds. I said, "Do you know what, girls? We have a rule in this house, but I've never obeyed that rule myself. When I've been angry at you I've never gone to your room with you and stayed there until we could forgive each other. I think that's wrong. So I'm going to stay in this room until you'll forgive me." Immediately they hopped out of their beds and were over on my lap kissing me, and we made friends.

Well, I learned a lot of lessons from that. But the one that sticks with me the most, because I'm a father, is that it's a father's job to repent first. That's what it means to me to be a father—to be the first one to repent and heal the relationship. My children were anxious and willing to forgive and be friends with me. But I had to start it.

It seems to me that that's the way relationships are healed. It's no more complicated than that. It may take longer in some cases, but there isn't much more to it than simply yielding your heart to what you know is the truth and saying, "I'm sorry."

The contention with his children shocked Richard into acknowledging his pride. What happened then sums up my recommendations about safeguarding our change of heart: Having glimpsed his fault, Richard made himself seek forgiveness—as quickly as possible. He spit the poison out.

It is by willpower that we strive to pay close attention to the telltale signs of self-betrayal and pride. It is by willpower that we refuse to allow ourselves to minimize them. And it is by willpower that we act as quickly, as boldly as we can, the very instant that pride, anxiety, or the sense of victimhood makes even the faintest appearance.

But willpower cannot supply the truth, nor is it our receptivity to the truth. Willpower plays its role by taking quick, vigorous, and resolute action to reject enticements to slip back into moral darkness and to keep our attention riveted on the light.

∽

A CAREER OF REPENTANCE

We have noted that after experiencing something of a change of heart, we are likely to encounter new occurrences of old emotional weakness and habits we thought we had conquered. Coming up against such challenges again does not itself indicate such a relapse. Rather, it presents us with a chance to decide whether we will continue to grow.

The same principles govern here as before. If we respond as we feel prompted, we remain free of any reason to justify or excuse ourselves and to blame others. And if we catch ourselves already in self-betrayal—criticizing, boasting, becoming angry, lying, indulging in self-accusation or self-pity or any other negative thoughts or feelings—we have a bona fide opportunity to decide whether we will continue to do so or turn ourselves about. We can do what we did before—we can ask, "Might I be in the wrong?" or "What is the right thing to do?" or "What is the other person struggling with?" and then let the truth guide our actions. Doing this sincerely is what it takes to stay on course, and it lies within our power.

Personal growth is not like the development of a skill. It does not take place in observable increments that can be measured and charted. Indeed, as we have seen, when we're growing in sensitivity, generosity, and compassion, we're not aware of it, because we're not focusing on ourselves. The recovery of emotional freedom simply does not have the quality, for most of us, of a controllable sequence of transformations. It's more a career of discovering further and further weaknesses and shedding them in turn.

We do well for a time. We slip. We have a truly dark day. We recognize how we've recently returned to our old, regrettable ways. We face up to a weakness. We resolve that this isn't how we want to live. We ponder what we must change and, if prayer is part of our lives, we seek for help. Perhaps we talk with a trusted friend, one wise enough not to tell us we're expecting too much of ourselves. We make a responsible move to do what seems most right to do. And so on.

The lapse is made temporary by our turnaround, when it

might have launched us on a downhill slide to depths even darker than those we knew before. In fact, in some ways our turnaround makes the lapse a strengthening experience that increases our ability to recognize and correct our falterings. This is how it goes for people who make consistent progress.

Laura (see chapter 11) told the story of a day when she was able simply to be herself rather than focus on herself, first with her students at the alternative high school, then with her two young friends, Daniel and Kristi, and finally with her mother. It was definitely the kind of day she would have wanted to continue. But like most of the rest of us, she hit a snag, and what happened then illustrates the kind of easy recovery I have been talking about.

After that day with Daniel and Kristi I had a brief relapse. My sense of "I" returned. I was getting ready to go home to write the paper, "On Being One," when I thought about how natural their affection towards me had been. I was struck with the thought, "I haven't done anything to deserve the love these children have for me." As if the children's affections could be my doing, my accomplishment! As if their love could be attributed only to my lovable qualities! I began to sense a lie hiding in these thoughts. I had made my relationship with the kids a matter of command and control. I've been a person who has maintained a death-grip hold on her control of situations. I had to be the one who was responsible, who would get the credit or the blame. But as I was sensing the lie embedded in my thoughts, I heard myself say aloud, "If I'm trying to take total responsibility for all that happens, then that's a lie." These words followed me to my car, lined up in front of me, and stared back. Accepting the children's love as not my own doing was the beginning of my letting go.

When I got home and sat down to begin writing, the words flowed. The ideas were there waiting for me to express them. As I got to the part about being one with

Mother over the phone, I noticed in myself a tendency to put the whole elaborate self-betrayal in the paper, under the pretense that it would make a good contrast with the oneness with her I had felt. I realized that wanting to put in the gory details was an attempt to glorify my repentance. I was trying again to control, to make sure of the impression I was making. By repeating my story of overcoming my victimhood single-handedly, I could reassure myself about how great I was. This was another attempt at control. This way of writing separated me from my mother. I began to think about her as I had before. It also separated me from my reader. After less than a paragraph, the flow was gone.

This startled me. Without pausing to consider, I pushed the backspace key on the computer, and began to erase the words backwards, letter by letter. As quickly as they disappeared from the screen, one line after another up the page, I could feel the spirit of love flow back to me. For a moment it seemed very strange that someone might think I had a normal relationship with my mother, with no particular hardship in it. This was a thought that just a moment ago I could not have allowed myself to have. Though it felt strange, letting go was sweet almost beyond belief.

As I ran the spell-checker over the finished paper, my computer froze, and I hadn't saved what I had written. It was 2 A.M. and there was no one awake to help. I considered leaving the computer on until morning in the flimsy hope that there might be some way to restore my paper. But all the fuss seemed unnecessary because the feelings I enjoyed while I was writing were still with me. I flipped the switch, restarted the computer, and retyped the paper. I think the rewrite is just about the same as the first version.

There was throughout this experience a serene joy I can't quite explain. Feelings of carrying a burden relaxed and untwisted. I recalled how I used to think of my mother as harsh and domineering. I had taken offense when I believed it was risky to be her daughter. Now I could see that I was never at serious risk except in those times when I did take offense.

The point of it all, the reason for our concerns about these matters, is not to polish ourselves to a nonhuman perfection, but to stand self-forgetfully and conscience-free in the light and to recover our balance quickly if we start to fall.

CHAPTER 13

CHANGING THE INFLUENCE OF THE PAST

Collusion Between Generations

Children born into a colluding family develop as persons not just by learning the family's language and adopting its ways, but also by entering into their family's ongoing collusions. In this way they become colluders themselves, starting at a very young age. They make the family's unpleasant emotional patterns their own. These patterns generally become so ingrained in them that they can seem impossible to break.

You will recall the story of Mandy from chapter 1. In her adult life, you may remember, she felt deprived of acceptance and attention and was frequently despondent.

> In her lonely hours she would remember bitterly the many times her father took her brother with him to work or on trips and left her home, or played with and kissed her little sister, Nessie, and not her. There was even one night not long before he died when she and Nessie switched beds for some reason, and when he got home late Mandy lay quietly awake, with only the top of her head out of the covers. He came into the dark room and kissed her forehead. When he realized she wasn't Nessie, he said, "Oh, oh, I'm sorry." Thinking about these things even as a child, Mandy would feel so brushed off, so minimized, that she would hide somewhere in the house so no one could see her crying, because when she cried her father would get cross with her. As she grew older she would often go off by herself, angry and dejected, and from time to time she

would attack with her sharp tongue some startled person who happened to say something she found offensive.

One other dimension of Mandy's story needs to be mentioned.

Mandy had matured very early, at about age eleven, and was strikingly attractive. Older boys, sometimes even men, paid her heavy attention. Her father was very displeased about this and got after her for it. He accused her of acting "like a slut."

He had stressed education for his children; they knew he wouldn't tolerate them slacking off in their schoolwork. She loved her school subjects and often competed in class discussions if she thought the teacher liked girls to participate. With her quick mind she had good insights to contribute. But she had a hard time writing term papers and seldom took an examination. A paper soon due would loom so large that it paralyzed her mentally with fear of failure. A coming exam would seem too formidable to attempt. She would get a sore throat or start vomiting or become so discouraged she couldn't bring herself to study. The problems got worse each successive year. Her college transcript was full of "Incomplete" grades, indicating that she still had to make up the course work in order to pass.

You will recognize the relationship between Mandy and her father as a collusion of a special kind. This collusion took place between parent and child, beginning so early in the child's life that it played a significant and decisive role in shaping her personality. Mandy's part in the collusion consisted of dwelling on and magnifying her victimhood; she thought of herself as a person doing the best she could to get on in life against obstacles so great she could never quite overcome them.

We can easily understand how she felt—always left at home

when her brother got to go out with Dad! Ignored while her father held and played with her little sister! Having the person she wanted most to please say she acted like "a slut"! Having teachers, whom she wanted to like and admire her, get down on her when it wasn't her fault that she couldn't complete her work! How could she shake herself out of her angry depression? What was she supposed to do—not care whether her father loved her?

Yet we need to notice in this story the accusatory elements we studied in chapter 4. Had Mandy allowed herself to stop focusing on her father's actions and looked instead at her own behavior, she might have seen how she was actively carrying on a collusion, and how this, her own behavior, was the source of her present problems. Like all self-betrayers, but in her own unique way, she bore the identity of a victim by seeing the awful things her father did to her (and make no mistake, some of them were wrong) as causes of her present unhappiness. By casting herself in the victim's role, she emphasized the monstrousness of what he had done and avoided having to consider her own role in her problems.

∾

COLLUSION HOOKS

You can imagine what Mandy's college roommates and teachers thought of her. She sought to be engaged in the life of the apartment and discussions in the classroom, but would back off quickly if she sensed that those present weren't accepting her. Her tendency to sulk resentfully put people off, which gave her reason to feel rejected yet again. Her physical attractiveness and quick mind drew people to her, including her teachers, but sooner or later they would come up against her failure to keep her commitments, her sometimes snappish manner, and her sulky moods. Then they would stop trusting her and, in the case of her friends, find more pleasant company to keep. And this would give her more reason to accuse and avoid them.

In this way, *the emotions and attitude with which she carried on her collusion with her deceased father tended to provoke the new people she would meet to react to her negatively. She would interpret these reactions as rejection, and thus she and they would create new collusions together.*

Let us call Mandy's original collusion with her family members her *primary collusion.* (I have emphasized only one dimension of this collusion. Other family members were involved, but that is a story too complex to detail here.) And let us refer to the other collusions as *satellites* of the primary collusion. A primary collusion is one that spawns various satellites and is not itself a satellite of any other collusion.

All but inevitably, we carry the I-It way we are with our primary colluders into our relationships with others. We *export* our attitude or way of being from a primary collusion and *import* it into a satellite one. In this manner the emotions and attitudes we have been maintaining in the deep background of our lives seep everywhere, like water colors on wet paper, darkening all our associations, activities, and even perceptions and muddying most if not all our other relationships.

We discussed this idea of importation in a positive context. In chapter 10 we spoke of how we are able to "activate" relationships in which we are considerate, even while carrying on collusive relationships elsewhere. We might, for example, recall the love or sacrifice of a parent, the example of a teacher, the loyalty of a friend or an animal, the goodness of God to us, or the need of someone in trouble, and as we do this we may feel ourselves moved to gratitude, sympathy, grief, or reverence. To the extent that we succeed in "dwelling in" such a relationship, our way of being is an I-You one. Then, in this open and considerate condition, we are able to turn our attention to those with whom we have been colluding and import into our relationship with them our more understanding and generous way of being.

In a similar way, we tend to export our way of being from our collusive relationships into other relationships. We may export anger, self-pity, suspicion, fear, sarcasm, or any other accusing, self-excusing attitude or emotion and thereby create a collusive satellite of another collusion carried on elsewhere. It's even possible by this means to turn formerly considerate relationships into troubling collusions.

Mandy's story demonstrates how the collusion from which we export an I-It way of being can be a primary one and how this primary collusion can spawn many satellite collusions. It showed us also the formative role that a primary collusion can play in the development of our personalities. We saw this too in the case of Eli, who carried forward into his marriage and work life his vindictiveness toward his father, treating every new person he met as a potential enemy. If our lives are as afflicted as Mandy's or Eli's, we become walking expressions of our ongoing troubled relationships with people who not only played a significant role earlier in our lives, but who continue to play this role, because *we* continue to walk through life displaying ourselves as their victims.

You can visualize being caught up in an oppressive primary collusion as carrying around an extra limb. This limb is made of emotion and attitude rather than flesh, and it's shaped like a hook. The hook is our I-It, insecure attitude or mentality—our defensive and accusing way of being. Subtly or blatantly we swing this hook in everything we do and everything we say. We cannot hide it no matter how we try, let alone amputate it; we swing it even in the manner in which we try to pretend it isn't there. And to the extent that other people have collusion hooks of their own, they sooner or later find us objectionable and react to us the way most other people have reacted for most of our lives. We and they catch each other with our hooks and create a new collusion, a satellite of primary collusions operating somewhere out of sight.

❧

"Just the Way I Am"

It was a number of years before Mandy began to comprehend the connection between feeling rejected by her father and her apparent inability to succeed and be happy. The way of being she maintained in relation to him expressed itself in almost everything she did, even though she didn't think she was portraying herself as a victim of his rejection. She thought her tendency to feel hurt was "just the way I am." "I'm not one of those people who stays on task very long," she would say. And "I don't handle pressure very well." And "When people reject me, I just want to get out of there."

What was true of Mandy is true generally. Because of our primary collusions, we often greet the world anxiously or angrily and do not comprehend how we became the way we are. We simply find ourselves beset by some inexplicable dislike, selfish desire, judgmental attitude, uncontrollable fear, despondent feeling, explosion of temper, or other mood, preoccupation, or impulse, without being able to explain why. We can't see that we have any responsibility for having this attitude or feeling. It seems to rise up in us whether we like it or not, like an alien force not subject to our will.

For this reason we tend to think of our negative emotions, attitudes, and moods as personality traits or character flaws or even disorders embedded in our natures. The more our negative feelings or attitudes push us to think and act in ways we regret, the more we say, "This is just the way I am." And this makes us feel that it's hopeless to try to change.

This hopelessness gets reinforced by the way in which our unwanted patterns of feeling and thought—our collusion hooks—tend to sabotage our relationships, even new relationships in which we want to start afresh with a new attitude. For a while we may manage to do a creditable job of pretending. But then the old fears or resentments anxieties reappear, and in spite of ourselves we find ourselves turning each new relationship into a repetition of all the rest.

How drearily, discouragingly predictable our life seems then! We feel certain that there's something within us that defeats all our efforts to be a better person!

Such are the kinds of observations we often make of ourselves when stuck in a primary collusion—observations of tendencies, emotions, and impulses that keep getting us into trouble, that we do not believe we've created, and that we can't seem to change. We resign ourselves to the belief that, for us, personal change is going to be limited to superficialities, like courtesies, various behavioral modifications, and image-creation—all outward, cosmetic stuff. As far as we're concerned when we think this way, the idea of changing our heart has got to be fantasy.

A RECOVERY, NOT A CHANGE

The description just given of how we self-betrayers often observe ourselves tells us how things often *seem*. But it is *not* how things are. Contrary to how we experience them, our accusing, self-excusing thoughts and feelings do not spring from the depth of our natures, and therefore they are not utterly beyond our control.

Such thoughts and feelings can often be traced to our primary collusions and the self-betrayals associated with them—even though we may not believe it at the time. You will recognize what great good news this is. If our self-destructive dispositions and impulses arise from our present self-betrayals and collusions rather than our natures, we're responsible for them and therefore can eliminate them. That is the diagnostic linchpin of this book. *The discovery that we are responsible for our troubles does not condemn us, but opens up a way of escape.*

To his amazement, Glen discovered that Becky did not value Christmas more than she loved him, and she learned that he did not prize his work more than he cared about her (see chapter 7). Christmas and career were pseudo issues. Glen's and Becky's offensive behavioral styles did not manifest unalterable personality traits or character flaws, but the false and fortunately temporary way they were being with their respective families of origin and with one another.

This suggests that when we escape our stuck, self-betraying condition, our nature does not change. The I-It mode of being is not our nature. It is this temporary condition into which we plunge ourselves by means of our self-betrayals. So in a very important sense, when we experience a change of heart we do not really change at all. We simply stop betraying and justifying ourselves. We stop feeling victimized. In short, we let ourselves be the person we would be if we were not "messing ourselves up" by trying to prove a point about ourselves.

We have compared being "stuck" in an emotionally troubled condition to physical illness. If people are ill, we do not expect them to be transformed into a different kind of physical specimen. We expect them to become as they used to be—healthy or whole (which, incidentally, mean the same thing). They need to "feel like themselves again." As we learned in chapter 11, that transformation does not "make us over" into a different kind of creature, but restores us to that nonconflicted, straightforward condition we sometimes call "being ourselves." It's misleading to speak of this recovery as a change. The turnaround moment in the life of the prodigal son, as told in the famous parable, is described in these words: "He came to himself."

∽

"My Beginning Will Not Dictate My End"

We have learned that if a primary collusion does not keep us from undergoing a change of heart, it is likely to lurk in the background after we have experienced the beginnings of such a change. It will wait there, ready to cause trouble. And sooner or later it will show itself unexpectedly in the form of some impulse, aversion, stubborn preference, fear, irritability, despondency, impatience, outbursts of anger, or similar behavior. When this happens, we lose the considerate feelings we had recently been enjoying, as Richard and Victoria both did when they reverted to their old ways. Then we either revive an old collusion or create a new one.

Such slippages should serve as signals that there's more work to do if we are going to obtain and sustain a change of heart. That work consists of tracing our "long-running" emotional and attitudinal habits to their source and rooting them out; this is sometimes called "unfinished business." *Unless we get ourselves engaged in and ultimately succeed at this business, we shall never fully resolve the satellite collusions that afflict us, for we shall never be rid of our collusion hooks.*

Every growing season on my property I battle a noxious garden weed called morning glory. It twines itself around anything in the vicinity and ruins desirable plants. You can pull as much of it as you possibly can out of the soil and still stupendously long pieces of root remain underground, sometimes miles long. These roots quickly push their way through the surface again. You can kill this weed, but only with a powerful herbicide that travels all the way to the ends of the roots. The absolute honesty of soul we have been discussing in this book can kill the perversity of an I-It way of being, but only if it penetrates to the deepest of its roots.

Transforming "The Way I Am"

We are now prepared to see how this works in ending a primary collusion. Recall the story of Mandy, the woman who felt constantly rejected because, as she remembered only too often, her father had spent his free time before his death with her older brother, Jeddy, or little sister, Nessie, but seldom with her. (You might want to look at this story again, on page 9).

Not long before, something extraordinary happened. It unfolded one evening when my husband had told me he would be home early, so we could have dinner together. For some time a resentment had been building up in me, especially over his preoccupation with work and with fixing up the yard. We didn't talk very much, at least in the way *I* wanted to talk. I had worked up my courage. I thought if I told him of my need he might understand and sympathize and we could spend the evening just talking about the things that mattered to us. I prepared a meal he liked and he thanked me for it, but then said he needed to get to the nursery for some bedding plants and potting soil before it closed.

This struck me like an ultimate blow. I had prepared myself to go out on a limb and almost beg for his kindness—and he had better things to do!

I went to the bedroom and started to cry. But suddenly

there came to me memories of myself as a girl with deeply hurt feelings, holding back tears. I remembered one episode after another of Daddy being too busy or telling me I couldn't go with him or saying I was too old for hugs and kisses. Right then I realized I was doing the same thing with my husband as I had done with Daddy, only now I was supposed to be grown up.

Then there came memories of more episodes of feeling hurt by people who wouldn't pay attention to me and thinking how cruel they were and not wanting to be anywhere near them. It seemed as I reflected on it that I've always been the hurt one, and always suspected people of wanting to close me out. If they wouldn't gush over me, I took that as rejection. One after another, I recalled these events and could see the truth, glowing and terrible, in front of me. I had always rejected others so they could not reject me! I felt so sorry. I felt I loved them all and wanted to find a way to make it up to them.

But I couldn't make it up to my father. He was gone. I wanted to apologize to him and ask for his forgiveness. Daddy, I wanted to say, I didn't know I was hurting you.

I went walking out in my husband's garden. It was so well cared for. Unbelievable as it sounds, this was the first time it occurred to me that he kept that garden nice for me!

And then a whole lot of memories came of Daddy and me together. He would have me help him with the lawn and the flowerbeds. On Saturday morning he often came to my volleyball games. It shamed and thrilled me to remember these things. I must have held his hand quite a lot, because I could remember very clearly how rough and hard it was and how he smelled when he got home from work—I knew that because I'd stand next to him in the bathroom while he washed his hands and fingernails and arms and face and neck before we had dinner. He would let me dry his mustache. I would make the bristles go upward and he would pretend it hurt him and we would laugh. And then I could remember we'd dry dishes together after dinner and he would ask me all about school and my friends. Our vacations came back to me, too, when Daddy would relax and we would play games and go to the country store for a treat. How could I have forgotten all these good things?

So focused are accusing feelings that they obliterate or shunt into irrelevance all other facts except those that support them. If, before her change of heart, someone had reminded Mandy of her father's kindness and frequent companionship, she would have said that she didn't remember it or that it wasn't much or that it couldn't make up for his neglect. But with that change came a revival of her memory of what he had given her, and she found it fully sufficient for her happiness.

What happened here? The past is the past, after all. The damage Mandy had sustained was done. How could that damage be undone?

Though none of us is responsible for the misfortunes that befall us, we are, thankfully, responsible for how we use those misfortunes. We cannot alter past events, it's true. Not having been responsible for them, we cannot take responsibility for them. But we *are* responsible for the effect they have upon us—for the meaning we assign to them and the way we remember them. And we can learn and grow from them.

This important truth is expressed in the subtitle of a book written by Wayne Muller, who has worked extensively with people abused as children. It reads: "The Spiritual Advantages of a Painful Childhood." *Whether past pain blesses or crushes us is ours to decide.* In working with abused women, I, like others, have taught them that the first step toward wholeness is to let go of all resentment and recrimination. When they no longer carry themselves in the world as victims, they can start on the road to recovery, but not until then. The fact that Mandy had many good memories to recover when she "came to herself" is inspiring but not essential. Even those who have few or none can make it.

Beginning at age six, Jacqueline had been abused sexually by several men during her childhood in the Detroit ghetto where she was born to a nineteen-year-old prostitute. After an uncle rescued her from that situation when she was a teenager, she worked hard to make something of her life. When I met her, she occupied a trusted, influential position in one of America's forty largest corporations. It was not hard to understand why—she was bright and incisive and had built a reputation for getting difficult things done. Besides that, everyone, including Susan and me, found her warm and welcoming, and she was so instinctively, artlessly therapeutic that at noon and after work people would wait outside her office for a chance to talk with her about their troubles. No anger or self-pity hobbled or confused this woman; she had vacated her horrendous past, taking with her its lessons without its liabilities.

Six months or so before we met, Jacqueline initiated a court proceeding against her former husband; long, long before that she had discovered that he had violated their two daughters from their childhood. In the first weeks of our association—she worked with the Arbinger Institute for a time—she allowed herself to acknowledge the abusive background from which he had come, and to see him forgivingly. With her daughters, she left all of her resentment, though not all of her sorrow, behind. On occasion she would tell her very moving and inspiring story publicly, always in the third person, as if she were talking about someone else. Then, at the end, she would add two sentences. The first: "That little girl whose story I have told you is me." And the second: "The mission statement for my life is 'My beginning will not dictate my end.'"

KILLING THE ROOT

Mandy's and Jacqueline's stories illustrate vividly the principle that we determine whether our past crushes or blesses us. So does the following story of a man named Samuel.

Since puberty Samuel had exhibited symptoms that would have led many therapists to assume childhood abuse even before talking to him about his history. Much of the time he was sunk in deep depression, a kind of utter darkness of spirit that would completely incapacitate him. He had been put up for adoption by his natural parents, and his adoptive parents were highly dysfunctional individuals who apparently could not relax their concern with their own personal agendas enough to nurture or to love him. Like many other victims, this was a child whose shocking introduction to this life was cold, systematic rejection and mistreatment.

So harsh was Samuel's self-loathing that he became involved in what he himself considered despicable sexual activities. Professionals labeled him an addict. He spent a great deal of time with psychiatrists who for a period of years medicated him heavily, with very limited success. One day he appeared at my door and asked me to help him. We talked about the ideas I have been presenting in this book, and then I suggested he talk also with certain others. The following week he recounted to me a significant event.

That very morning, he had been pondering a recurrent dream in which he found himself in an abandoned house—the furniture was gone; the windows were boarded up. The waning light of sunset filtered through the windows. He became aware of beings moving outside the house; they were vampires, scratching to gain entrance. As he continued in this reverie, he found himself reliving the dream, even though now awake. He realized this was the house of his grandparents. In the scene he was reliving, he went out on the veranda where he encountered his adoptive father, in his early thirties, smiling.

The two men walked together onto the lawn and sat down to talk. Samuel felt a desperate yearning for his father to provide something of the care and love and emotional sustenance of which Samuel felt he had been deprived. As they sat there, his father put his head on Samuel's shoulder and then, gradually, began to diminish in size, becoming smaller and more vulnerable than the adopted son sitting by his side. All of a sudden Samuel realized that his father was the one who needed to be loved. For the first time ever, he felt compassion for this man.

After this experience, Samuel spent the hours before he came to see me that day walking in the mountains, weeping profusely, in a release, both painful and joyous, of pent-up feelings for which he did not even have a name. "I anticipated that I would one day need to go through some sort of process of excusing my father for how he treated me," Samuel said. "But that is not at all what happened. Instead I came to the realization that he needed me even more than I needed him, and I had closed my heart toward him."

Samuel said that in a deep way that he could never before put into words he had always known this. Now he admitted it freely. "What left me at that moment was my conviction that my parents were to blame for my condition. Yes, in one sense they had misused me, but they could not have done better than they did. I remembered with great sorrow something I had once been told, that my father stuttered as he was growing up and that *his* father took him to the basement and beat him to get him to stop. Why had I not remembered this before now?"

This reminds us of Mandy's recovered memories when all accusation left her heart. Samuel allowed his father to be as he really was, a man deprived and mistreated. Previously he had refused to allow him this, and the way he refused was to insist on being the deprived and mistreated one himself. This shows clearly that his resentment of his father lay behind his depression; the depression was the way he carried on the resentment, just as Mandy's quickness to feel rejection and school failures were her way of doing the same sort of thing. Samuel said he realized that the depression "allowed me to excuse myself for closing myself to my father and his needs." It was in allowing the father he had so much resented to become real for him that he was healed. I call this *receiving the gift of his father's humanity.*

That day marked the turning point in Samuel's existence. Previously, with great determination he had achieved some control over his sexual behavior. But beginning with the day I have described, his depression began to lighten and his addictive cravings gradually disappeared.

Mandy's and Samuel's stories illustrate with a shimmering clarity the organic connection between primary collusions and the satellite collusions connected with them. *Healing a primary collusion helps to cut many satellite collusions at their source.* We kill the root of a present anguished emotional condition and then—but only then—it dies.

This doesn't imply, by the way, that the only way to end a satellite collusion is to heal the primary collusion from which it springs. Progress on a satellite, though incomplete, can soften us enough that we can at last work on the primary collusion successfully.

IF WE'RE RESPONSIBLE, WE CAN CHANGE

Most people think emotional injuries are like physical injuries and not our responsibility at all. According to this theory, our present-day emotional problems are the effects of emotional wounds inflicted in the early years of life. This we will call the "causal theory." It says the troubles that make life hard to bear occurred in the past—they were caused by something our parents or others did years ago that damaged us. The truth is that these troubles are always occurring *right now*. Our inner conflictedness and compulsive emotions are the ways we are colluding, *right now*, with our original caretakers or others of significance in our earlier lives. They are accusations we are making *now* against those caretakers for doing years ago what we continue to resent.

So, strictly speaking, what actually happened way back then is of no significance now; what is significant now are our *present* accusations against them. *Our emotional problems are the accusations we make of others <u>now</u>. They are not scars from the past but actions in the present.* They are actions of portraying ourselves as having been scarred in the past.

This, as we have already noted, is great good news. Whatever elements of our emotional and psychological suffering we are maintaining now—and these are the ones that make life hard to bear—we can simply stop maintaining. *We can determine the effects that our adversities have on us.*

The following story, which illustrates this principle rather vividly, presents a person courageously ending a primary collusion with someone who was not a family member or early caretaker, but a rapist. To this story I add the suggestion that you not draw from it any conclusions about how long this kind of healing takes (this healing happened quickly; for others the healing might take years), or what's required to initiate such healing (here there's a bold, forthright act which might be counterproductive in other situations). Thus I do not offer this story to show "how it's done," but rather, as with many other stories in this book, to instill hope. The author's name is Jay.

> After she had been married for several years, my sister Barbara came to me and said she was going to divorce her husband, Frank. She would have gone to our father, but he had died. She had discovered that Frank had committed adultery several times, well, quite a bit, actually, over the years. Her heart was broken. She was ashamed and hurt. She seemed to feel she couldn't do anything else but leave him. I could hardly believe it. I hadn't even guessed this kind of thing might be going on.
>
> I thought I should speak to Frank. When we got together, I sensed something was wrong. So I began to pry. Why had Frank done it? Barbara had expected so much more. And hadn't she been loving to him? As we talked I discovered something that stunned me. Throughout their married life she had almost always refused him intimacy. Well, I immediately thought of the tragedy that had happened to her when she was raped when she was twelve years old. It was a savage thing. But I had thought, and so did the rest of the family, that after a couple of years she pretty much got back to normal and grew up without a lot of scars. Now I realized she must have spent her whole married life terrified and sort of walled in.
>
> Frank said Barbara's excuse for her behavior was that she cared about him, and the physical part wasn't important. I was astonished.
>
> What she had done to her husband was terribly wrong, for him and for her. She knew about her problem

when she married him, and she blamed all that had happened on him! I knew I had to do something, but I didn't know what. I felt so sorry for her I couldn't stand it. She had been going through all kinds of trouble inside herself, and the rest of us in the family had more or less tried to forget about the whole thing. But I felt that if I didn't watch out I'd help her paint her situation in the darkest colors and she never would see her way out of it. If I really loved her I couldn't stand by while she ruined two lives because of her fears. Off and on for more than an hour, as I drove to Barbara's house, I sobbed uncontrollably.

When I got there she started crying and said, "He's shamed me so much. I can't do anything now but leave him, though I'm sure that in a way he feels he's already left me."

Then I said I understood she had never allowed her marriage to be consummated. Very defensively, she denied it. "Oh, no, that's not true!"

So I explained to her what I meant and she said, "Oh, but that isn't important. I have always let him lie close to me and tried to be affectionate."

So then I said, "I want to tell you something." I was speaking pretty forcefully, because my heart was breaking for her. "You knew of the challenges you would have before you married Frank. And you've put a terrible burden on him and blamed it on something that happened to you years ago. This doesn't need to be! What you did is worse than what he did, and what he did is reprehensible. You've been mean and stingy and shriveled and small and unwilling to love and willing to let him suffer because of it. If you don't go home with your husband tonight and love him as you're supposed to love him, I'm going to testify against you in the divorce proceedings. You go home and do right and get this thing behind you."

You can imagine how stunned she was and how angry. When I left she was so upset she could not speak. But I'll tell you, she came to my home the next morning before I even left for work. She hugged me and the tears were flooding down her face and she said that what I had told her had changed her life forever. "Jay, you're the first person who ever talked to me straight. Everyone else helped me think I couldn't do it. Last night I loved Frank with all the physical and emotional completeness that a person can, all of it, and I'm not afraid anymore. And Jay, it's hard to believe, but I don't hate the man who did that awful thing to me anymore."

When she wholeheartedly accepted the truth of what her brother had told her, Barbara liberated herself from the hatred she felt toward the man who had raped her. Prior to this, her hatred had discolored every thought she had of her husband and their relationship. Not being able to bring herself to love him completely was her way of continuing to say to the world, "See how badly abused I was, that long time ago! See how I haven't been able to recover even now!"

So self-absorbed had Barbara become in making a victim of herself that she couldn't—she *wouldn't*—admit to herself how she had withheld herself from Frank or how much he needed her. But yielding herself to the truth, first about herself and then about Frank, she let go of the proof against the rapist she had been clinging to. She abandoned her hatred. By that very stroke she ceased "horribilizing" her victimizer, "catastrophizing" her misfortune, and exaggerating her loss. *She let the event become exactly what it was—a very, very hard experience indeed, one of the worst a human being can suffer. But not an excuse.* Thereby her soul deepened in experience and wisdom and expanded in compassion. She broke out of her self-enclosure, opened to the interior reality of her husband, escaped the bondage of self-induced affliction, and discovered what it is to love another person.

The parts of our psychological history that make a difference now do not reside in the past. They are present. It is our *presently* held story of the past that is our bondage or our freedom. Strictly speaking, the rest does not exist for us. Even Sigmund Freud, who invented the term "primal scene" for the experiences in infancy that in his view leave a scar, acknowledged that such experiences do not have their scarring effect until the child *later* endows the remembered scene with significance. For Freud, too, it is the present story of the past that works destruction in the individual life, not the past itself.

The difference between the ideas of this book and the causal theory is of the utmost consequence. If we are victims of our history, we can do nothing to correct our problems. The past has already wrought its damage and cannot be called back. We may be able to work around and compensate somewhat for the searing events in our past, but we can never eradicate them. On the other hand, *if we are not victims but instead producers of our emotional problems, and if it is right now that we are producing them, then we can eliminate the problems at their source.* By the means we have discussed in this book, we can stop producing them.

∾

True and False Compassion

Some think it unfeeling, even harsh, to hold individuals responsible for their attitudes and emotions. Isn't this being judgmental? Doesn't compassion require that we excuse people for their unsavory behavior on the grounds that they're not ultimately responsible for it? After all, people start out in this world with a genetic makeup that's not their fault, and they develop into adults in response to examples and training they themselves do not choose. Clarence Darrow, the brilliant Chicago attorney, became well-known for arguing, in the celebrated 1925 "Monkey Trial," for John Scopes's right to teach evolution in Tennessee. A year earlier he had become famous for his position on the subject we're studying here: He defended the child murderers Leopold and Loeb on the ground that anyone with their backgrounds would have turned out the same way and done the same sort of dastardly things. He interpreted the French saying, "To understand all is to forgive all" to mean, "To understand all is to excuse all."

Though this point of view may be part of the intellectual fashion of our age, it is false, and not only false, but uncharitable as well. It says, "You can't!" rather than "You can!" Although those who hold this view think they're being compassionate and kind, they are only being indulgent. Indulgence is a punitive counterfeit of charity. It extends no hope at all for freeing ourselves of our emotional troubles. It takes the position that we are stuck with being the deficient vessels we think we are and are doomed to cope with our lot as best we can.

It is because we are responsible for whatever we have become that there is hope for us to change fundamentally. True compassion can be found only in extending this hope to others, never in denying it to them.

CHAPTER 14

FORGIVING, FORGOING, AND LIVING FREE

Forgiveness,
Correctly Understood

The process by which we open ourselves to the reality of others and thereby undergo a profound personal change can properly be called "forgiveness." Why so?

In a class I was teaching twenty years ago, an older, very concerned woman raised an issue about forgiveness she said had been bothering her all her adult life. She said: "If you forgive somebody, you more or less say, 'There's something that person needs to be blamed for, something he's done wrong to me, but I'm a big enough person to overlook it.' You have to keep in mind what they've done wrong or else you don't have anything to overlook. So you can't forgive and forget, can you? You have to remember the wrong they've done. That doesn't seem to be very charitable. So I don't understand forgiveness. I've always been suspicious when people say they forgive."

This comment exposes a flaw in our ordinary, self-betraying way of thinking about forgiveness. This woman was right to say that we do not, we cannot, accuse someone in our heart and at the same time forget about the wrong we're accusing them of doing. The best we can do, as long as we continue to accuse, is to counterfeit a pardon for them and try our best not to think about what they have done.

But overlooking or "letting pass" a grievance or an offense does not qualify as forgiveness. Forgiveness is something else entirely.

First, forgiveness responds to the real issue, the real reason why we have felt offended. And the real reason, as we know, is not any wrong that others have done to us, but the wrong *we* are doing to them. *Forgiveness concerns <u>our</u> wrongdoing, not theirs.* And our wrongdoing includes our failure to treat them as we ought, our finding them at fault for this failure, and our refusal to forgive them for this supposed fault.

Second, *our act of forgiving consists of repenting of this wrongdoing of ours,* or in other words, ceasing to accuse those we have been accusing.

Third, *when we cease to accuse them, we cease to feel there's anything on their part that needs to be forgiven!* We no longer find them offensive. We see that from their point of view they are struggling against perceived offenses and threats just as we have been. Thus forgiveness involves opening ourselves to the truth, letting our former offenders become real to us, and no longer believing there is anything for us to forgive. As they undergo a transformation in our forgiving eyes, we undergo a transformation ourselves.

This must be so. As long as we see others as needing our forgiveness, we will continue regarding ourselves as their victim and will remain accusing still. We live free of the bondage of accusing, afflicted feelings only by ceasing to find and take offense.

Desiring Forgiveness for Not Forgiving

We need to note one more element of genuine forgiveness. Just prior to forgiving someone, we will have been finding him or her offensive. But with forgiveness comes a realization of the offensiveness of this. How accusing we must have appeared to that person! Whatever he or she may have done that we previously found offensive has changed in our memory of it, as Mandy discovered when she thought about her father—the past is not what we had thought. Recently we wondered whether we could forgive that person. Now we wonder whether he or she can forgive *us.*

This is our new attitude toward having previously refused to forgive. We feel a desire to be forgiven for it. *Genuine forgiveness includes a desire to be forgiven and, if it is fitting, to seek that forgiveness.*

Of all the initiatives people can take who feel a devastating wrong has made them miserable, one stands above all others in effectiveness. It is actually seeking forgiveness for having refused to forgive. I have observed that when individuals have struggled for years to escape the effects of abuse and have tried everything they can think of to forgive their abuser, they rarely succeed. The reason is that the forgiveness they aim to produce is a counterfeit of real forgiveness. It could not be otherwise, because they continue to believe they have been offended. But when they recognize that the wrongdoing has been *theirs,* good things start to happen—but not until then.

We have already encountered significant examples of this self-recognition, such as Eli, Mandy, and Samuel, so I will add only two more. It happens that they are both intergenerational examples. That seems appropriate, for typically they are the most difficult and they lead to the most thoroughgoing changes of heart.

The first concerns Ellie, a notably energetic music teacher who took a course from me.

Four years before approaching me, Ellie had gradually begun to recall having been abused sexually by her father when she was still a girl. She had worked with a psychiatrist for much of those four years. In spite of her efforts she had gained no fundamental relief, no healing. "I feel as if I am a flute clogged up with sludge. I make all kinds of effort, but no music comes out of me." I asked whether she had forgiven her father. She said she had thought she had but wasn't sure, because she still had no peace.

Then I asked her: "Have you sought his forgiveness for your hard feelings toward him all these years?" She had not. It had never occurred to her to do so. I suggested that forgiveness consists not of forgetting what happened, but of repenting of unforgiving feelings about what happened, and if possible seek forgiveness.

A light went on in her face. She pondered for a few moments and said, "I'm going to do that." The next day she told me she had written a letter to her father the night before, asking his forgiveness. She said, "I saw that by blaming him I was refusing to forgive. I was refusing to admit that he too had suffered in his life and needed my compassion. And now that I have done this, I feel free for the first time in my life. This morning, music is flowing through me and it is sweet." Since that day, this woman has written me letters filled with happiness. In one she said of her father, "Last week I even asked his advice, and he was shocked and pleased."

It is often said that we need to forgive for our own sake, to rid ourselves of resentful feelings. That's what Ellie tried to do and couldn't. Forgiveness cannot be done from self-concern. It must be done for the truth's sake, or to right a wrong, or out of compassion for those we previously condemned by our refusal to forgive.

The second story unfolded when a twenty-nine-year-old woman named Margaret asked to attend one of my classes.

Margaret had been in counseling or therapy continuously for fourteen years, chronically depressed and almost non-functional. She blamed her inability to get on in life on her mother—though she claimed she would go for long periods without allowing herself to think of her mother (which is obviously an accusing thing to do, since it's a way of saying, "You're too despicable to think about, you upset me so much.") At any one time, she said, she had at most one friend, toward whom she would behave so possessively that after a few weeks or months the friend could not tolerate her anymore and would then leave her alone. Her lips trembled when she talked and were pinched in when she didn't, and almost always her eyes were downcast. I found it hard to pity her because she was obviously spending a lot of pity on herself already. In private I learned that her mother had frequently abused her sexually when she was a child and, as Margaret thought, ruined her forever.

The class extended over the Christmas and New Year's holidays. When we reconvened on January 10, Margaret was the only participant not present. We started anyway, and about twenty minutes into the session a woman whom I did not recognize entered the room and took a seat at one of the tables where the participants were sitting. As I usually do in situations like this, I let the discussion continue—interruptions can break the class's concentration. After a few minutes I realized with a shock who the woman was and whispered to the person next to me, "It's Margaret." Simultaneously, I noticed, others were doing the same thing. Margaret's face was relaxed, and there was a natural dignity in her bearing that had been completely absent before. And when she spoke, as she did presently, her lips did not tremble. The self-pity was gone. To me, her countenance seemed to be illuminated.

She asked to speak, and told us she had taken the train over the holiday to see her mother, whom she had freely forgiven. She told her mother that, more than anything else, she wanted her to have some peace before she died. She asked her mother's forgiveness for the hatred she had borne toward her through so many years. In the days following her return she often had tender feelings toward her mother, and called and wrote to her.

I have heard from Margaret periodically in the ensuing years. Her "cure" was far from instant, but that visit to her mother proved to be a turning point. After about a year, in which things

gradually improved in her relationships with roommates, her fear
of being betrayed by them finally disappeared. She has been able
to hold a job successfully. Each time I hear from her she seems to
be doing a little better.

Genuine Forgiveness Transforms the One Who Forgives

When we forgive genuinely, those we formerly accused suddenly become real for us—the experiences of Eli, Mandy, Samuel,
Ellie, and Margaret are all memorable examples of this. We sense
their insecurity and anxiety; we perceive something of their
struggle to show themselves as worthy and acceptable while fear-
ing that the opposite might be true. How much like ourselves they
are! A new emotion pushes out the old resentments and fears.
Preposterous as it would have seemed when we were stuck in self-
absorption and fear, we love them.

You might say, forgiveness has transformed us into beings
upon whom others are writing the truth about themselves, and
that truth awakens our compassion. We are like a tuning fork that,
by resonating to sounds all around, gives off pleasing sounds of its
own. The humanity we find in others becomes our own, measured
exactly. That is how human beings achieve depth of soul. Love is
the substance of any forgiveness worthy of the name.

⌀

AFFIRMING OTHERS'
FREEDOM SETS US FREE

You can see that in an unexpected and, to our ordinary way of
thinking, odd way, we owe to the people we are able to forgive a
very large debt. No matter how reprehensibly they may have

treated us, they have provided us with a gift. The gift is their humanity. Without their humanity, to which we are able to open ourselves, we cannot get ourselves emotionally unstuck no matter how we might try. We cannot do it by denying or repressing our feelings or by willing ourselves to feel differently—feelings are subject to our indirect but not our direct control. We are able to do it only by recognizing, respecting, and, yes, revering others as they really are, in the fullness of their humanity and vulnerability.

This insight makes connection with a principle we first encountered in chapter 3: We are I-You individuals only insofar as others become fully real to us. We need them in order to become authentic and genuine ourselves. We do this, as we first learned when we talked about yielding to the truth (chapter 9) and studied further in this chapter, by letting their inward reality—their needs and aspirations and fears—write themselves upon our hearts and guide our responses to them. This creates bonds with them that free us from the burdens of our self-absorption.

More needs to be said about this respectful and reverent act of accepting the gift. In one sense, it means recognizing that the choices others make are not *our* affair. Our concern must be limited to our own right conduct, not theirs; we need to concentrate not so much on the choices they make as on the choices *we* make. "Ours is only the trying," wrote T. S. Eliot. "The rest is not our business."

This does not diminish the care we have for others. On the contrary, it manifests the purest kind of love. *We care passionately about nurturing and protecting their right and their ability to choose for themselves,* which right and ability I like to call their *agency.* And therefore we recognize how inconsiderate and desecrating it would be for us to override or squelch their agency by trying to make their choice for them, and how it would invite defensiveness on their part and draw them into collusion.

In approaching her father to ask his forgiveness for her hard-heartedness toward him, Ellie had no concern about how he would react. She was concerned with her own wrongdoing. Therefore she did not apologize in order to obtain his apology; she left that part wholly up to him. It was only her own apology that she made her business. Consequently she no longer believed that her well-being depended upon what he did; she ceased to act as if his response could determine her feelings. By seeking his forgiveness, she liberated herself from this very unhealthy dependency.

In this way, setting *him* free to respond however he chose set *her* free to respond however *she* chose. She no longer gave him the power to control her and her happiness that we studied in chapter 5.

And when she did respond freely, to what did she respond? Not to his lifelong rejection of her but to his vulnerability and need. She did not feel it necessary to make her father understand her, to insist that she had been right, or to have the conversation turn out in her favor. She was no longer bound in those chains of insecurity.

This liberating element, which we might call *the power of respect* or *the power of compassion,* stands out even more unequivocally in Margaret's story, for Margaret got back no reciprocal apology from her mother. After Margaret asked for forgiveness, her mother just sat there, silent and cold. Yet Margaret's liberation from her self-enclosing thoughts and feelings did not lag behind Ellie's in any respect. In both cases, it was the act of setting another person free from accusation that set the erstwhile accuser free from her self-afflicting role as accuser.

We find the liberating element in Mandy's and Samuel's stories also. They allowed their fathers to be who they really were, rather than turning them into scapegoats responsible for their problems. Samuel said, in effect, that by insisting that he was the deprived and mistreated one, he would not let his father be deprived and mistreated—he would not let his father become real for him. Completely on his own, apart from professional opinion,

Samuel came to believe that his depression was his way of controlling his father's impact on his life—and making sure that impact would be a hardening and not a softening one.

Some people think that forgiving abusers means minimizing the offense committed and letting them get away with it—so that they won't have to suffer the punishment they deserve. This isn't true. Abusers suffer quite independently of being resented. They harbor wretched, hateful feelings, and if they one day admit to what they've done, they will also suffer exquisite guilt and sorrow. Our resentment cannot increase their torment; it harms only ourselves. And besides, it may give them an excuse to believe that we deserved whatever they did to us.

The acceptance, respect, and love that I am calling "forgiving" is one of the basic principles of all human flourishing. It frees us from the benighting, subtly controlling lies that structure the I-It world. Moreover—and by now this should go without saying—it invites those we accept, respect, and forgive to become accepting, respectful, and forgiving in their own right. We liberate ourselves from bonds of anguish by cultivating the purest form of love.

∽

FORGOING: THE EVERYDAY WORK OF LIBERATED PEOPLE

Return with me for a moment to Jane Birch's story of Elizabeth, that remarkable exemplar of self-forgetfulness in whose presence Jane could also be self-forgetful (this story appears at the end of chapter 9). It would not be accurate to give the name *forgiveness* to Elizabeth's ability to perceive no offensiveness in others. It can't be called forgiveness because during the episode that Jane recounted, Elizabeth did not perceive her insensitive companions as needing to be forgiven.

We can describe Elizabeth's responses in the story by means of a term that will distinguish them from forgiving. What she did was to *forgo* accusation, rather than to repent of it. If forgiving can be thought of as recovery from moral and emotional illness by means of a change of heart, *forgoing* is never falling morally and emotionally ill in the first place, never needing a change of heart. If forgiving helps us recover from relapses, forgoing keeps lapses from happening at all. It is prevention rather than cure. This is the daily manner of life of those free people who don't have to spend all their time suffering from, agonizing over, and repenting of their repeated mistakes.

Here is another example:

> Jeff and Robin have made for themselves one of the best marriages I know. They have complete respect for one another; they do volunteer work together; and their children, now grown, reflect their emotional healthiness and serenity. The road leading to this unity has had more than its share of obstacles and treacherous ruts, but they've handled these unselfishly and cooperatively, and this I think has had a formative impact upon the children.
>
> But their marriage didn't start out this way. In school, Robin had been the trophy girlfriend of the boys with status, and she reveled in this glory. She had picked out Jeff as the one she wanted most and, deploying all her instinctive wiles, caught him—much to his parents' concern. When the wedding ceremony ended, it quickly became clear that she had invested about as much in the relationship as she was going to. She lost none of her childish hedonism. She stayed in bed till noon, refused to acknowledge any domestic duties, shopped in the afternoon, and took off on her own at night for parties and dance-hall hopping with her old friends. Jeff's friends and family

mourned for him; what they had predicted had come to pass.

But Jeff didn't mourn for himself. Not once did he complain. In fact, he consistently showed his gratitude for Robin. He got up early to make breakfast and leave her portion for when she arose; he cleaned the apartment at night; he treated Robin with unwavering respect. He was an unflagging embodiment of the principle of forgoing the taking of offense.

A year went by, and then two. Robin started showing signs of disillusionment with her party life. She complained about the selfishness of her friends. She wondered why they couldn't be more like Jeff. Then she began to worry about the possibility that Jeff might leave her and told his mother he had every right to do so. His quiet, undaunted love didn't fit into "the world according to Robin," in which people acted only to please themselves. That confused her; she couldn't figure him out. Why didn't he ever tell her he'd had enough of her? For a while her worry became so great that she seemed almost depressed.

Then one day she announced that she wanted to accept Jeff's parents' invitation to Sunday dinners, which she had almost always refused, and a little later she started visiting his mother, asking her questions about their family and about making a home. In time, she told Jeff she wanted to become a mother and do it in the right way, and she did.

Jeff's early career success might have been slowed by his service to Robin. No one can know this for sure. In any case, Jeff did not seem concerned about that issue. He responded to the circumstance in which he found himself by simply doing what lay before him and needed to be done. No pity, no blame. Consequently he became the occasion for Robin's change of heart, in just the ways we have studied in this book.

In effect, without realizing this was what he was accomplishing, Jeff made it his work to help Robin overcome the primary collusion in her life, the collusion in which she played the role of a spoiled child. In response to this profoundly considerate and generous man, Robin became a different sort of person; she was able to leave behind entirely the sort of person she had been in relation to her early family and friends. When we think about the gift he gave her and its decisive impact upon her, upon their children, and (as I write these words) upon their children's children, we begin to see that he could scarcely have accomplished anything more significant in his life, no matter what else he achieved. As we discovered in chapter 9, *love is a power, greater than any other.*

Jeff's story teaches us about one of the precious fruits of true friendship, whether in marriage or out. He came into Robin's life so considerately that he invited her into a relationship in which she was able, after a good deal of resistance, to become considerate herself. And when she did, she broke free of her primary collusions with her own original family. Jeff helped her do this. He accomplished this by forgoing. Though others found in her much that they deemed worthy of blame, he did not. Violence of heart seemed alien to his emotional repertoire. He did not even think of himself as exercising patience.

We should note that Jay's gift to his sister Barbara—we read their story in chapter 13—was no less liberating than Jeff's. Some might think he acted harshly. On the contrary, his telling Barbara the truth was both compassionate and tender, and it was motivated strictly by love. That's why it touched her so. In their different ways, both Jay and Jeff show us that what love dictates may be easily misunderstood. It can't be put into a formula (e.g., "When such and such happens, do or say this"). It's never sentimental or indulgent, but instead compassionate. It may look wimpish or it may look harsh when in fact it's courageous. It may require end-less patience or decisive initiative, but not for advancing oneself. Understand the deep similarity of Jeff's and Jay's conduct and you have the secret of influencing people to yield their hearts to the truth.

Not As Preposterous As It May Seem

These points may seem difficult to swallow. What if Robin had never changed? You might ask, What if Jeff had made the sacrifices for nothing?

If that's your question, then I have a question for you. If in fact Robin had not changed, would Jeff have been better off to have dealt with her selfishness impatiently and angrily? Should he have left her when it didn't seem that she would change? Would that have made him happier?

Most of us will find it hard to resist answering, Yes, it *would* have made him happier. But we need to remember that *if he had reacted to adversity in this manner, he too would have been stuck in a self-absorbed way of being, just as she was. He would not have been cheerful and uncomplaining but angry, resentful, and full of self-pity.*

Still we may think: But look what he forfeited because of her! If this is our objection, we need to realize that it looks that way only through I-It eyes. Viewed through I-You eyes, the loss must be counted as next to nothing compared with the happy state of his spirit.

Let me explain what I mean by comparing two situations. You enter upon your day with your agenda all worked out. A neighbor calls. Will you help her jump-start her car? You feel disrupted and a little violated. You help her, though, hiding your agitation about your disrupted day, yet letting her know in little ways how hard you're working to hide it. Was her request an interruption? Yes.

On another day you get a different call, this one from a

neighbor who's observed *you* trying in vain to start *your* car and offering to give *you* a jump. Interruption? No. Why? Because you constructed the day's agenda with your self-interest in mind, and the offer of help furthered that self-interest—in contrast to the call asking *you* to be the helper, which did not.

Jeff's is the second kind of case, not the first. *He didn't consider serving Robin a deflection from his life's purpose because she <u>was</u> its purpose.* He let her needs dictate his days. He made serving her his work, not a disruption of his work. That's why, too, he never felt noble or heroic during those early years of marriage, and also why, when others felt sorry for him, he never felt sorry for himself.

Jeff's life answers his critics. They say, "Look what he gave up!" But he can say, "Look what I gained!" After all is said and done, he has been right, not they. He has been right about Robin. He and she have fashioned an extraordinary marriage and together created a remarkable family in which they find great joy.

❧

THE ONLY WAY TO START AFRESH

Still not quite convinced? Still thinking Jeff might have been better off bailing out early in his marriage and finding someone less selfish? Still thinking he wasted a lot of good years of his life? Still sure he was called on to sacrifice too much? If so, consider the following memorable images devised by that insightful Dane, Søren Kierkegaard.

Imagine, he says, two artists. One travels the world over to find a human subject worthy of his skill as a painter of portraits. But so exacting are his standards and so fastidious his judgment that he has yet to discover a single person worthy of his efforts. Every potential subject is marred by some disqualifying flaw.

The second artist, on the other hand, has no special admiration for his own skill. Consequently, he never thinks to look beyond his immediate circle of neighbors for his subjects. Nevertheless, he has yet to find a face without something beautiful in it, something eminently worthy to be portrayed.

Wouldn't this indicate, Kierkegaard asks, that the second painter is the real artist? Yes, he says, because this man "brings a certain something with him" that enables him to find in others that which is worthy to paint. The other man could not find anything worthy to paint anywhere in the world because he did not bring with him this "certain something."

So it is with love, says Kierkegaard. *Love is the expression of the one who loves, not of the one who is loved.* Those who think they can love only the people they prefer do not love at all. Love discovers truths about individuals—*any* individuals—that others cannot see (see Søren Kierkegaard, *Works of Love* [New York: Harper and Row, 1962], 156–57).

This same point can be made in terms of the principle of forgoing. *Forgoing the taking of offense is an achievement of the one who forgoes; he or she extends it to all, including those nearest by. It cannot depend upon what others do, or else it is not genuine forgoing.*

The lessons found in the story of two artists bring clarity to what Jeff's story has taught us. Here's one of those lessons:

Unless we change in our hearts toward the people we struggle with *here and now*, we are condemned to struggle with whomever we may find ourselves associating with.

It doesn't matter if we marry a different spouse, take another job, or move to another country. *We* will be the same: we will interpret our world the same way, and others will respond to us the same way. The details of our days may distinguish them from one another, but their substance will not change. "Wherever you go, there you are."

Nothing can change fundamentally until *we* change fundamentally. We shall never find a beloved until we become lovers.

This Is the Best of All Possible Situations?

A second significant lesson we can draw from Kierkegaard's
images:

> When it comes to seeking a change of heart, our starting
> place must include our present situation, with the people
> we live with right here and now. It is with these very
> people that we must learn to forgo all taking of offense.

I have sometimes called this principle BOAPS—when it comes
to seeking and maintaining a change of heart, we are in the Best
of All Possible Situations. You may be wondering, in a state of
alarm, how a principle so startling, so counterintuitive, can possibly be true. If so, you are not alone. A woman named Melinda
wondered the same thing when I taught the BOAPS principle in a
class she attended. Her husband had kept his secretary in a nearby
apartment, had a baby by her, attended the birth, named the baby
after himself, and put a birth announcement in the newspaper!
Melinda said, "When you said I am living in the best of all possible
situations, my nervous system got a charley horse. My whole body
stuck its tongue out at you."

But think about the principle: It doesn't say that our situation
could not be better. Many of us have serious needs, like too little
to eat or broken health; even those of us who are fairly comfortable could benefit from positive changes in our circumstances.
What the principle says is, *in matters that can affect our happiness,
we are in the best of all possible situations.*

Let me explain further. We have a special obligation to those
with whom we have been colluding. Since we, by our accusing
attitude, have supplied them excuses for their self-betrayals, we are

in a better position than anyone else to help them change, and we can do so by means of our own change of heart. Leaving them would be a way of *continuing* to accuse and collude with them—to say, in effect, "I can be happier if I get you out of my life." This does not mean there are no circumstances that require us to part from former colluders; for example, as in Melinda's case, from an incorrigibly unfaithful or abusive spouse. But that is different from abandoning such a person in order to seek what we fantasize will be better opportunities elsewhere. Leaving for the latter reason only continues the collusion; it's an act of refusing to forgive.

You might like to know that Melinda took the implications of the BOAPS principle seriously. She accepted her circumstance without resentment and concentrated upon this point: If she and her husband were to part because of his refusal to make a marriage with her, and she left without resentment or recrimination, she would be able to leave and live freely. Otherwise, she would remain tied to him by bonds of anguish even if he were to move to the other side of the world. They did part, because of the choices he continued to make, but she emerged a person completely free of self-pity, loving her life. She obtained an advanced degree and became a counselor, and she has made positive contributions to many people's lives.

We cannot be liberated from our burdensome feelings toward certain people unless we forgive *these very people;* without this, we leave unfinished the task by which we ourselves can be transformed. For wherever we go, we will remain accusing, self-excusing individuals who, fantasizing, think a change of circumstance will make a fundamental difference. Instead of leaving our problems behind, we will take them with us.

When happiness is the issue, the best possible situation for us is the one we're in now, and the people around us are the best we could be with.

Joy without Fantasy

We too easily assume that before Robin's change of heart Jeff must have considered his situation grim and that he persisted in his marriage by sheer grit. No, grim is how it would have seemed to a person stuck in an I-It mode of being. It was not grim to Jeff. Difficult, no doubt. And challenging. But not grim.

Sunk in our I-It resentments, we who are self-betrayers reject opportunities for joy by considering ourselves victims. Then we fantasize about the joys of which we have deprived ourselves. We think that if only certain things could be otherwise—if we could earn more money or change our spouse or move to a better location—then we could be happy. We're absolutely sure that the one situation in which we can *never* be happy is the present one, which is exactly opposite from the truth!

The story of the hardened businessman named Norm, introduced in chapter 1, illustrates the two ways of being—grimness and fantasy before his change of heart, and joy without fantasy after. Norm, you may remember, is the man so fixated upon his economic success, so thoughtlessly convinced it would bring him some sort of happiness, that he nearly destroyed the significant relationships of his life.

His story also exemplifies other ideas we have studied in this book, especially the difference a person can make by taking decisive action at the true choice point. Norm stopped his self-betrayal not by trying to fight against his lifelong judgmental and brusque tendencies, but by admitting to himself where he had been wrong and then doing what seemed to him most right.

To this day, I consider Norm to be among the most macho males I have ever worked with—an ex-boxer who had made it big by starting a company in a very competitive industry. He hadn't been the type who examined or even questioned his emotional reactions. His style was always to bull ahead. In the first session of the class he attended, I told the story of Marty, the fellow who stayed in bed after feeling he ought to get up and take care of the baby in the middle of the night. Norm blurted out, "That story doesn't apply to me." As the others present were discussing the story, Norm interrupted again with, "I'd just poke my wife and say, 'Hey, your kid's awake.'"

By the second session, Norm seemed worried. "This stuff's logical," he said. "I can see it in a lot of people I know, like my alcoholic brother-in-law, but I can't see it in myself. I can't see that I'm into any self-betrayals, though I suppose I might be." It's neither expected nor usual for participants in our classes to disclose themselves so unabashedly, but Norm was not a usual kind of person.

During the third session I told a story of a business leader whose primary aim was to help his subordinates grow as people and to take responsibility and initiative in their assignments. To the degree he helped them do this, the profits came naturally. He didn't run roughshod over people. Before I had finished my story, Norm erupted in his customary manner: "You just hit my button. You just got to me." A few minutes later, while someone else was talking, he suddenly started talking again, as if he was carrying on a dialogue with himself and we were getting bits of it. "You know when you talked about that guy who didn't get up to take care of his kid? And I said his story didn't apply to me?" He paused and then said, "It applied to me. I always knew, all the time my kids were growing up, that I should get up and help. I always knew." From that moment until the lunch break, it appeared that Norm wasn't tuned in to the class discussion at all. He sat staring into space.

"Let's go to lunch," he said abruptly. "I want to talk."

So my associate, Duane Boyce, and I sat across the table and heard a man tell the truth about himself in the very moments he was opening himself up to it. These are always remarkable occasions. Duane and I both felt we were in the presence of an unshielded human soul, standing in a sacred space.

Norm recounted the poverty of his childhood and his resolve to make money. Money had been such an over-riding passion, he said, that he had abused people for it, kept himself from having fulfilling relationships with the people he worked with day after day, and missed partici-pating in much of his children's childhood. He had told himself his hard work was for them, although that, he now realized, was just an excuse for not giving of himself. As people always do at times such as these, Norm was accepting the truth of what he had been and taking responsibility for it; and in that very process what he had been was disappearing.

That evening over a late dinner Norm reflected on his day. I wrote down what he said as soon as I got back to my room:

"All afternoon I've had the funniest feeling, a feeling I'm not used to. I feel I want to help people.

"At lunch, when I was talking, my body started relax-ing. I was relaxing so much I had to hold myself up with my arms to keep from sliding off the chair.

"For twenty-five years I have had a painful knot at the top of my back, here, right where my head goes into my shoulders. Twenty-five years, that's how long I've been running this business. Today, while we were eating, it went away. It feels really warm there, but not tense."

Several weeks later, Norm's chief financial officer confided that Norm had been the poorest executive he had ever met, in terms of understanding and working with people, but within a few short weeks he had become one of the best. Norm told us that he had never felt comfortable speaking in public, and now, in conducting management meetings, the words seemed to flow out of him, "as if I were being given the things to say." In his youth he had a photographic memory that he lost in adulthood. But since that day when he simply admitted to himself, emotionally, the truth about his life, this ability had returned. For many years he hadn't slept well because of preoccupations and worry. But now he wasn't sleeping "because I have so many great thoughts to think."

But these were not the things that impressed me most. Instead of taking weekends to play golf with his cronies, he was working in the yard with the two children who were still at home or gathering his children and taking them on trips and enjoying them completely. And whereas Norm had complained that the people who worked for him were not very competent—"I just don't have anybody who can take over the really important responsibilities except myself," he had said—now he described the amazement with which he discovered how many first-class people he had. They were responding to the changes in him and showing that they weren't really the kind of people their former behavior (which he had provoked) suggested they were. "What am I going to do with them all? There are just so many top positions in a company this size."

"I've got the secret of life," he'd say to people. "I've run into those people who try to make you feel better about all the crap in your life by telling you it's natural, it's the way everyone feels. That's all propaganda. It shortchanges you. The point is not to tell yourself you're okay when you're not. The point is to dump the garbage out. I know a person can. If I can just keep feeling the way I feel now, I won't do what I believe is wrong again for anything."

LIVING FREE

Norm became something of a free spirit, and he did it with the very people he had had so much trouble with before. He substantially freed himself from the burden of negative emotions, attitudes, or moods that had made his life so hard to bear. The value of the freedom he attained is this: by it, his life became more of what it was meant to be—difficult and challenging, but also, and often, sweet, fulfilled, and joyous.

All of us operate by some ideal of freedom or other, by which we believe we can make our lives better. Most of us in our Western culture have been subtly taught and have come to believe that freedom is being able to get whatever we desire. It doesn't make any difference if our desires are self-serving. We think that any prohibitions, constraints, or obligations that are put upon us block or diminish our freedom; we want to throw them off. That's perhaps the dominant popular idea of freedom.

Another widely accepted idea is that freedom has to do with being able to act *contrary to* our self-serving desires. According to this idea, in the moment between experiencing a provocation or temptation and our response to it, a choice presents itself. We can give in or hold back. You would think this the very opposite of the first idea, but it isn't. Both kinds of freedom leave our self-absorbed condition basically intact. Both assume that we are self-serving by nature and unable to change fundamentally. Therefore both kinds of freedom are defined in terms of what we are able to *do*. Neither of them touches on what we are able to *be*. It is not hard to see how limited human happiness would be if these were the only freedoms available to us.

In chapter 11 we introduced a third ideal of freedom, one that pins our hope upon the possibility of somehow remaking or reinventing ourselves. In this book we have repeatedly talked about the problem that defeats this hope: Trying to be a different kind of person without undergoing a change of heart can at best produce only a counterfeit. In spite of its lofty aspirations, this ideal, like the others, can bring about only changes in behavior, not a change of heart.

These notions of personal freedom are all based on fantasy— the fantasy that by our own wit or power we can somehow relieve ourselves of, distract ourselves from, or compensate for our bondage to our unwanted, burdensome emotional condition. That's one reason why most advice on how to live our lives makes little fundamental difference. Even if we follow it faithfully, we still carry with us the cloudiness of spirit we are trying to escape.

By contrast to this fantasy, freedom from this cloud springs from the most down-to-earth realism possible. Early in this section we noted that, as self-betrayers, we paint our world in threatening tones and then fantasize about fleeing to some other situation that we think will make us happy. This produces false optimism about our chances for happiness elsewhere or false pessimism about our chances for happiness here and now. The point is neither to accept the falsely threatening world nor to escape it, but to change it—or in other words, change the meaning it has for us. And that is done by undergoing a change in how we see the world, which is a change in ourselves.

The world we respond to and our response to it are one. We choose by our response whether the world will address us invitingly or threaten us menacingly. Herein lies our freedom from fear, anxiety, cynicism, and selfishness: Nothing can harm us emotionally, fundamentally, if we let the truth, especially the truth about the interior life of others and God's love for them, write itself upon our souls.

What I've written stands incomplete. It awaits its completion in your response. I have stopped short of offering "how to" instructions, because these would never quite fit your situation. The plans that will guide your actions will be supplied as you contemplate the stories and the principles I have shared. No doubt you have already felt summoned to do certain things in relation to various people in your life. I am counting on it; this book completes itself in your "uptake" of it; you serve as its co-author. Books are lifeless inscriptions on sheets of paper, but your living connections with others and with God speak to you the living truth. You will decide the steps you need to take.

Epilogue

When we're stuck in self-betrayal, we dedicate ourselves to finding or producing evidence to prove that we're acceptable and worthwhile. Whatever our particular outward style, from self-disparaging or fawning to arrogant or angry, we live as if we were defendants in a trial. The jury is composed of all the people whose opinions we think are important; they're the ones we've got to convince. Unsettled by our insecurities, we await their judgment.

But the jury members never come back with a final verdict. They hold us forever in suspense. Every hour or so, it seems, the foreman of the jury returns with a demand for more evidence. So we try again to win the jury's favor or at least to be found acceptable in their eyes, but nothing we can do will satisfy them once and for all.

Why? Because from their individual points of view, *they* are the ones on trial. They are as concerned to have us validate their self-image as we are to have them validate ours. *We* sit on *their* jury. Therefore what they want from us is not evidence that will establish our acceptability but evidence that will establish theirs. They can't give us their final stamp of approval because they never feel completely approved of themselves.

By contrast, doing the right thing no matter what others may think requires faith—faith of a peculiarly practical kind. It takes faith *not* to rely upon external evidences, or anything else that can be seen, for our sense of acceptability. We must trust instead in certain things we cannot see and cannot use for self-promotion, such as the light or guidance given us through our sense of others' needs and feelings. Signs of these needs flow to us from others without interruption and invite us to love them. We cleanse ourselves of insecurity and gain self-assurance when we do exactly as this love dictates, rather than constantly struggle to prop up a dubious, idealized image of ourselves. The key is to recognize the infinite supremacy of love over status.

We already know why this practical kind of faith works so well. It does not artificially calm our insecurities but instead frees us from them. Some people misguidedly think that faith is for insecure people who cannot stand on their own, and who use it as a crutch. Those who think this way do not appreciate how dependent we are upon each other, positively or negatively. Nor do they comprehend that theirs is the negative kind of dependency, a bondage maintained by comparisons, judgments, and generally unspoken mistrust. The dependency of faith, on the other hand—the faith of people like Rachael, Eli, Laura, Jeff, and Norm—is a linkage to others by means of love. Because this faith often requires standing undaunted against the disapproval of the majority, it manifests the purest kind of courage.

∾

Some people assume that because it's not combative, the life of faith I have described must be timid, weak, and ineffectual. On the contrary, I have found that, all things being equal, self-absorbed people never think as clearly or act as decisively as those whose conscience is clear. They see threats where none exist, often can't tell their enemies from their friends, and tend to surround themselves with allies who won't overshadow them. Invariably their plans are unduly complicated because, besides attaining their stated goals, they have to worry about who is going to get the credit. Moreover, they spur other people to resist them; they don't inspire people to get things done. They cling to others' failures, failures they have helped provoke, in order to excuse failures of their own. They talk of effectiveness but foster discord and waste.

After a good deal of consulting experience in organizations of every size, from families and schools to multinational corporations, I'm convinced that the judgmental, comparative, assertive, combative, and controlling way of life undermines itself at every turn.

Welcoming, resonant, generous people don't defeat their own efforts. Typically they have a disarming, childlike way of cutting through the smoke of double-minded logic and getting to the heart of issues. By their manner, example, and love, they invite cooperation and creativity, not resistance. The softening that Eli brought out in his pious enemy, the uncompromising and passionately caring correction Jay gave to his sister Barbara, the transforming patience with which Jeff served Robin—of such achievements as these, no self-absorbed person is capable.

Fable
The quality of life—the success we hope for—depends largely upon attaining what people have commonly called *the good life*. By this we mean competing for, obtaining, and securely holding on to certain externals—for example, pleasures, status, or possessions—which we regard as valuable, satisfying, and reflective of our worth.

Fact
The quality of life depends upon the choices we make, moment by moment, to do exactly what we sense is right toward all living things, including God. To distinguish this from pursuing the good life, I would like to call it pursuing *a life of goodness*. This means *a life of practical faith*.

In my experience, there is one personal characteristic upon which all else turns—one that clarifies, simplifies, and focuses us, that makes us effective when we're not even trying to be effective. It is not intelligence, wit, charm, or even stubborn determination, since all these become negative when we're self-absorbed. No, the key personal characteristic is *a consistent readiness to yield to the truth in all circumstances,* no matter what the apparent cost. This both requires and enhances our ability to have an undistorted sense of the inner concerns of others, including their perception of us. It guides us in how we ought to treat them. As we have learned in this book, great is the influence of those souls who are sensitive to how they affect others (which does not mean seeking to please others but doing what will actually help them), and who govern themselves according to that sense.

This personal quality, our allegiance to the truth and the sensitivity that accompanies it, makes consideration and true generosity possible. It invites others also to forget themselves and thus sets in motion the kind of collaborative creativity, work, and enjoyment that lead us to say, as I said on our memorable Idaho vacation, "This is how it's supposed to be."

∾

In this book I've suggested that this influence flows from beings who enter our lives to love us and to set us an example. In our relationships with them, we are reminded of what is right and gently taught how much we matter. Their power flows from their love, a love that absolutely requires them to be just. They love us and they love the truth so perfectly that they will not indulge us by collaborating in our lies and leading us to believe we're doing right when we're not. When we're mired in any degree of self-deception, we cannot fathom how desperately we need the solid, immovable truth that true friends revere.

I believe that the ultimate source of that influence is God. Without the constant intervention of his perfectly just love and loving justice, we would long ago have fallen by the wayside, one by one. We would have been left to draw our emotional nurture from other beings who are trying to draw their nurturance from the likes of us. The delicate emotional ecosystem upon which we all depend would have long since collapsed. Consideration would have given place to collusion everywhere and love would have turned to recrimination and then to hate. (Anyone who has lived in or observed a family going bad knows just how this happens.) In order for our species to have maintained a viable social existence—in order for there to have been renewals of kindness and hope from time to time, as surely there have been—a loving, just influence must have been everywhere available to those who've chosen to attend to it. We could not have thrived, we could not even have survived, without the gently disruptive nudges that encourage us even while pulling us up short in our arrogance and evasions.

Call this divine influence the spirit of truth, if you will. Call it the loving justice that governs the relationships we've talked about in this book. Whatever it be called, it seems to me a constant gift that intelligent organisms cannot produce on their own. This astounds and humbles me, as does the liberality with which the gift is given. It is abundantly available to each of us, whether or not we acknowledge its source. We are not only beneficiaries of more gifts than we can see; we are beneficiaries of more gifts than we can imagine.

This of course is my personal conviction and lies beyond the focus of this book. But there's a closely related principle not personal to me or separable from the ideas we have been discussing here. It is this: To the degree that we become receptive and responsive to the truth, life will keep instructing us. It will teach us all sorts of fresh things about matters we thought we already understood. This is partly because we will no longer perceive them distortedly. We will be more open to seeing things as they are instead of anxiously twisting them to validate any lies we may be living. Not only will the possibility of a practical faith take on new meaning, but so will goodness, nature, beauty, friendships, family, work, and many other dimensions of life.

I have perfect confidence in your ability and mine to harvest the truths that lie beyond the discussions of this book—provided only that we faithfully act according to whatever we sense is right to do, and continue steadily in this path.

Story Index

SUBJECT INDEX

Abstinence, 236–39

Accusation, 13; impossibility of hiding, 12–13, 103–4, 106–7; in emotions, 28; caused by mistreating others, 30, 63; as source of troubled feelings, 33, 285; as self-victimization, 60; collusion cycle and, 92–94, 103; moral blindness and, 108–11; in story lines, 112, 115–16; in self-disparagement, 118–21; impossibility of doing good with, 124–25; effect of the truth about the other on, 142–43; giving up, 143, 162, 167, 219, 275–77, 294; effect of giving up, 176; in trying to change others, 188; fear in, 203–4; forgiveness and, 293. *See also* Accusing feelings and emotions

Accusing feelings and emotions: lying with, 28, 203; self-betrayal as the cause of, 29–30; as signs we're in the wrong, 30; facts and fables about, 30, 31; as dishonest but genuinely felt, 30–31; as projecting an illusion, 31–33; as self-betrayal, 34; truth of the accusation and, 34–35; lack of specific self-betrayal in, 35–36; seeing oneself as a victim and, 60, 71–73; lack of malice in having, 79; letting go of, 79–80, 143, 200, 202–3, 204; impossibility of hiding, 83, 103, 106–7; role of, in forming collusion, 83–84, 92–94, 103; corruption of conscience and, 110; in story lines, 112, 115–16; in self-disparagement, 118–20;

responsibility for, 122, 274, 276; possibility of escaping, 122–23; necessity of letting go of, 203; false confession and, 203; fear in, 203–4; vs. trustworthy feelings, 230–31; collusions as source of, 275–76; as hiding contrary facts, 280. *See also* Accusation; Blaming emotions and attitudes; Troubled feelings and emotions

Addiction, emotional, 236–39

Advice, 12–13, 214

Agency, 299–301. *See also* Freedom

Anasazi Foundation, 216

Arbinger Institute, 214, 224, 281

Assertiveness, 112–13, 118

Attitude, 191

Attitudes. *See* Accusing feelings and emotions; Blaming emotions and attitudes; Troubled feelings and emotions

Attunement of souls, 129–31. *See also* Light

Baal-Shem, 22–23

Barksdale, Laura, 239

Being ourselves, 248, 275–77. *See also* Who we are

Betraying ourselves. *See* Self-betrayal

"Bigger box," 257–59. *See also* Self-image, false

Birch, Jane, 191

Black Elk, 103

Blame, 26, 204–7; self-betrayal and, as a single act, 34; and seeing oneself as victim, 62, 63, 78, 204; in relationships, 84; provokes blame,

PERSONAL AND READING GROUP GUIDE

The reflection (R) and discussion (D) topics and questions provided here can be used to enrich individual and group study of *Bonds That Make Us Free,* by C. Terry Warner. This book subtly draws the reader into seeing his or her own life and relationships from a new perspective that cannot co-exist with self-destructive emotions and attitudes. Reading, pondering, and discussing the material, you can experience an inner change taking place—a liberation from petty, insecure, and resentful thoughts and feelings. The process can be enhanced as you reflect on, write about, and/or discuss the items below, or any other questions or insights you're interested in.

One set of items is provided for each of the book's fourteen chapters. If you are working alone, you can begin with the reflection items and then ponder the discussion items by yourself, possibly writing your thoughts in a journal. If you are in a discussion group, it's best in many cases to start out by spending a few minutes on the reflection items individually, and then talking together about the discussion items and perhaps also the reflection items.

1. Life's Sweetness Lost

(R) Think (and if possible write) about the contrast in your life between the times when, within yourself, you have felt peaceful, loving, and delighted with your situation (you may have to go back to your childhood for this), and the times when you have felt insecure, anxious, wounded, angry, or simply hardened and unfeeling. During instances of the latter, did you feel you had become a person who was not really you?

(D) What strategies do we commonly use in trying to deal with our troubled feelings and what we think is causing them? What strategies do "experts" usually suggest? Do any of these strategies bring about deep, fundamental, and lasting changes? If so, under what conditions? If not, why not?

2. Living a Lie

(R) Individually, write (in bullet points if you want) a story of self-betrayal from your own observation or experience. Can you see in it evidence of self-justification, rationalization, and accusation?

(D) To the extent you feel comfortable doing so, share your stories with one another. Let the discussion focus on what you are discovering about self-betrayal and its consequences.

3. The Self-Absorbed Way of Being

(R) Call to mind the situations when you are, or have been, more self-absorbed (I-It), and the times when you've been more open and responsive to others (I-You). What do you learn from making this comparison?

(D) What is it like to live in the box? Does it have any redeeming value? What is it like to live out of the box? Is there any downside to it?

4. Making Victims of Ourselves

(R) Think of a self-betrayal story you've experienced, heard, or read, and find the self-victimization in it. Have you known people who seem to have made a lifestyle out of amplifying their victimhood? Do you see any of this tendency in yourself?

(D) Why do we embrace our miseries and preoccupy ourselves with our victimhood?

When we perceive that people are deceiving themselves, acting hypocritically, blaming others, and magnifying the damage they think others are doing to them, we might feel contempt for them and consider them very hard to live with. Does understanding why they are doing this change our estimate of them—or, in other words, does it change *us?* In what way?

5. Being False Together

(R) Write a story of collusion from your own observation or experience. You may want to do this by filling out a diagram like the one on page 167. Identify the ways in which each party is co-responsible for what he or she blames on the other.

(D) To the extent you feel comfortable doing so, share your collusion stories and the insights you've gained from them.

6. The Darkness of Our Eyes

(R) If possible, try to identify and make notes about one or more of the following:

An experience in which a "good" act of yours was actually a counterfeit of goodness.

An experience in which your conscience became corrupted— when you believed what was wrong to be right or what was right, wrong. To do this, you may want to briefly review the story of Jennifer on pages 47, 113, and 118.

Your characteristic style of self-betrayal. You might do this by imagining what those who know you best might say.

(D) Share some of the experiences you have identified and the insights you have gained. Let the discussion focus on what you have been learning and any changes you have noticed in your basic attitude and emotions.

7. The Light Beckons Always

(R) Try to recall the feeling you have when you sense that something is right or wrong to do. Is it burdensome or inviting? Do everything you can to ignore any impulse to limit yourself to what you've heard about this subject, or what you think you're supposed to think. Let yourself be open to your authentic experience.

(D) What do you think now of living faithful to the light? How do you think you can stay attuned to it?

Focus the discussion on what it might be like to have an experience like Glen's and Becky's, in which a very significant relationship is healed.

8. Opening Ourselves to Others

(R) Do the reconsideration exercise, pages 162–66.

Might there be, or might there have been, someone like Robby in your own life? What do you feel you should do about it?

(D) Share with one another the insights you gained from doing the reconsideration exercise. Talk together about these insights.

9. Influence

(R) What person has had the greatest influence for good in your life? Make a list of that person's predominant characteristics. Are these I-It or I-You characteristics?

(D) Share what you discovered in the reflection item for this chapter.

What have you observed about the influence of those who are absorbed in other's welfare rather than absorbed in themselves?

10. The Truth Dispels the Lie

(R) In thinking about and observing the power of being honest with yourself about your weaknesses and self-betrayals, what have been your insights? If you haven't been discovering weaknesses and self-betrayals in yourself, what do you think might be holding you back? What do you think holds others back?

(D) What difference does it make in the quality of our lives to be completely honest with ourselves about weaknesses and self-betrayals?

Is it possible to counterfeit self-honesty? What are we like when we do this?

11. Doing the Right Thing

(R) As you have read these chapters, what has come to you that you feel you ought to do toward certain other people? Is this something you have known for some time and not acknowledged? When you finally did acknowledge it, did you do it? If so, what happened?

(D) Share your insights as you thought about the reflection questions for this chapter.

Have you ever been in a situation like Benson's? Like Doug's? Like Rachael's? How did you respond? How do you think you might respond now?

12. What Comes After a Change of Heart?

(R) and (D) What have you learned from this chapter and your reflections on it about becoming more emotionally mature? Focus the discussion on the pitfalls you might meet and the effort it will take to hold on to your new understanding and maintain a change of heart.

13. Changing the Influence of the Past

(R) If you can, write a story of intergenerational collusion from your own experience, with you in the child's role. Is there any sense in which you might be carrying on that collusion now? What emotions does thinking about this relationship stir up in you?

(D) To the extent you feel comfortable doing so, share the insights you gained from working on the reflection items for this chapter.

14. Forgiving, Forgoing, and Living Free

(R) Consider a situation in which you need to forgive. Have you made the attempt before? What went wrong? What will genuine forgiveness require in this case? (Keep in mind the discussion in the first part of chapter 14.)

Is there anyone in your experience who seems to have lived the principle of forgoing, at least in part? What do you think has been the experience of living for this person? What kind of influence has he or she had upon others?

(D) Share the questions and insights you had working on the reflection items for this chapter. Focus the discussion on what living free is like, including the sacrifices it requires and the rewards it brings.